edited by
Michela Braga · Lucia Corno · Paola Monti

HOMELESSNESS

Data, Prevalence and Features

Typesetting: Corpo4 Team, Milan
Cover: Cristina Bernasconi, Milan

Copyright © 2024 Bocconi University Press
EGEA S.p.A.

EGEA S.p.A.
Via Salasco, 5 - 20136 Milano
Tel. 02/5836.5751 – Fax 02/5836.5753
egea.edizioni@unibocconi.it – www.egeaeditore.it

All rights reserved, including but not limited to translation, total or partial adaptation, reproduction, and communication to the public by any means on any media (including microfilms, films, photocopies, electronic or digital media), as well as electronic information storage and retrieval systems. For more information or permission to use material from this text, see the website www.egeaeditore.it

Given the characteristics of Internet, the publisher is not responsible for any changes of address and contents of the websites mentioned.

First edition: October 2024
Revised edition: January 2025

ISBN Domestic Edition	979-12-80623-34-8
ISBN Digital Domestic Edition	978-88-238-8895-1
ISBN International Edition	979-12-81627-08-6
ISBN Digital International Edition	979-12-81627-09-3

Table of Contents

Introduction	VII
Acknowledgments	IX

1 Homelessness and its definitions 1
    1.1 Who is a homeless person? Several definitions of homelessness ... 1
    1.2 Definition of homelessness adopted in Europe ... 3
    1.3 Definition of homelessness adopted in the United States ... 6
    1.4 Definition of homelessness adopted in Australia ... 7
    1.5 Concluding remarks ... 9

2 Methodologies to count and survey homeless individuals ... 11
    2.1 Service-based administrative data ... 12
    2.2 Service-based estimation strategies ... 14
    2.3 Point-in-time counts and surveys ... 15
    2.4 Imputations with non-standard sampling methods ... 17
    2.5 Data from the general population census ... 18
    2.6 Longitudinal data on homelessness ... 19

3 The volume of the homeless population ... 23
    3.1 A new cross-country dataset on the homeless population: the International Homelessness Dataset (IHD, 2024) ... 24
    3.2 Homelessness prevalence across countries ... 30
    3.3 Homelessness prevalence across cities ... 37

4 Over-time trends in homelessness across European countries ... 51
    4.1 Trends at the country level ... 51
        4.1.1 European countries ... 51
        4.1.2 Australia and the US ... 63
    4.2 Trends at the city level ... 67

5	**What does contribute to homelessness?**	73
	5.1 Data on a country's institutional characteristics	74
	5.2 Correlation between the volume of homeless and socio-economic factors Europe	75
	5.3 Correlation between homelessness and welfare generosity in Europe	76
	5.4 Correlation between homelessness and the labor market	80
	5.5 Correlation between homelessness and political orientation	84
	5.6 Homelessness and social housing	88
6	**Who are the homeless and those at risk of homelessness?**	103
	6.1 The characteristics of homeless individuals: Evidence from an original point in time survey in Italy	103
7	**The costs of homelessness and potential policies**	121
	7.1 The costs of homelessness	121
	7.2 What types of interventions might help to reduce homelessness?	124
	7.2.1 Theoretical considerations	124
	7.2.2 Available evidence on effective programs	126

Final remarks   129

Appendix Tables   131

Bibliography   139

About the Authors   149

Introduction

Extreme poverty and housing deprivation are central issues on the policy agenda of many industrialized countries. "*Europe 2020*," the ten-year socio-economic plan proposed by the European Commission in 2010 to emerge from the economic crisis, has identified homelessness and housing deprivation as first-order priorities to be tackled by European Member States. Ten years later, in November 2020, the European Parliament adopted a set of recommendations to tackle homelessness and end housing exclusion. Indeed, the number of people living without adequate shelter is alarming. In 2022, approximately 896,430 people in Europe and 582,462 people in the US experienced homelessness on any given night, and these figures have increased over the past decade (FEANTSA 2023, HUD, 2022). Recently, the Covid-19 outbreak seems to have exacerbated the problem. As a result, in June 2021, the European Commission launched the so-called European Platform on Combatting Homelessness, which aims at promoting policies to strengthen cooperation and mutual learning among all actors involved in the fight against homelessness.

But what do we know about homeless people (i.e. who are they, why do they become homeless, etc.), and about homelessness prevalence rates across different European and non-European countries? Can policy interventions mitigate the phenomenon?

The goal of this book is to shed light on homelessness from various perspectives, by consolidating all available economic research on the topic and by compiling data on the number of homeless individuals and their characteristics, using a comparative approach across countries. Our objective is to offer a comprehensive view of the phenomenon from an international perspective. This book is intended not only for social scientists, but also for a broader audience of policy makers, NGO operators, service providers, advocacy, organizations, and readers interested in a data-driven and analytical examination of homelessness. Furthemore, the data reported in this volume are accessible to all researchers and policymakers seeking a deeper understanding of the homelessness phenomenon. We hope is that these data will be broadly used for economic research.

Interesting insights can be drawn from this volume. First of all, although the pattern of homelessness is not exactly the same in all countries, a common feature in many contexts is the lack of reliable, comparable and systematic data on the homeless population across and within countries. Comparable data are important to start rigorous empirical research on the topic. Indeed, despite the fact that homelessness is one of the most extreme forms of poverty in the developed world, economic research on the phenomenon is extremely scarce. For these reasons, despite data limitations we try throughout the book to provide robust evidence based on available and comparable data. The second message of this volume is that policies and institutional features matter. In particular, welfare assistance schemes should be re-designed to encourage homeless people to leave the streets and to help the most vulnerable individuals to avoid becoming homeless. The third message is that policies must be updated to face new forms of homelessness. The Covid-19 pandemic, together with the austerity measures imposed by international standards, produced non-negligible effects in many countries, even in those that were adopting consolidated and integrated policies to reduce homelessness in the long run. The typical traditional homeless person (middle-aged single man) is still present in many countries, but we are seeing increasing numbers of women, young people and families with children living in inadequate housing. The changing profile of homelessness calls for changes in policies and interventions. Finally, the fourth message is that it is necessary to examine how individual risk factors interact with local structural and institutional factors in contributing to homelessness. Longitudinal data, when available, provide local and international researchers the opportunity to answer some of the fundamental questions that have interested and eluded homelessness researchers for many years. Both individual and structural factors can lead to homelessness. Depending on the prevailing cause, different interventions are needed. Individual factors call for specific *ad hoc* solutions, while structural factors call for long-term policies and structural changes.

The book is organized as follows. In **Chapter 1** we discuss the possible definitions of homelessness currently adopted by the European Union, highlighting the (unfortunate) lack of a unanimous and shared view of who is a homeless person across European countries. We also analyze the definition of homelessness used in the US and Australia. In **Chapter 2** we analyze advantages and disadvantages of all the methodologies used so far to count and survey homeless people. In **Chapter 3** we have undertaken a rigorous exercise to assemble all available data to provide a new cross-country and cross-city dataset on the homeless population. Through our data collection efforts, we were able to gather information on 36 OECD countries and 123 cities. **Chapter 4** analyzes the time trend in the number of homeless people in the European countries for which data are publicly available. Overall, we observe a general decrease of the phenomenon in Northern European countries (i.e. Finland, Norway) but an increasing trend in others (i.e. UK, Germany, Spain). We also observe a high variability in the evolution of homelessness within countries. In **Chapter 5** we have made the interesting exercise of correlating institutional factors, such as the *Gini Index* or the political orientation of a given country, with the prevalence of homelessness. **Chapter 6** uses available micro data we collected in three major Italian cities to describe the characteristics of a homeless person, the dynamics of the phenomenon and of the duration of a homeless spell. Finally, **Chapter 7** is devoted to the discussion of the policy approach to fight homelessness.

Acknowledgments

We wish to thank all those who attended the XVI European conference of the Fondazione Rodolfo Debenedetti and who actively contributed to the discussion. In particular, we wish to express our gratitude to Tito Boeri, Luigi Guiso, Andrea Ichino and Chiara Saraceno. Some chapters of this book benefit from the contribution of Brian O'Flaherty, Guy Johnson, Gavin Wood, Rosanna Scutella and Yi-Ping Tseng.

We are very grateful to all the volunteers who participated in the data collection among homeless people in Milan, Turin and Rome. Gabriele Borg, Serena Cocciolo, Simone Ferro, Elisa Facchetti, Matteo Marti, Arianna Savo, Carolina Marsiglia and Chiara Serra provided excellent research assistance.

Financial support from the Empirical Research in Economics (ERE), Bocconi University, the Municipality of Turin and the Fondazione Rodolfo Debenedetti is gratefully acknowledged.

1 Homelessness and its definitions

1.1 Who is a homeless person? Several definitions of homelessness

Homelessness is a complex and dynamic phenomenon. Individuals often go through phases of homelessness that may be temporary, recurring, or prolonged. It is not uncommon to move in and out of homelessness frequently, reflecting a pattern of residential instability where transitions occur within short timeframes (Sosin et al., 1990; Pickering et al., 2003; Stax, 2004). Moreover, it is somehow difficult to establish a clear boundary between roofless individuals, those living in extreme poverty, and socially marginalized people. This complexity contributes to the absence of a single, universally accepted definition of homelessness across countries.

Defining what constitutes 'homelessness' is a challenging task. Typically this includes, for sure, people who may be staying in shelters, transitional housing, or places not meant for human habitation, such as streets, parks, or abandoned buildings. The common image of a person sleeping on the street during winter is widely recognized as homelessness. However, situations may be more nuanced when considering someone temporarily without a home or an individual without a stable, adequate place to live. Moreover, cultural factors influence the definition of homelessness, particularly the notion of what is considered 'adequate housing.' The political orientation and policy priorities of local and national authorities may also influence the definition of a homeless person (Cordray and Pion, 1991; Bogard, 2001). As a result, definitions of homelessness may reflect broader or narrower views of the issue, often shaped by policy preferences.

For years, researchers, practitioners, and various institutions have debated the adoption of a uniform definition of homelessness. Beyond semantics, this issue carries significant practical importance, as any chosen definition delineates the scope of the target population. Consequently, it significantly impacts data collection methods and policies aimed at addressing homelessness. Additionally, the absence of a precise definition of homelessness results in a scarcity of comparable measures and reliable data, both within and across countries. This lack of clarity has contributed to the limited presence of empirical economic research on homelessness in the literature.

In many countries today, including the United States, there is a tendency to adopt a fairly literal approach when categorizing homelessness. Specifically, the homeless population is narrowly delineated as those individuals who fall within the category of the 'street-and-shelter-population', often referred to as 'literally homeless' (Rossi, 1991; HUD, 2008) or 'primary homelessness' (UNSD, 2008). This definition typically includes individuals sleeping in places not meant for human habitation, such as streets, parks, cars or abandoned buildings, as well as those staying in emergency shelters and other temporary accommodations for homeless people. Given the clear and objective condition of the lack of a suitable place to sleep, at least within a well-defined timeframe, there is almost unanimous consensus that these extreme cases of poverty and housing deprivation should be included in the reference population. In its simplicity, this definition clearly reflects the typical – and somewhat stereotyped – image of a homeless person as perceived by the public or depicted in the media.

There is much more disagreement about where to set the boundaries for a broader definition of homelessness. This broader view typically acknowledges a continuum of housing situations, with some individuals residing in a 'grey area' on the edge of homelessness. Sometimes institutions or researchers adopt a more inclusive approach in their definition of homelessness, including people who are, for example, 'precariously housed'. More comprehensive perspectives can take into account various living conditions that put people at risk of homelessness, such as individuals living temporarily with family or friends, those at risk of eviction, households spending an extremely high proportion of their income on rent, or individuals in institutions such as prisons, psychiatric hospitals, or women's shelters because of domestic violence.

While opting for the broadest possible definition of homelessness may be appealing in theory, this choice remains controversial for several reasons. Firstly, it can be somewhat counterintuitive and challenging to communicate a very broad definition to the general public, as it may encompass people who are currently housed but deemed 'at risk' of homelessness, some of whom may never actually become roofless. Secondly, where the line is drawn significantly impacts the estimated size of the homeless population, with a broader definition mechanically resulting in higher numbers. Thirdly, broadening the definition can also lead to confusion about the appropriate strategies and policies to address the issue, given the increased heterogeneity of the target population. Finally, expanding the target population from rough sleepers to the precariously housed also increases the methodological challenges associated to data collection (as discussed by Cordray and Pion, 1991), as the range of settings where homeless individuals can be found expands exponentially. As we will discuss in the next chapters, counting the 'literally' homeless people has proven to be very difficult. The attempt to include those at risk of homelessness poses additional challenges in devising effective methods to track them.

The choice between a restrictive or a broader definition of homelessness is closely tied to the objectives for which it is adopted by researchers, policy makers, or practitioners. A narrow definition focusing on specific groups may suffice for practical purposes and be more cost-effective when addressing short-term needs, such as determining the number of beds or meals required for emergency interventions. However, when the focus shifts to long-term planning and prevention measures, a broader definition encompassing groups 'at risk' of homelessness may be more beneficial.

Additionally, defining homelessness is politically sensitive, as it involves deciding who should be counted as homeless, thereby revealing the extent of extreme poverty in a given area. Consequently, any attempt to estimate the homeless population implicitly displays the costs society must pay to address this issue. Homelessness estimates can have significant implications for various stakeholders, including local and national policymakers, service providers, advocacy organizations, mass media, and the general public. Each group may have different interests and reasons for supporting a more or less inclusive definition of homelessness (Williams, 2011; Berck et al. (2008). Politicians, for instance, may react to the perceived magnitude of the problem based on voter concerns and the political feasibility of increasing spending on homeless individuals. Data on the number of homeless individuals can influence the demand for policies to address the issue and the allocation of resources, with policy makers often preferring a narrow definition to minimize public responsibility and portray the problem as manageable, while advocacy organizations and service providers would typically lobby for a broader definition to increase political relevance and resource allocation (Busch-Geertsema, 2010; Williams, 2011).

In the US, for example, the Department of Housing and Urban Development (HUD) regularly carries out counts of homeless individuals through local planning bodies coordinating homelessness services, the so called CoC ('Continuums of Care'). Despite the fact that the HUD imposes methodological standards for the count, it also explicitly states that collecting data on homeless people is a key element of the process associated with applying for CoCs program funding as well as a way to justify requests for additional resources (HUD, 2008). Consequently, the HUD's survey is largely carried out by interested parties.

Finally, the cost of collecting information on homeless individuals is another highly debated issue. Particularly in contexts with limited resources, where providing adequate services to homeless people can be challenging, service providers may view costly data collections as a misallocation of funds. Conversely, advocacy organizations often see such projects as opportunities to inform public opinion and raise awareness, and they are typically inclined to use research findings to advocate for expanding existing services and resources. Similar pressures and diverging interests in the design and implementation of enumeration projects are far from being unusual, as reported by many researchers in this field (Berry, 2007; Williams, 2011).

In what follows, we briefly review the alternative definitions of homelessness currently used to collect data in many OECD countries, with a special focus on differences between Europe, the US and Australia. We also explore how these definitions have evolved over time, often in close relation to changes in the policy agenda of each country.

1.2 Definition of homelessness adopted in Europe

Achieving a unified definition of homelessness across Europe remains elusive, with the European Union yet to consolidate a common social policy for addressing housing issues and homelessness. The variability in legislative frameworks and welfare systems across Europe further complicates the pursuit of a standardized definition and its implementation in national assessments and surveys.

Despite the lack of an uniformly or officially adopted definition of homelessness, the European Typology on Homelessness and Housing Exclusion (ETHOS) is a widely acknowledged and used 'common language' for assessing and comparing different living situations of people experiencing homelessness in Europe (Feantsa, 2024a).

The ETHOS framework was developed by the advocacy organization FEANTSA (European Federation of National Organizations Working With the Homeless) in the 1990s. ETHOS aims to provide a comprehensive view of homelessness, capturing its physical, legal, and social dimensions to identify what constitutes adequate, safe, and secure housing. According to ETHOS, a person experiences homelessness or housing exclusion when lacking at least one of three dimensions: physical (the actual lack of housing), legal (the rights to remain in accommodation), and social (the quality of living situation, such as insufficient privacy or physical insecurity within the household). This typology distinguishes between different states of homelessness (rooflessness, housing exclusion or social isolation), viewing homelessness not only as housing issue but also as a broader social problem including social exclusion.

Although ETHOS serves as a theoretical framework for understanding homelessness, translating it into practical data collection and analysis has posed challenges. Put simply, ETHOS was never designed to serve as a 'statistical definition'—a tool for quantifying the actual number of individuals in each category. The original framework, comprising 13 conceptual categories and 24 living situations, made it exceedingly complex to differentiate between different statuses. In an effort to introduce a more manageable definition, and following consultations with the European Commission, a condensed version of ETHOS was developed in 2007, referred to as 'ETHOS Light' (Feantsa, 2024b). The revised definition kept the same structure of the original version, but omitted most of the categories related to inadequate and insecure housing, which were seen as the most controversial and difficult to quantify (Busch-Geertsema et al., 2014)[1].

The ETHOS typology has never been formally adopted by EU institutions. Data collection remains decentralized, with countries employing different definitions influenced by their own policy developments. Some countries integrate ETHOS into their national policies, while others use it as a reference point alongside their own definitions.

Nevertheless, in March 2021, the European Commission in the European Pillar of Social Rights Action Plan announced the establishment of a European Platform on Combating Homelessness to trigger dialogue, facilitate mutual learning, improve

---

[1] ETHOS Light excluded categories such as accommodations and reception centers for immigrants (living situations 5.1 and 5.2 of ETHOS) and long-term accommodations for formerly homeless people (7.1 and 7.2 of ETHOS). It also left out most living situations described as insecure (categories 8.2 and 8.3, occupation of dwelling/land with no legal rights; categories 9 and 10, people living under the threat of eviction or violence) or inadequate (categories 12 and 13, unfit and extremely overcrowded housing).

Table 1   **The ETHOS classification**

Conceptual category		Operational category	Living situation
Homelessness	Roofless	1 People living rough	1.1 Public space or external space
		2 People in emergency accommodation	2.1 Night shelter
	Houselessness	3 The People living in accomodation for the homeless	3.1 Homeless hostel
			3.2 Temporary accommodation
			3.3 Transitional supported accommodation
		4 People in a women's shelter	4.1 Women's shelter accommodation
		5 People in accommodation for immigrants	5.1 Temporary accommodation, reception centres
			5.2 Migrant workers' accommodation
		6 People due to be released from institutions	6.1 Penal institutions
			6.2 Medical institutions
			6.3 Children's institutions/homes
		7 People receiving longer-term support (due to homelessness)	7.1 Residential care for older homeless people
			7.2 Supported accommodation for formerly homeless persons
Housing exclusion	Insecure	8 People living in insecure accommodation	8.1 Temporarily with family/friends
			8.2 No legal (sub) tenancy
			8.3 Illegal occupation of land
		9 People living under threat of eviction	9.1 Legal orders enforced (rented)
			9.2 Repossession orders (owned)
		10 People living under threat of violence	10.1 Police recorded incidents
Inadequate		11 People living in temporary, nonconventional structures	11.1 Mobile homes
			11.2 Non-conventional building
			11.3 Temporary structure
		12 People living in unfit housing	12.1 Occupied dwelling unfit for habitation
		13 People living in extreme overcrowding	13.1 Highest national norm of overcrowding

Source: FEANTSA
Notes: rooflessness = lack of fisical, legal, and social dimension; houselessness = lack of legal and social dimension; insecure housing = (mainly) lack of legal dimension; inadequate housing = (mainly) lack of social dimension.

the evidence base, and strengthen the cooperation among the different stakeholders involved in tackling homelessness in the EU.

In general, adopted definitions of homelessness tend to be narrower than ETHOS, except in some Northern European countries (Finland, Sweden, and Denmark) that closely align with its broad categorizations. Countries like France, Hungary, Poland, and the United Kingdom employ narrower definitions, typically focusing on rough sleeping or emergency shelter residency. However, wider definitions are used in countries such as Luxembourg, Lithuania, and Ireland, encompassing individuals residing in institutions or facing imminent discharge without available housing.

Variations in definitions often reflect differing perspectives on homelessness as either primarily a housing issue or a broader result of social exclusion. For instance, France emphasizes housing standards to prevent stigma, while Norway views homelessness along a continuum of residential arrangements. In the UK, homelessness encompasses not just housing deprivation but also poor living conditions, reflecting a broad understanding of 'home.' In Italy, homelessness is often framed within the more general concept of social exclusion, where the lack of housing only represents one aspect of a multidimensional problem.

1.3   Definition of homelessness adopted in the United States

In the United States, the discussion about the definition to be adopted has been closely linked to the federal policy to fight against homelessness. Funding rules and shifts in government priorities regarding homeless people have somehow shaped the definitions of homelessness over time, as well as enumeration efforts.

Until 2010, the Department of Housing and Urban Development (HUD) used a relatively narrow definition of homelessness, first mandated by the McKinney-Vento Act of 1987. This major piece of federal legislation provided funding for a wide range of homeless programs and services and therefore introduced a definition used by most state and federal programs. The definition focused on a limited number of observable housing conditions and identified a homeless person based on the characteristics of their sleeping place during the night. In particular, the homeless is:

> *"an individual who lacks a fixed, regular, and adequate nighttime residence; and an individual who has a primary nighttime residence that is: a supervised publicly or privately operated shelter designed to provide temporary living accommodations (including welfare hotels, congregate shelters, and transitional housing for the mentally ill); an institution that provides a temporary residence for individuals intended to be institutionalized; or a public or private place not designed for, or ordinarily used as, a regular sleeping accommodation for human beings."*

Therefore, the definition included all the 'streets-and-shelters population,' but did not take into account precariously housed individuals. It excluded, for example, those at risk of eviction or those living with another individual or family in regular housing for a short period of time, the so called 'doubled up' people (Williams, 2011). This definition was mainly centered on individuals using emergency services and the priority group for policy was the chronically homeless people.

In recent years, a shift in US policy has occurred, moving the focus from chronicity to homelessness prevention (Culhane et al., 2011). This change in priorities translated into a new definition of homelessness introduced in 2009 by the Homeless Emergency Assistance and Rapid Transition to Housing (HEARTH) Act. The new definition, in principle, included also individuals 'at risk' of homelessness, such as those who are doubled up, facing eviction, and precariously housed. The new legislation also tasked the Department of Housing and Urban Development (HUD) with updating regulations on the definition of homelessness to be used for statistical purposes and in the implementation of assistance programs. After receiving extensive stakeholder feedback, HUD released the new definition in 2011, which remains quite narrow, only partly including 'at risk' populations (National Alliance to End Homelessness, 2012; Sullivan, 2023). According to the current HUD definition, a person is experiencing homelessness if at least one of the following criteria is met:

- People who are living in a place not meant for human habitation or people in emergency shelters.
- People imminently losing their primary nighttime residence.
- Unaccompanied youth and families with children and youth who are defined as homeless under other federal programs.
- Individuals and families who are fleeing domestic violence or other dangerous conditions.

Despite the legislative change and a stronger emphasis on prevention, this final definition only marginally includes groups going beyond the 'streets-and-shelters population,' and their inclusion in official statistics is still controversial. This reluctance is due, on the one hand, to the fear that a broad definition would inflate numbers of homeless people and draw funding away from rough sleepers and those living in shelters, on the other hand, it would complicate the design of enumeration strategies (Williams, 2011; Sullivan, 2023).

1.4 Definition of homelessness adopted in Australia

Research on homelessness in Australia emerged in response to significant changes in the social and economic landscape, including deindustrialization and reduced welfare protection, experienced in Australia and elsewhere in the 1970s. This period witnesses the release of two important reports in Australia: Report of Working Party on Homeless Men and Women (1973) and Homeless People and the Law (Sackville, 1976). These reports highlighted that homelessness was no longer a problem confined to 'derelicts' and 'bag ladies' in inner-city areas, but included young people, families, and women. They anticipated the emergence of what researchers around the world would subsequently consider 'contemporary homelessness.' At that time, interest in homelessness among Australian researchers was limited, but it began to change in the late 1980s. By the mid-1990s, there was a significant increase in the number of studies and government reports on the subject. Some of these studies were particularly influential. For instance, in 1989, the Human Rights and Equal Opportunities Commission released its report titled "Our Homeless Children" which raised awareness about youth homelessness among a wider audience. Another notable contribution came in 1992 when Chris Chamberlain and David MacKenzie published "Understanding Contemporary Homelessness." In this work, they proposed a definition of homelessness based on minimum community housing standards. Their approach was grounded in the idea that there are shared community standards regarding the minimum level of accommodation individuals are expected to achieve in contemporary society (Chamberlain and Mackenzie 1992; ABS, 2011; Chamberlain, 2014). The minimum accommodation for a single person (or couple) was described as:

> *"a small rental flat – with bedroom, living room, kitchen, bathroom and an element of security of tenure – because this is the minimum that most people achieve in the private rental market."*

This classification has led to the identification of three main categories: 'primary,' 'secondary' and 'tertiary' homelessness. Primary homelessness includes all people without conventional accommodation, such as those living on the streets, or using cars or other vehicles for temporary shelter. Secondary homelessness includes people who frequently move between different forms of temporary shelter and emergency accommodations. Tertiary homelessness refers to people staying in boarding houses on a medium to long-term basis, defined as 13 weeks or longer.

Over the following two decades, their definition, later recognized as the 'cultural definition' of homelessness, gained widespread acceptance among researchers, policymakers, and service providers. In 1992, "Homelessness in Australia: Causes and Consequences" by Neil and Fopp (1994) was published, offering a comprehensive overview of the issues surrounding homelessness at that time. In 1998, Chamberlain and Mackenzie conducted another influential study, this time focusing on youth homelessness (Chamberlain and Mackenzie 1998; Johnson and Chamberlain, 2008). This research, which drew on the idea of homelessness as a process of biographical change and adaptation, provided both empirical and theoretical foundations for early intervention efforts. One year later the Australian Bureau of Statistics (ABS) released its first attempt to enumerate the homeless population based on the 1996 census results (Chamberlain 1999).

By the turn of the century, a broad consensus had emerged regarding the definition of homelessness, accompanied by substantial evidence on the characteristics and scale of the homeless population. Policy directions were also becoming clearer, with a focus on assisting young people, women, and families, and prioritizing early intervention for both ethical and economic reasons.

The 1995 House of Representatives Report on Aspects of Youth Homelessness stated that early intervention is 'probably the one area of public policy which could deliver to the community the greatest returns in terms of increased social cohesion through the reduction in the levels of family breakdown and long term welfare dependency' (House of Representatives 1995:360).

Prior to releasing data from the 2011 Census, the ABS began reviewing the process and methods to enumerate homeless people, which included a revision of the definition of homelessness. This review led to the development of a new 'statistical definition' of homelessness, which takes into account the adequacy, tenure security and control of the dwelling (ABS 2012b). According to this new definition, individuals are considered homeless if they live in a dwelling that is inadequate, if they have no security of tenure (or a short and non-extendable initial tenure), or if they do not have free control over or access to space for social interaction. The current notion of homelessness under this definition is broader than the cultural one, as it includes people living in conventional houses and flats who lack privacy, safety, and security of tenure. Therefore, the definition emphasizes the concept of 'home' and includes elements such as a sense of security, stability, privacy, safety, and the ability to control one's living space. Moreover, it includes people living in severely overcrowded houses or flats.

The concrete applicability of such definition has been questioned by researchers, since it requires gathering information about how much space people have in their accommodation and whether they feel safe and secure in their residence (Chamberlain, 2014). Despite the methodological challenges raised by this new focus on precariously housed people and 'at risk' categories, the new definition reflects a shift in policy priorities from emergency measures toward early intervention and prevention.

1.5 Concluding remarks

As discussed earlier, defining homelessness is a complex and politically sensitive issue. A broad definition of homelessness is associated with methodological problems related to data collection, while a narrow definition may fall short in addressing broader policy needs when the focus moves away from emergency interventions. The recent attention on people precariously housed or 'at risk' of homelessness experienced in the US, Australia and some Northern European countries may reflect a shift toward prioritizing early interventions and prevention measures. However, this approach requires the development of new data collection strategies that will potentially encompass all individuals facing living and housing problems, even those who may never experience outright homelessness, and the ability to monitor their situations over time.

2 Methodologies to count and survey homeless individuals

Over the years, many methodological approaches have been used to produce counts of homeless people at local or national level. Yet, no universally accepted methodology has emerged. Different methods have been used depending on the specific segment of the homeless population to be tracked, the geographical scope or available resources. Each method has its strengths and weaknesses, and there is no consensus as to the optimal approach for obtaining an accurate estimate of the homeless population.

These difficulties in establishing common methodological standards stem from several factors. Firstly, there are difficulties associated with counting a transient population that frequently moves in and out of homelessness, has no fixed residence, and may be reluctant to be identified. Secondly, as we have seen in the previous chapter, issues related to the definition of homelessness make it difficult to produce comparable estimates across studies. Third, there is a lack of established best practice regarding operational decisions such as the reference period of the count (i.e. which season of the year?) or its duration (i.e. one night? one week? one month? one year?). Lastly, practical obstacles include the costs associated with implementing different methodologies.

In this chapter, we will examine the most common methods used to count and survey the homeless population. We will delve into the specifics of each method, discussing their strengths and weaknesses, and explore the different contexts in which they have been employed.

To the best of our knowledge, six major approaches have been adopted so far:

1. Service-based administrative data.
2. Service-based estimation strategies.
3. Point-in-time (PIT) counts and surveys.
4. Imputation with non-standard sampling methods: snowball sampling and capture-recapture.
5. Surveys aimed at the general population (census).
6. Administrative data or surveys aimed at collecting longitudinal data on homelessness.

Table 2 provides a concise summary of the strategies outlined in the chapter, considering: i) the geographical scope at which they are most appropriate: local (i.e. city)

Table 2 Overview of counting methods by scope, target group, and costs

Methodology	Geographical area	Target group			Costs
		Rough sleepers	Sheltered	At risk/ doubled up	
1 Service-based administrative data	local, regional, or national		FF	F	low
2 Service-based estimation strategies	local, regional, or national	F	FF	F	high
3 Point-in-time (PIT) counts and surveys	local (urban areas)	FF	F		high
4 Imputation with non-standard sampling methods	local or national	F	FF		low
5 Surveys aimed at the general population (census)	national		F	F	high
6 Administrative data or surveys aimed at collecting longitudinal data	local or national		F	FF	high

Notes: F = focus on target group; FF = strong focus on target group

or national; ii) their primary and secondary target populations; iii) a general assessment of the associated costs. The cost level is simply categorized as 'low' or 'high,' reflecting methods that rely on administrative data or a limited number of observations (low cost) versus those requiring more resources, especially in terms of the staff involved in the data collection process (high cost). When selecting a methodology, there is a clear trade-off to consider between costs, implementation complexity, and comprehensiveness. There is no single best method applicable to all situations; rather, different counting strategies are suitable for different purposes.

2.1 Service-based administrative data

This counting method relies on data from specialized services for homeless people such as shelters, soup kitchens, drop-in centers, warming centers, and social service agencies. Valuable information can be obtained directly from administrative records, since service providers often collect information about their service-users for operational purposes. This approach involves identifying a comprehensive list of service providers that homeless people are more likely to use and then asking them to report the number of people they are assisting and their demographic details over a specific period of time.

Service-based data collections were first developed in the US, but also many European governments have used registers and carried out counts by service providers to collect information about homelessness. Data collections based on administrative registers were initially developed in the United States, but they have also been adopted by numerous European countries. Scandinavian countries, in particular, have implemented extensive service-based counts, including a wide range of social and health service providers as well as local authorities. In Denmark, for example, the national statistical office has collected information on services available to homeless people and their use since the 1980, typically over the course of an observational week. Over time, this approach evolved to include personal identifiers, making it possible to track individuals accessing homeless services and to collect socio-demographic data and service use patterns. Moreover, the use of personal identifiers made it possible to match service-based data with general population registers, thus incorporating details on employment history, education, and medical records (Benjaminsen, 2005). Other significant examples of data collection based on administrative registers are the Central Electronic Registration of Service Users (the KENYSZI database) in Hungary, a centrally managed registration system that collects information on service providers and users on a daily basis through an online platform, and the publication of quarterly data on 'statutory homeless'[1] individuals by the Department for Communities and Local Government (DCLG) in England.

Using service-based administrative data is one of the least expensive approaches to counting homeless people, making use of existing administrative archives and recording systems. Moreover, both short and long observation periods are feasible, as data extractions from administrative archives can be repeated over time or users followed over specific time spans (for example, recording the number of days an individual spent in shelters over the course of a year). However, if only aggregated data are collected, individual-level information may be limited or not available. Thus, data quality will crucially depend on the standards employed in recording user information. Furthermore, harmonization issues may arise when integrating data from different service providers (Busch-Geertsema et al., 2014; HUD, 2008).

Another common issue with this approach is that numbers may be inflated by duplication across services. The risk of double counting is significant because the same homeless individuals may access a variety of services on a daily or weekly basis. Therefore, enumeration efforts based on this methodology should include a strategy for assigning a personal identifier to each individual and checking for duplication (Fitzgerald et al., 2001). An additional limit of service-based data collections is that a substantial number of people who use services targeted for homeless people may not be, in fact, homeless. This issue is particularly common when the count includes services used by both homeless and non-homeless people (such as soup kitchens) or

---

[1] According to the definition of the UK public authorities, statutory homeless are households which meet specific criteria of priority needs set out by the law, and to whom a homeless person's duty has been accepted by a local authority. Such households are rarely homeless in the literal sense of being without a roof over their heads, but are more likely to be at risk of losing or unable to maintain their current housing.

conventional social services (such as healthcare facilities or hospitals). In that case, a simple count of service-users may overestimate the number of homeless people. In principle, to address this problem, all individuals seeking services should be screened for homelessness by collecting individual information on their housing status (HUD, 2008; Fitzgerald at al., 2001).

Lastly, a significant problem with this approach, and one that is unlikely to be solved, is its inherent exclusion of homeless individuals who are not in contact with service providers, typically the most vulnerable among them. Specifically, the count will not include unsheltered homeless who do not have access to services. Unlike previous scenarios, this problem will lead to underestimating the actual number of homeless people. Additionally, it will also lead to estimates that are not representative of the overall homeless population, as they are likely to be biased towards service users.

2.2 Service-based estimation strategies

A somewhat different yet similar approach is using service providers to construct a sampling strategy for carrying out surveys on homeless people. The idea is to sample locations where homeless individuals are likely to be found (such as homeless shelters, soup kitchens, and outreach services) and then sample users from those places. Information from administrative data (such as the number of dedicated services and users during a given period) is then supplemented by individual questionnaires administered to a representative sample of service users. The initial part of the questionnaire usually includes screening questions to determine the person's homeless status. In the case of large geographical areas, the survey is typically carried out in a representative sample of municipalities to estimate of the total number of homeless people at regional or national level.

These service-based estimation strategies have been successfully used in cities, suburban areas, rural areas, and across countries both in the US and Europe (Busch-Geertsema et al., 2014; HUD, 2008).

An example of national surveys targeting homeless people accessing hosting facilities or other dedicated services are the ones carried out by the INSEE (National Institute of Statistics and Economic Studies) in France, respectively in 2001 and 2012. In this case, 80 urban areas were randomly sampled, and a complete register of accommodation and hot meal distribution services in these areas was compiled, collecting information on the types and characteristics of services provided. Subsequently, during the survey implemetation, a sample of beneficiaries were selected for face-to-face interviews over a one-week period. Similar surveys have been conducted in many European countries, such as Spain (2005, 2012), Italy (2011 and 2014) and Portugal (2009). Observation periods typically range between one week and a few months.

Certainly, service-based estimation strategies are less costly and require fewer human resources than headcounts carried out during one single night, as described in the following paragraph. However, they have a significant drawback: they tend to underestimate the real size of the homeless population because people who do not regularly use the selected services will not be accounted for. Moreover, the overall representativeness of the data crucially depends on the types of homeless service chosen. For instance, if the data collection primarily focuses on housing facilities and emergency accommodations, the sample will predominantly represent the sheltered homeless population. In constrast, if soup kitchens and outreach services are included, the likelihood of capturing rough sleepers, individuals doubled up, and those at risk of homelessness will be higher.

2.3 Point-in-time counts and surveys

One of the most common methods to enumerate homeless people is their headcount. Counts – also called point-in-time surveys – usually take the form of one-day census during night hours, the time span in which homeless people are less likely to move across different locations. The strategy consists of visiting all the streets of a metropolitan area (or a sample of them), to identify all the people sleeping rough. The short observation period and the reduced mobility of people during night hours are key conditions to minimize the probability of double counting. Counts typically take place in winter months, when the demand for homeless services is rising (especially shelters) due to the harsh weather conditions, thus reducing the number of people sleeping outdoors. However, in recent years, some countries have also started to regularly collect data during the summer months to gain a better understanding of the seasonal variations of the phenomenon and how needs change in each season, ensuring that appropriate shelters, supplies, and support are available. In addition, having more information during the year allows for better resource planning, and by comparing the counts in different time periods, service providers can evaluate the impact of some seasonal programs, such as winter shelter initiatives or summer food distribution, making necessary adjustments[2]. Sometimes individual questionnaires attached to the census, as screening device between homeless and non-homeless people or to collect information on essential characteristics of the homeless population.

The primary focus of this enumeration strategy is on rough sleepers, people who sleep outdoors in places like streets, doorways, parks or bus shelters, as well as those living in buildings or other locations not designed for habitation. Additionally, people staying in temporary and emergency shelters are typically included in the counts, following approaches like the S-Night method (Shelter and Street Night), first developed in Chicago in 1985 (Rossi, 1991) and gradually expanded to other US cities since the 1990s (Wright and Devine 1992; Berk et al. 2008). This method involves simultaneous counting of street and sheltered homeless individuals during the same

---

[2] In 2023, for example, the Fondazione Rodolfo Debenedetti and the Laboratory for Effective Antipoverty Policies (LEAP) conducted a winter and summer point-in-time count in Milan, following a similar initiative in Barcelona the previous year.

reference night across a defined geographical area. Conducting the count of sheltered homeless people on the same night is essential to prevent double counting of the same individuals who may alternate between sleeping in a shelter and on the street on different nights.

Unlike service-based approaches, point-in-time surveys have the key advantage of potentially recording homeless people who do not use any services. However, this method also has its limitations. Point-in-time counts face criticism for failing to consider that many homeless people remain hidden from public view during late-night hours, which increases the likelihood of them being overlooked by the teams tasked with observing those visibly sleeping outside at night. Audit studies carried out in a number of US cities suggest that point-in-time counts miss between 30% to 70% of rough sleepers, primarily because they are not seen by the enumerators. These studies used 'decoys' (fake homeless people) to estimate the proportion of visible homeless people missed by volunteer teams (Edin 1992, Cousineau and Ward 1992, Devine and Wright 1992, Martin 1992, Stark 1992, Hopper et al. 2008). According to the authors, incomplete enumeration of visible street homelessness is mostly due to organizational problems, such as incomplete lists of 'quasi-shelters,' insufficient training of enumerators, violations of the census protocol, and volunteer teams feeling unsafe going out at night (Wright and Devine 1992, Koegel et al. 1996). In other studies, different approaches were used to estimate the number of 'hidden homeless' who retreat from public spaces at night into hard-to-find places. Hopper et al. (2008) carried out a survey of service users the days following the 2005 New York City's count of homeless people in order to estimate the number of unsheltered homeless who slept in places that would be missed by enumerators. They found that from 31% to 41% of service users were in locations considered not easily visible to counters, or not legally accessible to enumerators. In Los Angeles, a general population phone survey was implemented to estimate the number of unsheltered homeless people who were hidden from view during the point-in-time count (Agans et al. 2014). They estimated between 22% and 41% additional hidden homeless with respect to the total estimates from the point-in-time count.

Another limitation of this approach is its inability to capture the seasonal fluctuations in the size and characteristics of the homeless population, unless the count is conducted multiple times throughout the year. If interviews are used as screening device, this process can become quite time-consuming. Conducting counts exclusively during the winter, for instance, may not accurately represent the homeless population's dynamics in other seasons. Conversely, conducting counts in the summer presents its own challenges, as the streets are often crowded with non-homeless individuals, making it time-consuming to distinguish between homeless and non-homeless individuals through interviews.

Point-in-time counts are typically carried out in urban contexts, where the concentration of homeless people is higher. Counts may cover an entire city or geographical area, or they may target a representative sample of specific sub-areas. While covering the entire city provides a more accurate count than focusing on selected areas, it comes with significant costs and organizational challenges. The approach of covering the entire city area was followed, for example, by the authors in carrying out the count of homeless people in some major Italian cities between 2008 and 2018 (which will be further described in Chapter 6 of this book). In most cases, however, point-in-time counts rely on a sample of locations within a city or a predetermined geographical area. These areas may be chosen randomly or through selection procedures that target areas with a higher concentration of homeless individuals. The total figures regarding the homeless population are then extrapolated as an estimate from the data collected in these sampled locations.

The use of statistical methods to estimate the number of homeless people offers a clear advantage in constructing more cost-effective estimates, particularly when the sampling strategy takes into account the available information on locations where homeless people tend to concentrate (Rossi, 1991; Berk et al., 2008).

Adequate planning is essential for point-in-time counts to be successful, given the limited time frame to carry out the count and the high number of actors involved. Typically, to secure collaboration from local organizations and keep the costs under control, counts are participatory, engaging service providers, advocacy organizations, local experts, volunteers, former homeless individuals, and so on (Farrell and Reissing, 2004). However, this approach can generate problems, such as the lack of training and experience among volunteers, and potential conflicts between researchers and local homeless organizations due to different priorities and methods of work.

The point-in-time approach is widely used in the United States, where the US Department of Housing and Urban Development (HUD) mandates Continuums of Care (CoCs), the local planning bodies responsible for coordinating the full range of homeless services in a geographical area, to conduct annual counts of sheltered homeless persons and biennial counts of unsheltered ones. HUD sets standards for conducting the Point-in-Time (PIT) counts counts, requiring CoCs to employ approved methodologies (Dunton et al., 2014; HUD Exchange, 2024).

In Canada the point-in-time counts have been frequently employed to estimate the number of homeless people in major metropolitan areas such as Toronto, Calgary and Vancouver. Similarly, this approach has been used in various studies across European cities, a topic that will be explored in detail in Chapter 3. However, unlike in the US, there are no standardized guidelines or definitions for city counts in Europe and Canada, making it very difficult to compare results across different geographical areas. Counts are typically carried out by a variety of actors (NGOs, local authorities, research institutions) and results are often published in national languages.

In Chapter 3 we will present the results of an extensive data collection carried out by the authors to collate and harmonize available point-in-time counts of the homeless population in several European and non-European cities.

2.4 Imputations with non-standard sampling methods

Two alternative approaches have been used to estimate the size of the homeless population using non-standard sampling methods: respondent-driven snowball sampling and capture-recapture (CR). The search for alternative methods was driven by implementation issues and the high costs associated with the traditional service-based and point-in-time estimations, respectively. However, the use of these alternative methods remains contentious since both approaches require strong assumptions for valid estimates.

For instance, David and Snijders (2002) used a snowball sampling method to estimate the homeless population in Budapest. This method collects information on the target population by allowing the sampled units to provide information on other population members with whom they have contact. However, both the lack of information on inclusion probabilities in different waves of the snowball sample and the fact that the social networks of homeless people are typically spatially clustered and age stratified tend to produce inaccurate estimates (Berry, 2007).

The CR method was originally developed to estimate the size of an animal population (La Porte, 1994). Researchers use two or more independent observations of the same 'hidden' population to generate estimates of the overall population. In particular, the CR method uses the information on individuals observed in multiple samples and those observed in just one sample to estimate the number of people not observed in any of the samples. The size of the total population is then calculated as the sum of the population actually observed and an estimate of the unobserved population. The method is clearly attractive since repeated observations can be funded with a limited budget and the involvement of fewer people with respect to traditional counts. Most studies relying on the CR approach use multiple lists of service users (shelters, hospitals, etc.) from administrative records to estimate the total homeless population (Ficher et al. 1994, David and Snijders 2002). However, list-based studies have been criticized for using data that typically compromise the assumptions necessary for valid CR estimates (such as independency between samples, population closure, no 'lost tags,' and having a non-zero capture probability)[3]. For example, many of them assume that individuals identified as homeless remain homeless for long periods of time (such as a year), despite the fact that people may move in and out of homelessness quite frequently. Moreover, lists of service users are typically not independent since doctors are likely to refer their patients to specific services or hospitals.

2.5 Data from the general population census

Population censuses offer extensive population coverage and are in principle suited to study small populations. They are also conducted by professional and disinterested parties. However, traditional census methods, whether interview-based or reliant on population registers, largely fail in tracking homeless individuals due to their assumption that everyone lives in a standard residential setting and may be reached at

---

[3] For a detailed discussion of the necessary assumptions for valid CR estimates of the homeless population see Berry (2007).

a specific address for an interview. Consequently, homeless populations, particularly rough sleepers and those living in doubled-up arrangements, are often underrepresented. Moreover, the high costs associated with censuses lead to infrequent data collection, typically every ten years, and limited information about individuals.

Some countries worldwide have made specific attempts to cover the homeless population in conjunction with their general population censuses. Each country adopted one or more of the approaches outlined in the previous paragraphs, and no specific methodology was developed. The peculiarity of these counts is that data collections on homeless people are carried out within the broader framework of a population census, typically coordinated and funded by national statistical institutes.

In Europe, during the 2011 census, several countries made targeted efforts to enumerate the homeless population. Some of the countries with register-based census, such as Denmark, Finland, Sweden, and the Netherlands, conducted *ad hoc* surveys to estimate their homeless population. In countries like Germany, Hungary and Portugal, specific measures were taken to count homeless people staying in hostels, night shelters, and accommodations for homeless people. In Ireland, Poland, and Portugal census counts tried to include rough sleepers. In most EU countries, however, homeless people were simply not counted, despite EU recommendations (Baptista et al., 2012; Busch-Geertsema et al., 2014).

In the US, the census does count residents of homeless shelters. According to the US Census Bureau, the 2010 census includes individuals in emergency and transitional homeless shelters in one specific day of the year (Smith et al., 2012). The 2020 census made attempts to count also people receiving services from shelters, soup kitchens, and mobile food vans, as well as people living in certain previously identified outdoor locations and other places where people are known to sleep (United States Census Bureau, 2024). In Australia, enumerations of homeless people have been attempted in every census since 1996. As we have seen in Chapter 1, this investment was key in developing an operational definition of homelessness.

2.6 Longitudinal data on homelessness

Longitudinal data on homelessness attempt to follow the same person over time and typically focus on the mechanisms leading people into and out of homelessness. In this type of data collection, the focus is not on enumerating homeless people, but on understanding the factors that influence the probability of becoming homeless, the duration of homelessness, and the likelihood of transitioning to stable housing.

In other words, longitudinal data are important to address questions such as: can homelessness be predicted? What information or individual factors may predict it? What interventions are more effective in preventing homelessness? Which factors affect exits and returns to homelessness? What measures are more effective in leading people out of homelessness?

Despite the importance of such questions, longitudinal data on homeless people, particularly individual micro-data, are exceedingly rare. Collecting longitudinal data presents additional challenges compared to point-in-time estimates, as individuals must be tracked over time. However, the transient nature of homelessness and the absence of a permanent address make it difficult to follow individuals across various locations and over time. Thus, a fundamental methodological challenge for this type of data collection is sample attrition, which is the gradual loss of participants in subsequent survey waves or in administrative records. Moreover, sample attrition among homeless people is typically non-random, since most mobile and 'instable' individuals are also more difficult to track over time. People who remain engaged with a longitudinal project for an extended period often differ significantly from those who drop out of the project. Therefore, systematic tracking techniques must be developed to keep relatively high retention rates. Indeed, there is considerable variation in the reported retention rates of existing longitudinal studies (see Scutella, 2012 for a review).

Administrative data can be a source of longitudinal insights, although they only provide information on people while they use homeless services. For example, several US studies focus on homeless people entering the New York City shelter system, which allows for tracking exits and re-entries to homeless facilities using a unified database. Studies by Weitzmann (1990) and Shinn (1998), for instance, follow families in New York City receiving Aid to Families with Dependent Children (ADFC). One group of families was homeless at the time of selection into the study, while another group was not, thus representing one of the few research designs to include a comparison group. Additional longitudinal studies focusing on the NYC shelter system include Wong et al. (1997) and Caton et al. (2005). Additional US-based longitudinal studies using administrative data from service providers include Sosin et al. (1990), which examines homeless adults using services in Minneapolis, and Wong & Piliavin (2001), which focuses on homeless adults either residing in shelters or being served by agencies providing meals to people in poverty in Alameda County, North California.

Brakenhoff et al. (2015) implemented a somewhat different strategy, using a nationally representative sample of youth (NLSY-97) to investigate individual and family characteristics during adolescence (ages 12 to 18) that predict homelessness by age 25. Respondents were interviewed annually beginning in 1997, when they were between the ages of 12 and 18, and continuing into their late 20s and early 30s. However, the use of a national survey raises some problems. A standard national survey may overlook certain segments of the homeless population, such as individuals and families living on the streets or in homeless shelters.

Most survey-based longitudinal studies tend to focus on specific locations or particular demographic groups. They often employ administrative data from service providers as a sampling framework to select study participants, who are then tracked for follow-up interviews (Caton et al. 2005; Craig et al. 1996; O'Callaghan et al., 1996). Typically, respondents are followed for relatively short periods, rarely exceeding 18 months, and interviewed only twice. For instance, Craig et al. (1996) conducted a longitudinal study of young people in London who were in contact with social services, some of whom were homeless. The authors employed comprehensive tracking methods to interview participants twice over a 12-month period. Similarly, Caton et al. (2005) interviewed adults without children upon entry into the NYC shelter system and at 6-month intervals for 18 months.

One of the most comprehensive and noteworthy longitudinal data collections is the Australian survey 'Journey Home,' conducted from 2011 to 2014, which focused on individuals vulnerable to homelessness. This survey consisted of six waves of data collection, spaced six months apart. It followed 1,600 income support recipients across Australia. Interestingly, participants in this survey were chosen from among disadvantaged Australians receiving any form of income support who were either homeless or at risk of homelessness during the observed period. The Journey Home survey had national coverage, allowing for the examination of both macro factors and individual circumstances contributing to homelessness (Scutella et al., 2017).

Finally, in recent years, a novel longitudinal data collection method has emerged in the US known as the 'by-name list' approach. This innovative method was introduced by the organization Community Solutions as part of the Built for Zero (BFZ) methodology, aimed at eradicating homelessness (Grainger, 2022; Community Solutions, 2024a).

The 'by-name list' approach is a systematic strategy aimed at gaining a comprehensive understanding of homelessness within a community and effectively addressing it. It involves maintaining a database that is regularly updated to provide an up-to-date list of people currently experiencing homelessness within a specific area. The database captures essential person-specific information such as names, homelessness history, health, and housing needs (Community Solutions, 2024b). The frequent update of information should in principle facilitate the identification of tailored housing solutions by enhancing coordination among service providers.

Methodologically, by-name lists enable the tracking of both inflows (individuals newly experiencing homelessness or returning to it) and outflows (individuals exiting homelessness through housing placements or becoming inactive within the system). Clearly, this dynamic insight into population size, composition, and transitions is potentially very useful for allocating resources efficiently, evaluating intervention effectiveness, and making well-informed policy decisions (Community Solutions, 2018). However, the creation and maintenance of a by-name list necessitate intensive collaborative efforts among local authorities and homelessness service providers. They should agree to use a standardized assessment method for all affected individuals, regularly share information through a common system, and use the unified database for ongoing support coordination.

Despite its organizational complexity, this approach is gaining popularity in the US, where several local planning bodies coordinating homelessness services, also known as CoCs ('Continuums of Care'), are currently developing it (Grainger, 2022). Similar experimentations are also underway in Canada (Community Solutions, 2019; BFZ-C, 2024) and Australia (Tually and Goodwin-Smith, 2019).

3   The volume of the homeless population

Empirical research on the size of homeless populations has historically encountered significant challenges due to the lack of standardized and comparable data across countries. Existing studies have primarily concentrated on nations with well-established frameworks for consistently collecting data on homelessness, notably the United States, Australia, and some Northern European countries. For instance, comprehensive data collection efforts have been operational in the United States since 2007, led by the Department of Housing and Urban Development (HUD), which annually provides consolidated estimates of both sheltered and unsheltered homeless individuals.

Conversely, in Europe, the lack of official statistics on homelessness has resulted in a scarcity of quantitative data. National initiatives have often been irregular, lacking coordination across borders and consistent methodologies. Differences in counting methods and definitions further complicate cross-country comparisons, making available data on homelessness incomplete and difficult to compare over time and across different regions.

Despite these challenges, recent years have witnessed a marked improvement in data availability regarding homelessness, as an increasing number of European countries and cities have developed their own data collection systems. The launch of the *European Platform on Combatting Homelessness* by the European Commission in Lisbon in 2021 represents a significant step forward in addressing homelessness across the European Union, including issues related to data availability. With all Member States committing to ending homelessness by 2030, there is a strong emphasis on fostering effective cooperation within the European Commission and across national governments, and stakeholders. This cooperation strategy entails supporting efforts to enhance data collections on homelessness, allocating funding to address this issue, and promoting mutual learning among EU Member States. Additionally, *Eurocities*, a network encompassing over 200 European municipalities, has demonstrated its commitment to the Lisbon declaration by implementing various local initiatives aimed at improving the quality of data collections and promoting more informed policy-making at local levels.

Leveraging on this emerging trend, we have embarked on compiling a novel dataset integrating homelessness statistics from several European countries and cities. We have also incorporated data from four non-European countries: Australia, New Zealand, Canada, and the United States. In this chapter, we provide a comprehensive overview of the methodology employed to construct the International Homelessness Dataset (IHD, 2024) dataset, along with the underlying assumptions. Furthermore, using these newly assembled data, we provide evidence on the prevalence of homelessness across such countries.

3.1   A new cross-country dataset on the homeless population: the International Homelessness Dataset (IHD, 2024)

The first effort to collect standardized data on homelessness across Europe occurred in the mid-1990s through the initiative carried out by FEANTSA, the European Federation of National Organizations Working With the Homeless (Avramov, 2018; Edgar and Meert, 2006). Notably, the 2006 report "Fifth Review of Statistics on Homelessness in Europe" by Edgar and Meert (2006) stands as a significant contribution from this period. The authors utilized the European Typology of Homelessness and Housing Exclusion (ETHOS) framework, developed by FEANTSA in the 1990s, to examine and categorize the approaches taken by different European countries in collecting data on homelessness. Their efforts marked an early attempt to standardize homelessness data across Europe.

Subsequently, FEANTSA, along with Busch-Geertsema et al. (2014), released a follow-up publication delving into the available data on homelessness within European countries. This report involved experts from fifteen EU Member States who examined existing statistical information regarding homelessness in their respective nations. Furthermore, FEANTSA has continued to issue annual and country-specific reports, known as FEANTSA Country Fiches, offering comprehensive insights into the prevalence of homelessness and related policies across EU Member States in recent years. In the "8th Overview of Housing Exclusion in Europe 2023," a report by FEANTSA and Fondation Abbé Pierre, it is noted that, although local and national-level statistical studies have been developed in recent years, their coverage is currently insufficient for a complete mapping of the homeless population across Europe. Despite these limitations, the report attempts to catalogue available homelessness data at the country level, estimating that at least 895,000 people are homeless in Europe. However, this estimate is based on incomplete and 'patchy data,' primarily capturing the most visible forms of homelessness. The report explicitly acknowledges the challenges associated with collecting comprehensive data on this population.

To compile a comprehensive cross-country dataset on homelessness in Europe, we built upon this previous work. We integrated data provided by FEANTSA with several additional sources, including national and city-level statistical offices, research projects, administrative sources, non-governmental organizations (NGOs), and local agencies. Extensive work has been done, trying to reconcile estimates from diverse sources. Within our dataset, we document the methodologies employed for data collection and try to assess the reliability and comparability of the available figures to the fullest extent possible.

Our dataset also includes Australia, Canada and United States, three countries that conduct regular homeless counts. Australian data come from five national censuses (from 2001 to 2021) by the Australian Bureau of Statistics, which include a wide range of homeless groups. Canadian data were taken from "The National Shelter Study" carried out by Human Resources and Skills Development Canada. Data were collected through a software tool used in homeless shelters across Canada over several years from 2005 to 2018. The study thus provided estimates of the number of Canadians using emergency shelters, but did not consider rough sleepers. The dataset also includes the 2016 first coordinated PIT Count across Canadian provinces and territories. Data for the US come from the Annual Homeless Assessment Report (AHAR) published regularly by the U.S. Department of Housing and Urban Development since 2005 (HUD, 2024). They cover both sheltered homeless and rough sleepers. In addition, our dataset has been expanded to include recent data from New Zealand, where the Ministry of Housing and Urban Development (HUD) commissioned the University of Otago to estimate New Zealand's homeless population using 2018 Census data.

Our final dataset, the **International Homeless Dataset (IHD, 2024)** consists of **340 country-level observations, covering 36 countries, and 884 city-level observations for a total of 123 cities**. To the best of our knowledge, this is the most comprehensive attempt to create an internationally comparable dataset on the homeless population.

Nevertheless, this data collection effort does come with certain limitations. First, the countries and cities included in the dataset may not offer a representative sample at the European level, as inclusion was based solely on data availability. Second, ensuring comparability across different data collections poses significant challenges. As previously discussed, various countries and cities employ different methodologies to estimate homeless populations, as well as different definitions of the target population. Lastly, data collection methods often differ even within the same country or city.

To enhance comparability across countries and over time, we make an effort to transparently outline the similarities and differences between various data collections. More precisely, our assembled data adheres to the following rules. Firstly, we provide details for each data collection included in our dataset, such as how the data was collected, the length of the observation period, the years of the data collections, and the data sources. We categorize data collections into five categories: service-based administrative data, service-based estimation strategies, point-in-time (PIT) counts and surveys, imputation with non-standard sampling methods, and general population census, following the classification described in Chapter 2.

We also make sure to specify which groups of homeless people each data collection is focusing on. In order to do that, we use categories from the European Typology of Homelessness and Housing Exclusion by FEANTSA whenever we can. Lastly, when gathering aggregate estimates on homeless people, we differentiate between rough sleepers and sheltered homeless individuals. Specifically, our estimates are categorized as follows:

i) *rough sleepers*: all individuals living in outdoor areas not intended for human habitation, such as cars, parks, sidewalks, or abandoned buildings (following definition 1.1 of ETHOS, see **Table 1**);
ii) *sheltered homeless*: individuals living in emergency shelters, temporary accommodations and transitional supported accommodations (definitions 2 and 3 of ETHOS, see **Table 1**);
iii) *reported total*: the overall number of homeless people reported in original data collections that adopt a broader definition of homelessness. This category of estimates may encompass individuals temporary living with family and friends, women seeking refuge in accommodations for victims of domestic violence, individuals facing eviction risk, or those in penal institutions without housing available before release, among others. Within this last category, comparability between different countries or cities is notably more challenging than for the other two categories, as there is considerable variability in the target groups included in different data collections. In our datased, we assemble all available information on which groups are included within the *reported total* category. However, in many cases where a broad definition of homelessness is applied, target groups are often vaguely defined. Consequently, reconciling these target groups with ETHOS categories 4.1-12, especially when not clearly defined in the source documentation, has proven to be quite difficult. Therefore, we do not separate sub-groups within the *reported total* category.

Table 3 tracks the evolution and geographical spread of data collection on homelessness across Europe and a selection of non-European countries over time, both at the country and city levels. From a temporal perspective, there is a clear upward trend in data availability, with data collection initiatives starting in the late 1980s and increasing steadily into the early 21st century. Data collection efforts reached a peak during the five-year period leading up to 2015, an acceleration that can be attributed to a series of data collection efforts that were often aligned with national censuses conducted around 2011.

In Europe, the first nationwide data collections started in 1987 in Finland and in 1993 in Sweden. At the beginning of the 1990s, Finland stood as the only European country generating annual estimates of homeless people. In 1996, the Norwegian State Housing Bank commissioned the first nationwide survey of individuals using homeless services. Subsequent to this, other countries such as Austria, France, and Germany started providing service-based estimates of homeless populations in the late 1990s. The progression into the late 1990s marks the beginning of a more systematic approach. Since then, a growing number of European countries have initiated data collection efforts on homelessness. Presently, our dataset encompasses aggregated national estimates for 32 European countries.

This period also sees the initiation of city-level data, starting with Paris and extending to Oslo, Helsinki, Dublin, and Munich. Two decades later, the landscape has transformed significantly, with the number of European cities providing data expanding to 123, indicating a significant effort to track homelessness in urban contexts.

City sizes offer further insights, with the most significant data collection efforts concentrated in the largest cities— capital cities and those with populations exceeding one million inhabitants. In contrast to Europe's national-level data, the United States embarked on city-level data collections earlier, with notable studies like the one carried out in Chicago in 1987, which is also one of the first examples of Point-In-Time estimate of homeless people (Rossi, 1991). Moreover, data on homeless individuals residing in shelters in New York City have been available since the early 1980s, while in 1990 five US cities – Chicago, Los Angeles, New Orleans, New York and Phoenix – conducted the "Shelter-and-Street Nights" data collections in conjunction with the national census. This initiative, known as "S-Nights," involved implementing point-in-time counts of both sheltered and unsheltered homeless people.

Overall, it can be observed that endeavors to gather data on homelessness have evolved progressively over time, gradually expanding in scope and depth. Recent developments underscore a transition from earlier, sporadic initiatives to a more systematic approach, evident both in Europe and the United States.

However, there is still significant variation in the frequency of data collections across countries, as can be seen in **Table 17**, **Table 18** and **Table 19** in the Appendix. Some countries, like Finland, Norway, Estonia, Hungary, and the United States, conduct regular data collections either annually or at fixed intervals. In contrast, in some other contexts, we continue to rely on sporadic attempts to estimate homelessness. Additionally, changes in data collection methods over time, can complicate comparisons between different periods.

In this regard, **Table 4** provides further details on data collection methods used across the coutries in our dataset. In particular, the table reveals a high variability of methodologies and observation periods at both country and city levels, reflecting the absence of a common approach in the efforts to quantify homelessness.

Country-level data collections primarily rely on administrative data or estimates based on users of homeless services, with such methods accounting for the majority of data collections (62%) in our dataset. In contrast, point-in-time estimates, which provide a snapshot of homelessness at a specific moment, represent a smaller fraction of the methodologies employed (20%). At the city level, however, point-in-time estimates are the most frequent method (47%), suggesting a preference for instant captures of the homeless population at a specific moment.

Table 4 also shows variability in observation periods, even within similar estimation methods, highlighting the absence of standard procedures in data collection on homelessness. This lack of uniformity makes it difficult to make measurements that can be compared across different situations and times. The number of homeless people on a given night is not easily comparable, for example, with the number of people who have been homeless at least once in a year. Similarly, the few countries using a one-month observation period – such as the one used by the Italian National Institute of Statistics in 2011 and 2014 – face challenges in comparing their data with that of other countries.

At the city level, there is a tendency toward shorter observation periods, with a significant majority using a single day or night (63%). An additional 13% use a one-week observation period. This aligns with the point-in-time strategy often used in urban contexts and is likely driven by the need to plan the provision of emergency services at the local level. City-level data also tend to concentrate on individuals who are literally homeless, typically including rough sleepers and people in emergency accommodations, further reflecting the operational focus of these data collections.

Despite the challenges in data collection discussed in previous chapters, **Table 4** also shows a clear interest, particularly at the national level, in expanding the definition of homelessness. This reflects a desire to capture a more comprehensive picture of homelessness, going beyond those who are literally homeless. However, assessing the effectiveness of these broader definitions is difficult due to often unclear operational rules for data collection and issues with data comparability.

In countries like Finland, Denmark, and Norway, which have a longstanding his-

Table 3 **Homelessness data collections by year and geographical area, at country and city levels**

	Country-level data		City-level data	
	Countries	Data collections	Cities	Data collections
Years				
1987-1994	2	9	2	13
1995-1999	6	10	6	12
2000-2004	10	20	14	26
2005-2009	24	60	73	164
2010-2014	33	103	89	297
2015-2019	30	98	68	208
≥2020	24	40	78	164
Area				
Northern Europe	8	98	31	224
Western Europe	9	121	26	138
Central and Eastern Europe	9	52	24	105
Southern Europe	6	29	12	50
Extra Europe	4	40	30	367
City dimension				
< 250,000 people			40	240
250,000 - 1 million people			43	251
> 1 milion people			40	393
Capital cities			25	195
Total	36	340	123	884

3   The volume of the homeless population

tory of data collection on homelessness, there is a preference for shorter observation periods and broader definitions. These choices are likely influenced by a more systematic approach to homelessness policy, which includes the monitoring of trends over time.

Table 4   Homelessness data collection methods, at country and city levels

	Country-level data collections	City-level data collections
Method of data collection (%)[1]		
PIT	20%	47%
service-based admin	34%	29%
service-based estimate	28%	16%
census	9%	3%
na	9%	6%
Total	*100%*	*100%*
Observation period (%)[1]		
1 night/day	26%	63%
1 week	10%	13%
2 weeks	1%	1%
1-2 months	5%	5%
4-6 months	2%	1%
1 year	34%	6%
na	22%	11%
Total	*100%*	*100%*
Definition (%)[1]		
rough sleepers (ETHOS 1.1)	52%	89%
rough sleepers and sheltered (ETHOS 2.1-3)	69%	85%
broad definition[2]	40%	11%
broad definition (including people temporarily living with family/friends)[3]	10%	26%
na	13%	3%

Notes:
[1] Comparable data collections that are consistently repeated over time are counted only once.
[2] Broad definition of homelessness including not only rough sleepers and sheltered homeless, but also at least one additional group from ETHOS categories 4.1 - 12 (such as, for example, people in women's shelters, people due to be releaesd from penal or medical institutions, etc.), with the exception of people living temporarily with family or friends (ETHOS 8.1)
[3] All ETHOS categories 1.1 - 12, including category 8.1 (people living temporarily with family or friends).

Finally, the presence of missing information is a recurrent issue in the dataset, denoted by the "na" (not available) category in the Tables. This occurs when the methodologies and operational rules are not clearly documented in the sources consulted or by the institutions conducting the data collections. Such omissions hinder the understanding and interpretation of homelessness data, emphasizing the need for more transparency and standardization in data collection practices.

In conclusion, the information from **Table 3** and **Table 4** illustrates the substantial progression in data collection on homelessness over the last decades, characterized by both an expansion in scope and a diversification in methodology. There has been a clear shift from initial, sporadic data collection to more frequent and systematic efforts that span across continents and encompass a wide array of urban and national contexts. However, despite advancements, significant inconsistencies remain. The range of data collection methods, the variability in observation periods, and the adoption of different definitions of homelessness across countries and cities highlight a fragmented landscape lacking standardized practices. This not only challenges the comparability of data but also makes it more difficult to effectively inform policy. Clearly, there is a pressing need for harmonized data collection standards to ensure clarity, continuity, and comparability in future research and policy-making efforts related to homelessness.

3.2 Homelessness prevalence across countries

Table 5 and **Table 6** present a detailed picture of homelessness prevalence across various countries, segmented by the length of observation periods and capturing the most recent data available. The number of homeless people in each country is converted into a proportion per 10,000 inhabitants to facilitate comparison, and this is presented by distinct categories of rough sleepers and sheltered homeless, as well as their sum and the *reported total* category. Finally, estimates are broken down by length of observation period.

Most of the countries included in **Table 5** focus on data collection over short observation periods, typically a single day or night, or a week. In contrast, **Table 6** focuses on countries collecting data over longer periods, where data are more sparse and comparability of estimates is more problematic.

In the United States, the most recent survey conducted in 2022 by the Department of Housing and Urban Development found that 582,462 people were homeless on a single night, which translates to 17.5 people per 10,000 inhabitants. Of these, 40% were located in unsheltered locations. In Australia, a comparable point-in-time estimate for 2021 reported a homeless population of 122,490 individuals, with 24% being unsheltered, equating to approximately 12.4 people per 10,000 inhabitants (ABS, 2023). FEANTSA recently estimated that around 895,000 individuals were homeless in Europe in 2023, corresponding to 0.17% of the total population. This calculation was based on point-in-time counts across 13 Member States from 2017 to 2022, with the percentage then applied to the entire European population. Our data confirm that

3   The volume of the homeless population

Table 5   Size and prevalence of the homeless population by country, short observation periods and last available year

Country	Number of homeless people			Homelessness rate (per 10.000 people)				Share of rough sleepers (%)	Last available year
	Rough sleepers	Sheltered homeless	Rough sleepers and sheltered	Reported total	Rough sleepers	Sheltered homeless	Rough sleepers and sheltered	Reported total		

Panel A - Lengh of observation period: 1 day, 1 night, 1 week

Country	Rough sleepers	Sheltered homeless	Rough sleepers and sheltered	Reported total	Rough sleepers	Sheltered homeless	Rough sleepers and sheltered	Reported total	Share of rough sleepers (%)	Last available year
Belgium	216			7912	0.2			6.8		2022
Croatia		364		1000		0.9		2.4		2018
Czech Republic	11915	5957	17872	23825	11.2	5.6	16.8	22.3	67%	2019
Denmark	535	2984	3519	5789	0.9	5.0	6.0	9.8	6%	2022
Finland	492	630	1122	3686	0.9	1.1	2.0	6.6	2%	2022
France	9746	108290	118036	141500	1.5	16.6	18.0	21.6	18%	2012
Germany	32467	178145	210612	262645	3.9	21.3	25.1	31.3	15%	2022
Greece	374	1271	1645		0.3	1.2	1.5		2%	2018
Hungary	2104	5500	7604	17534	2.2	5.7	7.8	18.1	8%	2020
Ireland		8369								2023
Italy			17000				3.0			2000
Lithuania		2447		4957		8.2		16.6		2012
Luxembourg		240				4.1		36.8		2017
Netherlands				32000				18.3		2021
Norway	102	1101	1203	3325	0.2	2.0	2.2	6.2	2%	2020
Poland	9600	14500	24100		2.5	3.8	6.4		40%	2021

Table 5 Size and prevalence of the homeless population by country, short observation periods and last available year (continued)

Country	Number of homeless people			Homelessness rate (per 10.000 people)				Share of rough sleepers(%)	Last available year
	Rough sleepers	Sheltered homeless	Rough sleepers and sheltered	Reported total	Rough sleepers	Sheltered homeless	Rough sleepers and sheltered	Reported total		
Portugal	4873	4731	9604		4.7	4.5	9.2		9%	2021
Slovakia	5196	1863	7059	71076	9.5	3.4	13.0	130.6	13%	2021
Spain	4508	11498	16006	28552	0.9	2.4	3.4	6.0	3%	2022
Sweden	990	7757	8747	33300	1.0	7.7	8.7	33.1	9%	2017
United Kingdom	3069				0.5					2022
Australia	7636	24291	31927	122490	3.0	9.5	12.4	47.7	24%	2021
Canada	2880	14400	17280	35000	0.8	4.0	4.8	9.7	17%	2016
New Zealand	3624	7929	11553	102000	6.8	14.9	21.7	192.0	31%	2018
USA	233832	348630	582462		7.0	10.5	17.5		40%	2022
Mean Europe					2.7	5.8	8.8	24.4		
Mean Extra Europe					4.4	9.7	14.1	83.1		

Notes: For each country we only consider the last available year of data collection. The share of rough sleepers is computed over the total number of rough sleepers and sheltered homeless.

3 The volume of the homeless population

Table 6 Size and prevalence of the homeless population by country, longer observation periods and last available year

Country	Number of homeless people			Homelessness rate (per 10.000 people)				Share of rough sleepers(%)	Last available year
	Rough sleepers	Sheltered homeless	Rough sleepers and sheltered	Reported total	Rough sleepers	Sheltered homeless	Rough sleepers and sheltered	Reported total		

Panel B - Lengh of observation period: 2 weeks, 1 month, 2 months

Bosnia	313				0.9					2013
Italy	20746	29978	50724		3.4	5.0	8.4		41%	2014
Serbia	445				0.6					2011
Slovakia		9771				18.0				2016
Mean					*1.6*	*11.5*	*8.4*			

Panel C - Lengh of observation period: 5 months - 1 year

Austria				19900				22.3		2020
Czech Republic		10225		11311		9.7		10.7		2016
Estonia		1546				11.7				2017
Germany	45000			256000	5.4			30.8		2021
Ireland				2348				5.1		2013
Italy				96197				16.3		2021
Latvia		5644				30.0				2021
Lithuania		1681				5.9				2022
Luxembourg				864				14.8		2016
Malta	6				0.1					2018

Table 6 Size and prevalence of the homeless population by country, longer observation periods and last available year (continued)

Country	Number of homeless people				Homelessness rate (per 10.000 people)				Share of rough sleepers(%)	Last available year
	Rough sleepers	Sheltered homeless	Rough sleepers and sheltered	Reported total	Rough sleepers	Sheltered homeless	Rough sleepers and sheltered	Reported total		
Poland		16735				4.3				2012
Portugal	1443	1953	3396	9535	1.4	1.9	3.3	9.2	3%	2018
Romania		2976				1.5				2017
Slovenia		1047				5.0				2020
United Kingdom	17042	69246	86288	242432	2.6	10.4	12.9	36.3	20%	2019
Canada		123000				33.2				2018
Mean Europe					2.4	8.9	8.1	18.2		

Notes: For each country we only consider the last available year of data collection by length of observation period. The share of rough sleepers is computed over the total number of rough sleepers and sheltered homeless.

estimates are available for a subset of European countries and indicate significant diversity in homelessness prevalence across European countries. Consequently, **Table 5** offers statistics from recent data collections in different countries rather than providing total estimates for Europe.

On average, however, European countries for which we have information seem to have a lower rate of homelessness than non-European countries in the dataset. For instance, the United States stands out with a significant homelessness rate (17.5 homeless people per 10.000 inhabitants), and a considerable share of rough sleepers compared to the total homeless count (40%). Looking within Europe, the rates of homelessness present a varied picture, with France showing the highest prevalence (18 homeless people per 10.000 inhabitants), comparable to point-in-time figures observed in the United States and Australia when combining rough sleepers and sheltered homeless. France's rate is heavily influenced by a substantial number of sheltered homeless, whereas the proportion of rough sleepers aligns more with the European average. Notably, Slovakia, Czech Republic, the United States, and New Zealand report the highest numbers of rough sleepers per capita for short observation periods within this data set.

Despite significant differences among European countries in our dataset, existing research indicates that in Australia and the United States, the spatial variation in homelessness is substantially greater than in European countries. In Australia, 2016 census data found homelessness to be highly unevenly distributed, with the highest rates predominantly in geographically isolated areas in the central, northern, and western parts of Australia and in the downtown areas and their immediate vicinities of the larger capital cities. This was analyzed using Statistical Area Level 3 units (SA3), which showed a stark contrast: the areas with the highest homelessness rates had about 13 times more homeless persons per 10,000 inhabitants than those with the lowest rates (Batterham et al., 2022). In the United States, homelessness also shows significant geographic concentration, with more than half of the homeless population found in just five states, as reported in the 2022 Annual Homeless Assessment Report to Congress. California alone had 29% of homeless people in the country.

The percentage of rough sleepers relative to the total homeless population varies significantly among countries. Some countries exhibit a higher proportion of sheltered homeless individuals compared to rough sleepers, possibly reflecting differences in social services and accommodation facilities available. France and Finland serve as notable examples in this regard. Despite France having one of the highest rates of homelessness in Europe (18 people per 10,000 inhabitants in 2012), only 8% of homeless individuals in France are rough sleepers (equivalent to 1.5 people per 10,000 inhabitants). In contrast, Finland, with a homelessness rate of 2 people per 10,000 inhabitants in 2022, has a much higher proportion of rough sleepers, accounting for 44% of the total homeless population. Consequently, the composition of the homeless population varies significantly across countries. In Europe, some nations have a rough sleeper percentage below 10% of the total homeless population (such as Norway and France), while others have a percentage exceeding 50% (such as the Czech Republic, Portugal, and Slovakia).

In **Figure 1** and **Figure 2**, we illustrate the prevalence of rough sleepers and sheltered homeless individuals across European countries. To enhance comparability, the data is based on short observational periods (1 day, 1 night, or 1 week). **Figure 3** and **Figure 4** expand the geographic scope to include Australia, Canada, New Zealand, and the US. Darker shades represent a greater prevalence of homelessness relative to each country's total population. Interestingly, the countries with the highest numbers of rough sleepers may not necessarily coincide with those having the largest populations of sheltered homeless individuals. This disparity can be observed, for example, when comparing **Figure 1** and **Figure 2**.

It is important to stress that when interpreting estimates on homelessness, it is crucial to approach them with a degree of caution. Taking France as an example, the data presented in **Table 6** indicates that homelessness appears more prevalent in France compared to other European countries included in the dataset. While this could suggest that France is facing a particularly severe homelessness problem, alternative explanations exist. The higher reported numbers in France could reflect a greater effort to track the elusive homeless population or the country's wider availability of homeless services. Notably, the prominence of homelessness in France is largely due to the considerable number of individuals in accommodations for home-

Figure 1   **Rough sleepers across Europe**

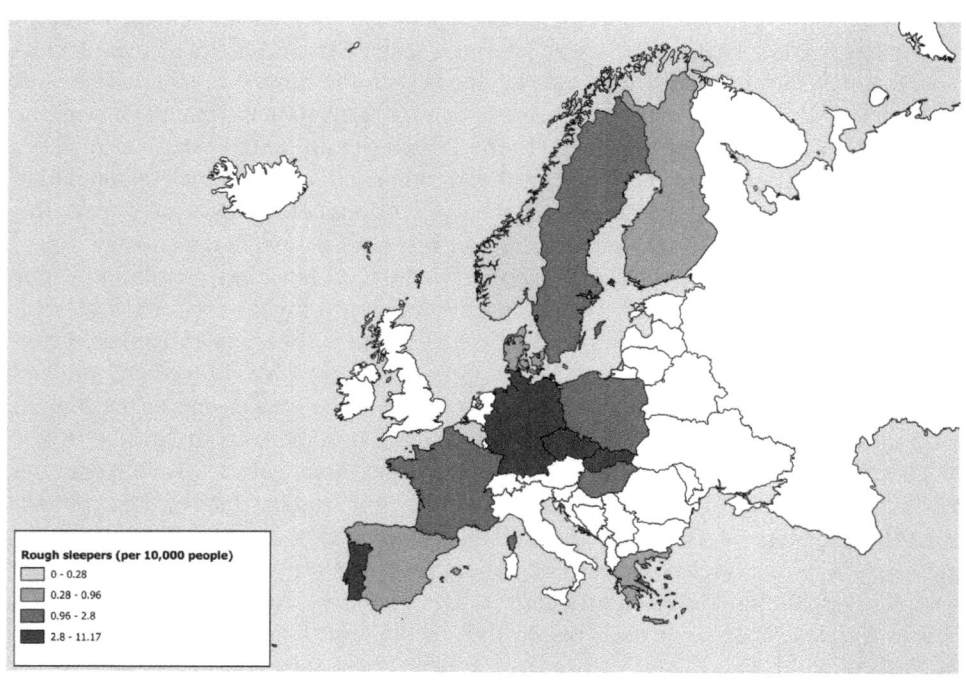

3 The volume of the homeless population

Figure 2 **Sheltered homeless across Europe**

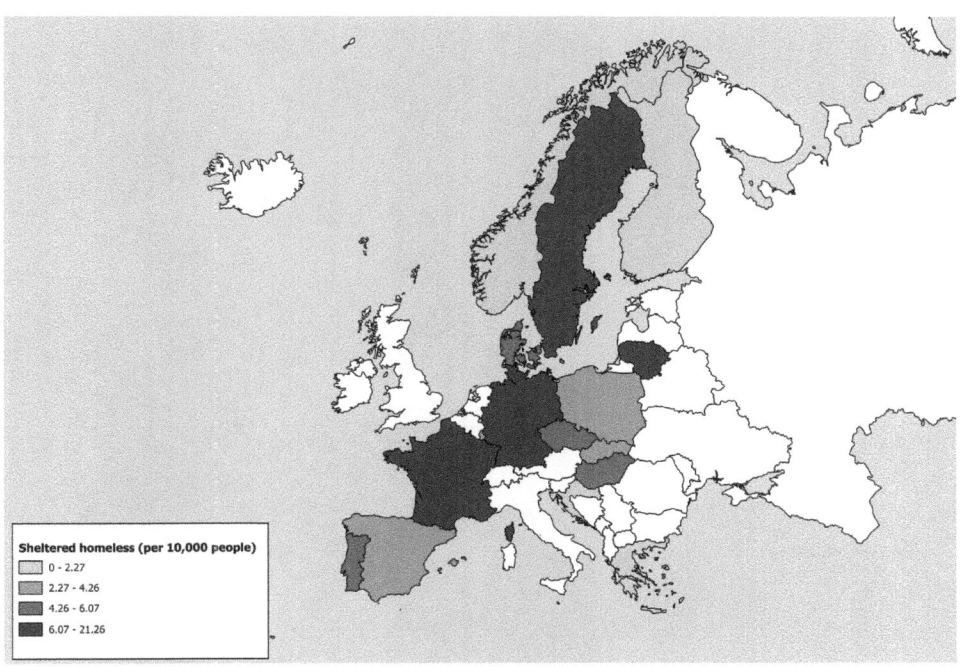

less people. The relative abundance of these services may render homelessness more visible by bringing into emergency shelters those who might otherwise be in less visible situations, like living temporarily with family or friends or those in severe cases of housing instability.

Despite the issues with data comparability, the figures provided in this chapter remain the best resources currently available for the countries in our dataset. They serve as the current benchmark for understanding the scale of homelessness, even as we acknowledge the constraints of this comparative analysis. It is hoped that ongoing efforts in data collection and methodology refinement will lead to more accurate and comparable estimates in the future.

3.3 Homelessness prevalence across cities

An important component of our homelessness dataset is the inclusion of city-level data. Through our data collection efforts, we acquired information on 123 cities (refer to **Table 3**). Specifically, the dataset includes information on 93 cities in Europe, 20 in the United States, 4 in Canada, and 6 in Australia. The majority of cities in our

Figure 3   **Rough sleepers across the world**

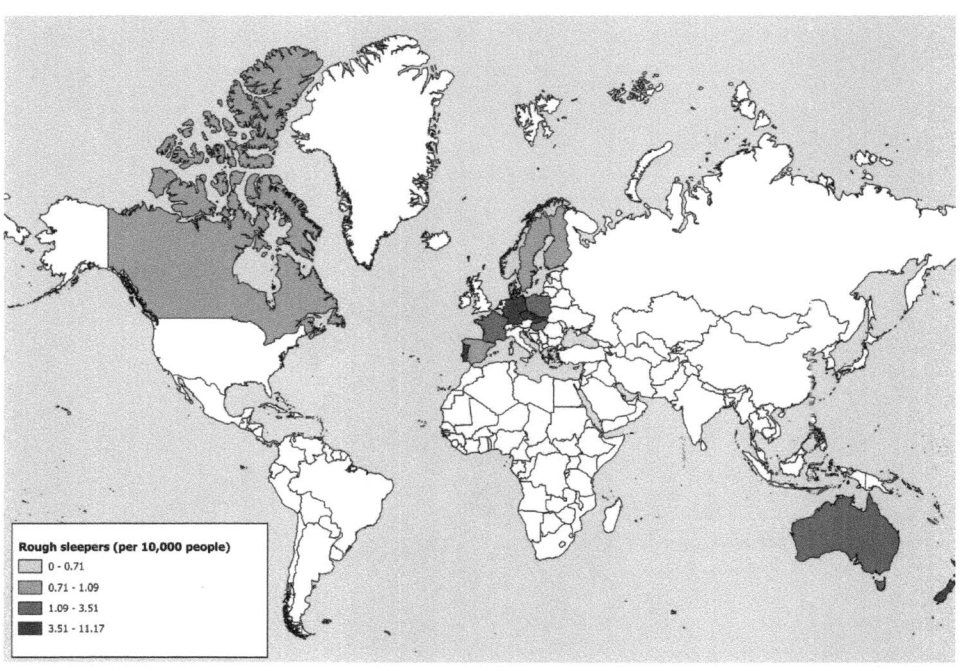

dataset are medium to large in size, with 33% having populations exceeding 1 million and 35% falling within the range of 250,000 to 1 million. Additionally, 25 of these cities are national capitals.

In **Table 7** and **Table 8**, we present the latest estimates of rough sleepers and sheltered homeless individuals at the city level, alongside calculating the prevalence of homelessness (per 10,000 inhabitants) based on the total population in each city. To ensure comparability across cities, our analysis focuses on data collected over a short observation period of one night, one day or one week, and includes cities where we have both counts and population statistics at the city level rather than at the county or metropolitan area level, resulting in 92 out of the 123 cities in our dataset being analyzed. Homelessness prevalence estimates are summarized in **Table 9,** with data delineated by city dimension and geographical area. Additionally, **Figure 5** and **Figure 6** depict homelessness prevalence across European cities, based on the PIT counts or estimates derived from short observation periods, while **Figure 7** provides a comparison between European cities and cities in the US, Canada, and Australia.

Across Europe, cities in Northern Europe tend to report both lower rates and lower proportions of rough sleepers, while those in Southern and Eastern Europe show higher proportions. Generally, European cities exhibit lower and less variable rates

3 The volume of the homeless population 39

Figure 4   **Sheltered homeless across the world**

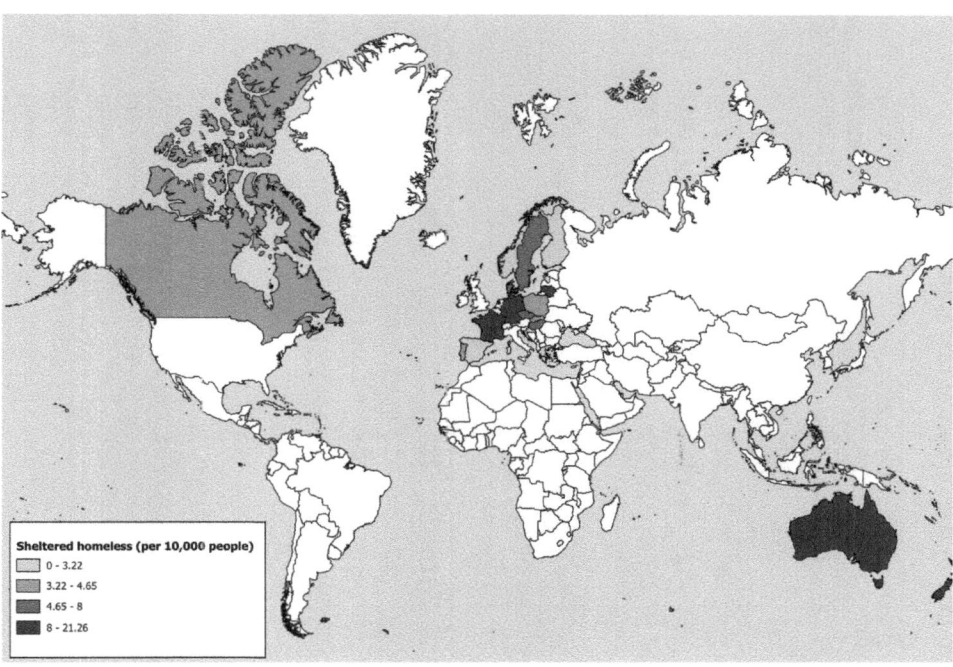

of homelessness compared to the US, where certain cities, notably Los Angeles and New York, have particularly high rates, especially among rough sleepers. Conversely, Canadian and Australian cities typically have lower rates of homelessness compared to their US counterparts, with Australia showing the lowest rates overall.

Table 9 also illustrates city-level homelessness rates by city size. Medium-sized and larger cities tend to have higher rates of homelessness compared to smaller cities with populations under 250,000. However, the proportion of rough sleepers to the total homeless population shows no significant variation with city size. This suggests that while overall homelessness rates are influenced by city size, the proportion of homeless individuals sleeping rough may be more influenced by local policies, such as access to accommodation facilities. This may also explain why homeless people tend to be concentrated in large urban areas, where they likely have access to various dedicated services like shelters, soup kitchens, drop-in and warming centers, which may not be as readily available elsewhere.

Finally, our data reveals that homelessness prevalence tends to be higher at the city level than at the country level. For instance, the average homelessness prevalence in European *cities* within our sample is 21.2 homeless individuals per 10,000 inhabitants (refer to **Table 9**), whereas the average homelessness prevalence across Europe-

Table 7   Size and prevalence of the homeless population at the city level in Europe, last available year

City	Nr. homeless people				Rate (per 10.000 people)				Share of rough sleepers (%)	Last available year	Method of data collection[1]
	Rough sleepers	Sheltered homeless	Rough sleepers and sheltered	Reported total	Rough sleepers	Sheltered homeless	Rough sleepers and sheltered	Reported total			
Aalborg	29	198	227	291	2.4	16.5	18.9	24.3	0.13	2022	SBA
Aarhus	61	233	294	507	2.1	8.2	10.3	17.8	0.21	2022	SBA
Amsterdam	70				0.9					2013	SBA
Barcellona	1147			4899	7.0			29.9		2022	PIT
Basel	80				4.6					2020	SBE
Bergen				402				14.1		2020	SBA
Berlin	807			1976	2.3			5.5		2020	PIT
Bern	603				5.8					2020	SBE
Bilbao	205	611	816		5.8	17.3	23.1		0.25	2010	PIT
Bordeaux	213	273	486	554	8.0	10.3	18.3	20.8	0.44	2023	PIT
Bratislava	615	681	1296	2064	14.5	16.0	30.5	48.6	0.47	2016	PIT
Brno	515	1173	1688	1950	13.7	31.1	44.8	51.7	0.31	2014	PIT
Budapest	737	2330	3067		4.2	13.3	17.5		0.24	2020	SBA
Copenhagen	155	846	1001	1370	2.4	13.1	15.5	21.3	0.15	2022	SBA
Cork				536				23.9		2023	SBA
Debrecen	193	228	421		9.5	11.2	20.6		0.46	2013	SBA
Dublin	118			5946	2.0			99.2		2023	SDA
Dunaújváros	0	74	74		0.0	15.5	15.5		0.00	2013	SBA
Espoo				373				12.2		2022	SBE
Frederiksberg	14	36	50	80	1.4	3.5	4.8	7.7	0.28	2022	SBA

3   The volume of the homeless population   41

Table 7   Size and prevalence of the homeless population at the city level in Europe, last available year (continued)

City	Nr. homeless people			Rate (per 10.000 people)			Share of rough sleepers (%)	Last available year	Method of data collection[1]
	Rough sleepers	Sheltered homeless	Rough sleepers and sheltered	Reported total	Rough sleepers	Sheltered homeless	Rough sleepers and sheltered	Reported total			

City	Rough sleepers	Sheltered homeless	Rough sleepers and sheltered	Reported total	Rough sleepers	Sheltered homeless	Rough sleepers and sheltered	Reported total	Share of rough sleepers (%)	Last available year	Method of data collection[1]
Geneva	1059				21.0					2020	SBE
Győr	92	306	398		7.1	23.8	30.9		0.23	2013	SBA
Göteborg				3221				54.0		2022	SBE
Hamburg	1920	4600	6520		10.1	24.3	34.5		0.29	2018	PIT
Helsinki				896				13.5		2022	SBE
Joensuu				43				5.6		2020	SBE
Jyväskylä				106				7.3		2022	SBE
Kecskemét	76	138	214	.	6.8	12.3	19.1		0.36	2013	SBA
Kuopio				125				10.2		2022	SBE
Lahti				92				7.7		2022	SBE
Lausanne	209				15.0					2020	SBE
Lisbon	465			3145	8.3			56.0		2019	PIT
London	858				1.0					2022	PIT
Lucerne	45				1.1					2021	SBE
Lugano	24				3.8					2020	SBE
Lyon	220				4.2					2022	PIT
Madrid	427				1.3					2020	PIT
Malmö				1782				49.9		2022	SBE
Marseille	455				5.2					2022	PIT
Milan	1001	1020	2021		7.4	7.5	14.9		0.50	2023	PIT

Table 7 Size and prevalence of the homeless population at the city level in Europe, last available year (continued)

City	Nr. homeless people			Rate (per 10.000 people)				Share of rough sleepers (%)	Last available year	Method of data collection[1]
	Rough sleepers	Sheltered homeless	Rough sleepers and sheltered	Reported total	Rough sleepers	Sheltered homeless	Rough sleepers and sheltered	Reported total			
Miskolc	212	387	599		13.1	23.9	37.0		0.35	2013	SBA
Montpellier	185	955	1140	2859	6.0	30.9	36.9	92.5	0.16	2022	PIT
Nagykanizsa	20	82	102		4.1	16.7	20.8		0.20	2013	SBA
Nice	195				5.6					2022	PIT
Nyíregyháza	69	164	233		5.8	13.9	19.7		0.30	2013	SBA
Odense	5	76	81	117	0.3	4.2	4.5	6.5	0.06	2022	SBA
Oslo				821				11.8		2020	SBA
Ostrava	442	448	890		14.9	15.1	29.9		0.50	2012	PIT
Oulu				123				5.8		2022	SBE
Paris	3015				14.4					2023	PIT
Plzen	119	53	172		7.0	3.1	10.1		0.69	2009	PIT
Porto	404			592	17.0			25.0		2019	PIT
Prague				3251				25.7		2019	PIT
Pécs	306	216	522		20.8	14.7	35.5		0.59	2013	SBA
Rome	1587	1747	3334		5.7	6.3	12.1		0.48	2014	PIT
Rotterdam	10				0.2					2013	SBA
Seville	253				3.6					2010	PIT
St. Gallen	41				0.8					2020	SBE
Stockholm				2379				24.4		2020	PIT
Szeged	113	130	243		6.98	8.03	15.01		0.47	2013	SBA

3 The volume of the homeless population

Table 7 Size and prevalence of the homeless population at the city level in Europe, last available year (continued)

City	Nr. homeless people			Rate (per 10.000 people)			Share of rough sleepers (%)	Last available year	Method of data collection[1]
	Rough sleepers	Sheltered homeless	Rough sleepers and sheltered	Reported total	Rough sleepers	Sheltered homeless	Rough sleepers and sheltered	Reported total			
Szolnok	74	60	134		10.05	8.14	18.19		0.55	2013	SBA
Szombathely	35	138	173		4.51	17.80	22.31		0.20	2013	SBA
Székesfehérvár	150	145	295		15.10	14.60	29.70		0.51	2013	SBA
Tampere				307				12.33		2022	SBE
Tatabánya	88	122	210		13.07	18.13	31.20		0.42	2013	SBA
The Hague	15				0.30					2013	SBA
Turin	288	477	765		3.24	5.36	8.50		0.38	2010	PIT
Turku				377				19.05		2022	SBE
Utrecht	2				0.06					2011	SBA
Valencia	352	402	754		4.46	5.09	9.55		0.47	2021	PIT
Vantaa				291				11.98		2022	SBE
Veszprém	100	139	239		16.32	22.68	39.00		0.42	2013	SBA
Zalaegerszeg	21	63	84		3.55	10.64	14.18		0.25	2013	SBA
Zaragoza	120				1.80					2018	PIT
Zurich	446				2.90					2021	SBE
Ústí nad Labem	11	53	64	92	1.17	5.62	6.79	9.76	0.17	2011	PIT
Mean					*6.47*	*13.79*	*21.18*	*25.81*	*0.34*		

Notes: We only include data collections with observation periods of 1 day, 1 night, or 1 week, focusing on cities where we have both counts and population statistics at the city level rather than the county or metropolitan area level.
[1] Method of data collection: PIT = Point-in-Time counts; SBA = service-based administrative data; SBE = service-based estimates; CEN = Census data

Table 8 Size and prevalence of the homeless population at the city level in the US, Canada, and Australia, last available year

City	Nr. homeless people			Rate (per 10.000 people)				Share of rough sleepers (%)	Last available year	Method of data collection[1]
	Rough sleepers	Sheltered homeless	Rough sleepers and sheltered	Reported total	Rough sleepers	Sheltered homeless	Rough sleepers and sheltered	Reported total			
USA											
Atlanta	738	1941	2679		14.8	38.9	53.7		27.55	2023	PIT
Boston	169	1599	1768	5202	2.6	24.6	27.2	79.9	9.56	2023	PIT
Chicago	990	5149	6139		3.7	19.3	23.0		16.13	2023	PIT
Los Angeles	28458	13522	41980		74.5	35.4	109.8		67.79	2022	PIT
Miami	970	2470	3440		21.6	54.9	76.5		28.20	2022	PIT
New York	3455	58385	61840		4.1	70.0	74.2		5.59	2022	PIT
Phoenix	994				6.3					2015	PIT
Portland	1438				22.8					2015	PIT
Seattle	3738	4428	8166		50.5	59.8	110.3		0.46	2020	PIT
Mean					*22.3*	*43.3*	*67.8*	*79.9*	*22.2*		
Canada											
Calgary		3112		2782		23.8		21.3		2022	PIT
Toronto	742	6605	7347		2.5	22.3	24.9		0.10	2021	PIT
Mean					*2.5*	*23.1*	*24.9*	*21.3*	*0.1*		

3   The volume of the homeless population

Table 8   Size and prevalence of the homeless population at the city level in the US, Canada, and Australia, last available year (continued)

City	Nr. homeless people				Rate (per 10.000 people)				Share of rough sleepers (%)	Last available year	Method of data collection[1]
	Rough sleepers	Sheltered homeless	Rough sleepers and sheltered	Reported total	Rough sleepers	Sheltered homeless	Rough sleepers and sheltered	Reported total			
Australia											
Adelaide	103	113	216	623	0.8	0.9	1.7	4.9	0.48	2011	PIT
Brisbane	67	304	371	1944	0.3	1.5	1.9	9.8	0.18	2011	PIT
Canberra	27	610	637	821	0.8	17.1	17.9	23.0	0.04	2011	PIT
Perth	188	168	356	909	1.0	0.9	1.9	5.0	0.53	2011	PIT
Mean					*0.7*	*5.1*	*5.8*	*10.7*	*0.3*		

Notes: We only include data collections with observation periods of 1 day, 1 night, or 1 week, focusing on cities where we have both counts and population statistics at the city level rather than the county or metropolitan area level.
[1] Method of data collection: PIT = poit-in-time estimate.

Table 9   City-level homelessness prevalence with short observation period

City characteristics	Number of cities	Homelessness rate (per 10.000 people)				Share of rough sleepers (%)
		Rough sleepers	Sheltered homeless	Rough sleepers and sheltered	Reported total	
City dimension						
<250K people	33	7.9	13.2	20.7	12.6	33%
250K - 1milion	37	8.1	23.2	34.2	40.6	30%
1 milion people	22	8.1	18.8	28.8	14.6	34%
Capital city	17	4.9	13.2	18.7	32.9	28%
Geographical area						
Europe	77	6.5	13.8	21.2	25.8	34%
Northern Europe	28	4.9	9.1	10.8	16.9	17%
Western Europe	15	4.3	21.8	29.9	48.4	30%
Eastern Europe	22	9.2	15.1	24.2	34.0	37%
Southern Europe	12	6.1	8.3	13.6	37.0	41%
USA	9	22.3	43.3	67.8	79.9	29%
Canada	2	2.5	23.1	24.9	21.3	10%
Australia	4	0.7	5.1	5.8	10.7	31%
		8.0	17.8	27.0	25.5	32%
Total nr. of cities	**92**	**73**	**47**	**46**	**38**	**46**

Notes: We only include data collections with observation periods of 1 day, 1 night, or 1 week, focusing on cities where we have both counts and population statistics at the city level rather than the county or metropolitan area level.

an *countries* in our dataset is 8.8 homeless individuals per 10,000 inhabitants (refer to **Table 5**). Moreover, in line with earlier observations, larger cities exhibit higher rates of homelessness compared to smaller ones. These findings reinforce the notion that homeless individuals are more concentrated in urban centers rather than in small towns or rural areas.

3   The volume of the homeless population

Figure 5   **Prevalence of rough sleepers across European cities (PIT counts)**

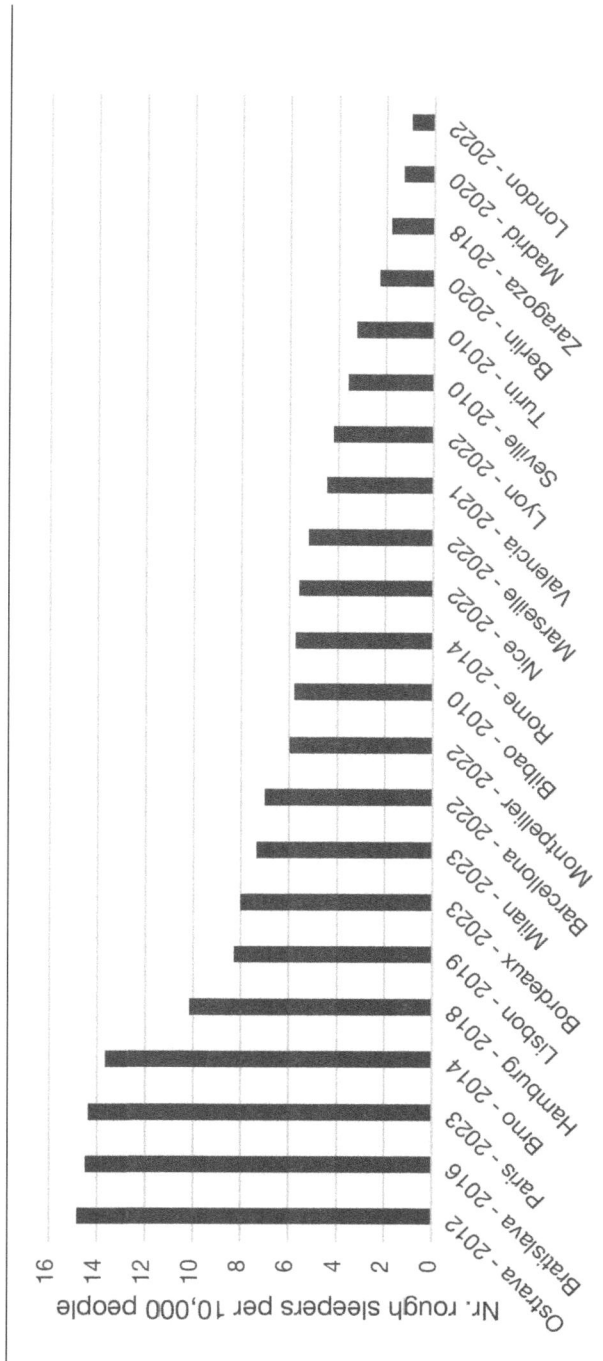

Notes: Homeless prevalence is computed as the proportion of homeless people per 10,000 inhabitants. We only include PIT counts, focusing on cities where we have both counts and population statistics at the city level rather than the metropolitan area level.

Figure 6   **Homelessness prevalence across European cities**

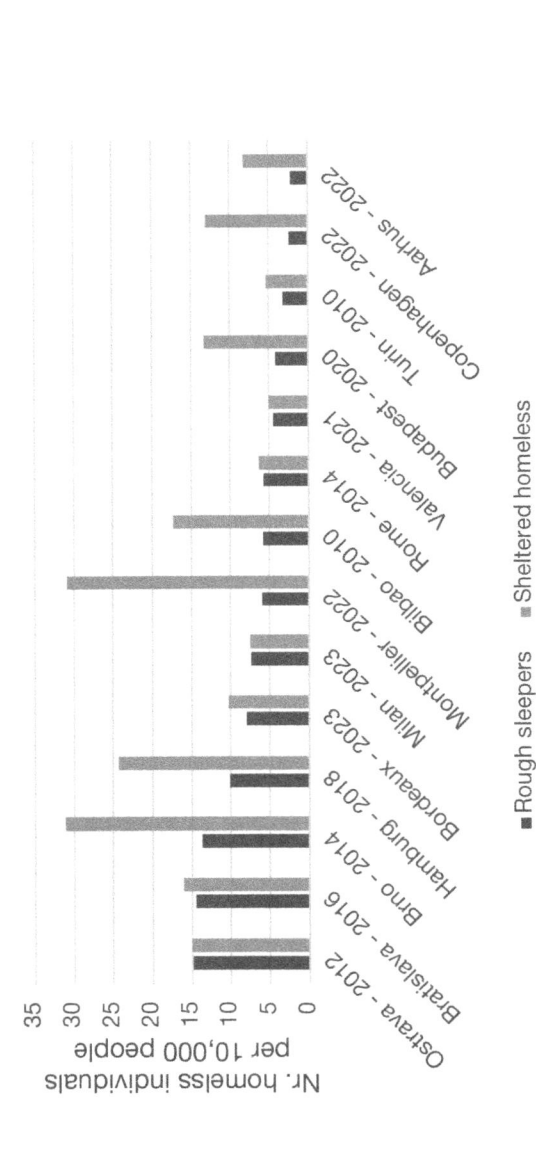

Notes: Homeless prevalence is computed as the proportion of homeless people per 10,000 inhabitants. We only include data collections with observation periods of 1 day, 1 night, or 1 week, focusing on cities where we have both counts and population statistics at the city level rather than metropolitan area level.

3   The volume of the homeless population

Figure 7   **Homelessness prevalence across cities in Europe, USA, Canada and Australia**

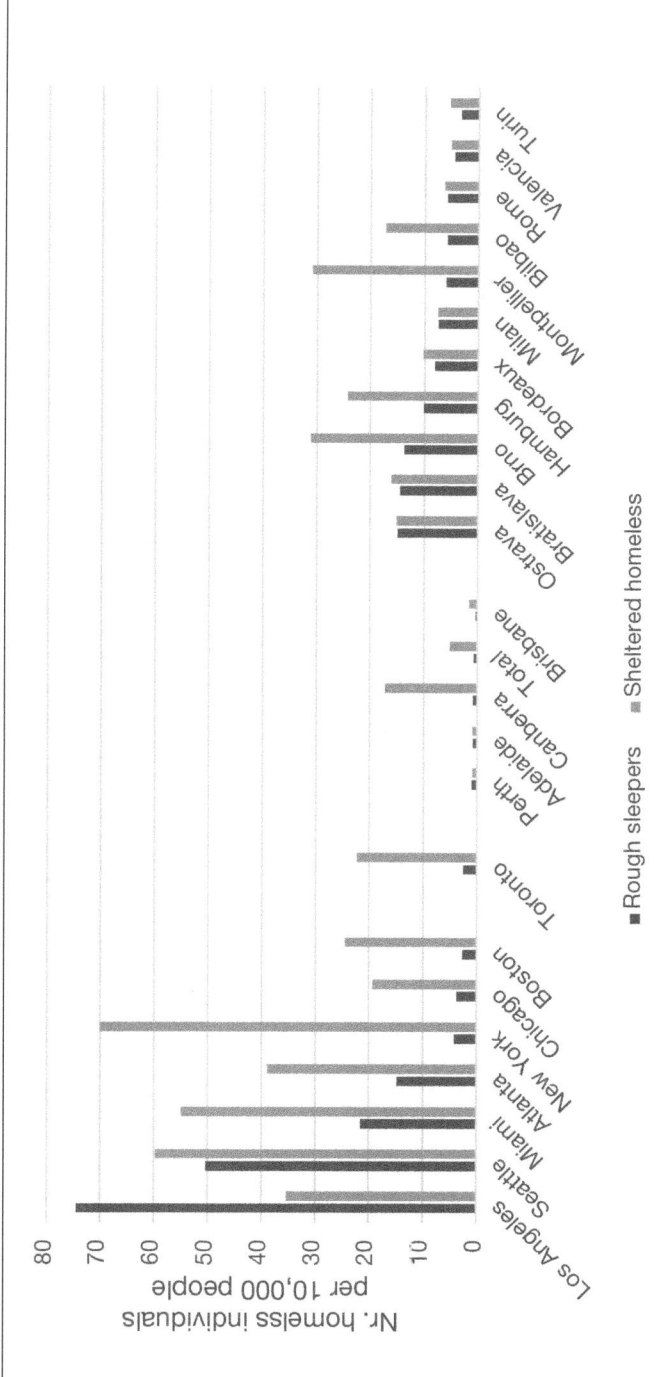

Notes: Homeless prevalence is computed as the proportion of homeless people per 10,000 inhabitants. We only include PIT counts, focusing on cities where we have both counts and population statistics at the city level rather than the county or metropolitan area level.

4 Over-time trends in homelessness across European countries

Gaining a comprehensive understanding of the evolution of the number of homeless in Europe over time is challenging due to the scarcity of sufficiently long time series data. Typically, the longest time series data come from northern European countries, where robust social welfare systems and extensive data collection efforts have historically been in place. In contrast, for much of the rest of Europe, comparable data collections are either recent or sporadic, stemming from a variety of factors including different methodologies, resource constraints, and varying levels of governmental prioritization. Consequently, in this chapter, we will not present overarching trends for Europe as a whole. Instead, we adopt a more nuanced approach, focusing our analysis on those European countries where relatively long time series data are accessible, based on the dataset meticulously compiled and described in the preceding chapters of the book. Focusing on regions with more comprehensive data coverage, we aim to provide a more accurate and insightful picture of the evolving dynamics of homelessness, taking into account all the differences and peculiarities across the continent. Furthermore, for comparison purposes, we include data from Australia and the US. Finally, in the last part of the chapter, we report the homelessness trends across cities in Europe, the US, and Canada, where comparable data collections are available over time. Local data allow us to shed light on the interplay between urbanization, socio-economic dynamics, and homelessness prevalence, providing valuable insights into the local factors driving homelessness and potentially suggesting interventions and policy initiatives.

4.1 Trends at the country level

4.1.1 European countries

This section offers an overview of over-time data on homelessness, focusing in particular on Finland, Norway, Denmark, Germany, and Hungary. For some of these countries, the data reveal a general downward trend in homelessness in recent years, which may be attributed to targeted national strategies.

In **Finland**, efforts to address homelessness have been comprehensive and systematic. The Housing Finance and Development Centre of Finland (ARA) conducts an annual survey on housing exclusion since 1987. The survey adopts a very inclusive definition of homelessness since it considers people sleeping rough or in emergency accommodation and hostels, but also people living in institutions, such as supported housing units, rehabilitation units and hospitals, or those living with relatives or friends. In addition, information is collected from various sources including social services, landlords, and housing application management bodies. According to the most recent data, 71% of Finnish cities and municipalities participated in the survey in 2022 (ARA, 2023). One of the main advantages of the Finnish approach is that it allows to cover the full range of living situations listed by the ETHOS typology.

Initial estimates in 1987 revealed over 17,110 homeless individuals in Finland, marking 34.7 homeless per 10,000 inhabitants. However, over the ensuing 35 years, this overall figure has drastically decreased. In 2022, Finland recorded a substantially lower count of only 3,686 homeless individuals, corresponding to 6.6 homeless per 10,000 inhabitants. Among them, 492 were rough sleepers, while 630 stayed in homeless shelters. This translates to 0.9 rough sleepers and 1.1 sheltered homeless per 10,000 inhabitants, respectively.

Homelessness estimates from 1987 to 2022 are displayed in **Figure 8** illustrating three distinct categories: "Reported Total" in the top graph, and rough sleepers and sheltered homeless in the bottom graph. Despite some fluctuations, there is a clear downward trend in all categories over time, with the most substantial decline observed in sheltered situations. Following a reduction in the 1990s, the rough sleeper category has remained relatively small and stable throughout the years, with a slight increase in the most recent data. Following a surge in rough sleepers in the aftermath of the Covid-19 crisis, there has been a recent decrease in homelessness, with the share of street homeless returning to its previous pattern. Instead, no significant changes in the trends emerge when considering the years following the great global recession.

Finland's success can be attributed to its integrated national strategy, which combines financial assistance, targeted support services, and the development of rental accommodation. In particular, Finland support services prioritize the Housing First approach, which focuses on providing permanent housing to the homeless as a primary solution before other interventions. Additionally, Finland has invested significantly in housing specifically for homeless individuals, converting existing shelters into residential units and constructing new apartments. Indeed, the last big emergency shelter in Helsinki was closed in 2012 and converted in supported housing units (Busch-Geertsema, 2010; Feantsa, 2023).

The global economic crisis did not affect Finland as severely as some other countries, although GDP declined, unemployment rose, and government budget deficit increased (Anderson et al., 2015). In response, Finland promptly implemented fiscal stimulus packages and structural reforms to stimulate economic growth and mitigate the impact on the population. As a result, also homelessness incidence did not increase.

Instead, the economic impact of the Covid-19 crisis in Finland, as elsewhere, was significant. In response to the pandemic, the country adapted its strategies to safeguard vulnerable populations: the government implemented emergency measures to

4 Over-time trends in homelessness across European countries   53

Figure 8   **Over-time trends in homelessness in Finland**

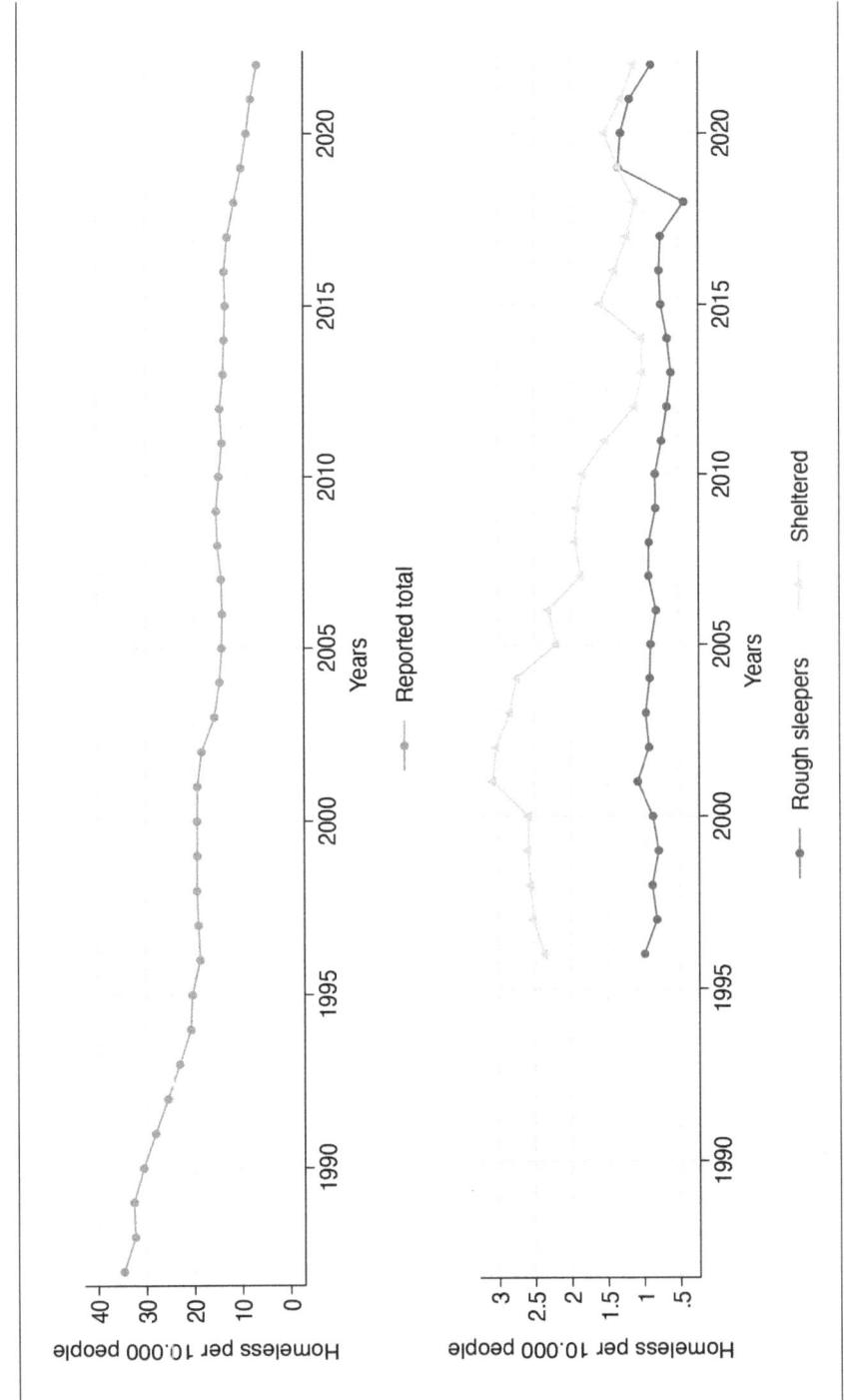

Note: Service-based estimates, 1 day

provide temporary accommodation, healthcare access, and social support to homeless individuals. As a result, the Finland's support system for homeless individuals demonstrated resilience during the 2020 and 2021 social and health crisis, which may be also attributed to the high number of vulnerable individuals already housed and supported in self-contained units (O'Sullivan, E. (2022). However, it is important to highlight that the country's approach during the pandemic extended well beyond providing immediate relief to people. On one hand, according to the IMF Fiscal Monitor Database of Country Fiscal Measures in Response to the Covid-19 Pandemic, the country invested resources in emergency intervention, such as increasing sanitation in food services and shelter for the homeless (IMF, 2021). On the other hand, in a more holistic approach, the government focused on addressing the underlying causes of homelessness exacerbated by the crisis, in particular unemployment, housing, and mental health problems. For example, the government invested (about US$ 250.9 million) in a housing scheme for the homeless. In addition, local communities and NGOs designed and implemented targeted interventions to alleviate pandemic-related economic hardships, also thanks to public resources allocated by the Ministry of Social Affairs and Health to projects for the development of new health and social services that would reduce homelessness[1].

Overall, the country's success in tackling homelessness seems to be related to its strong social system, where social welfare policies are comprehensive, healthcare coverage is universal, and housing is considered a fundamental right.

Norway is another country for which information is available both over time and across different categories of homeless people. Although at irregular intervals, seven nationwide surveys among homeless people were carried out between 1996 and 2020. Data on the homeless population was collected through individual questionnaires, completed by various service providers who interact with homeless individuals, over a one-week reference period. The primary respondents were municipal social services, often supplemented by additional services in larger urban areas. Other respondents include departments within healthcare facilities, correctional institutions, non-governmental organizations (NGOs), and private agencies that offer support services to homeless individuals.

Homelessness estimates from the different data collections are shown in **Figure 9**. Until 2008, there is a general trend of a slight increase in the total number of homeless people. Additionally, the number of sheltered individuals increases, while the number of rough sleepers remains relatively stable. After 2012, the total number of homeless individuals, as well as the subcategories, begins to decrease. By 2020, there is a notable reduction in both the total homeless population and the number of sheltered and rough sleepers compared to previous years. There were 14 homeless people per 10.000 inhabitants in 1995, whereas in 2020 this number decreased to only 6 per 10.000 inhabitants.

---

[1] More information can be found on the Ministry of Social Affairs and Health website https://stm.fi/en/reducing-homelessness-with-better-targeted-health-and-social-services

4 Over-time trends in homelessness across European countries

Figure 9   **Over time trends in homelessness in Norway**

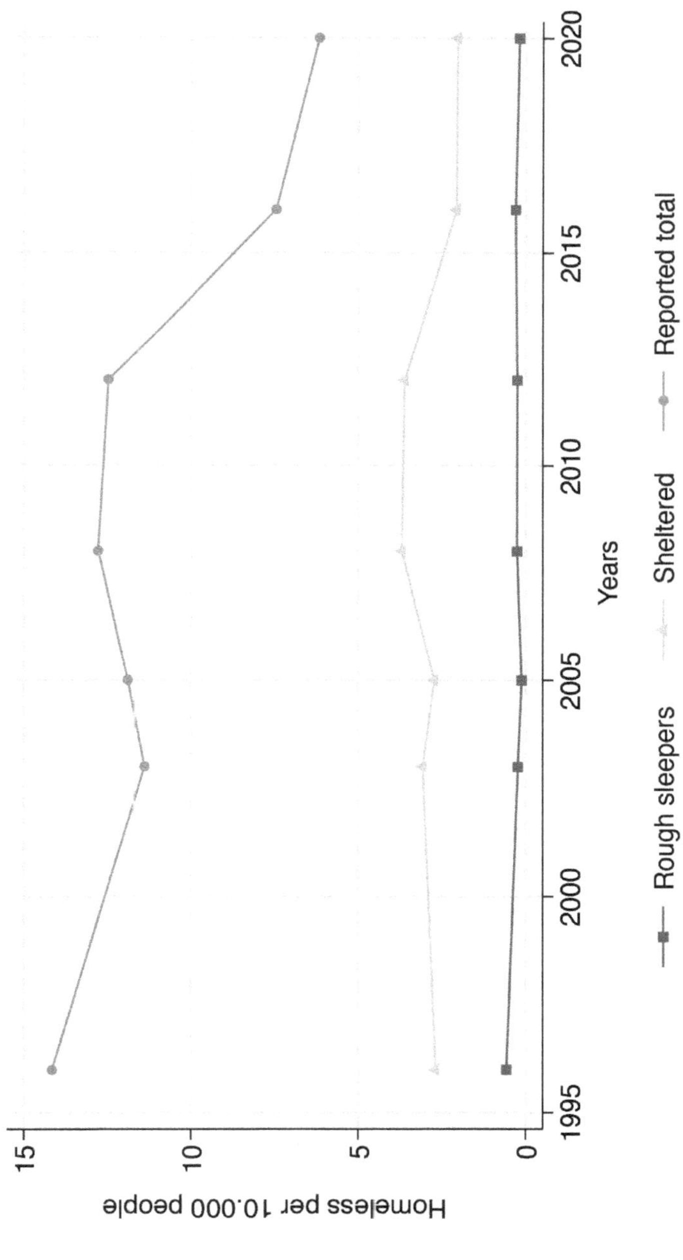

Note: Service-based administrative data, 1 week

Based on Eurostat data, the impact of the 2008-2009 economic crisis was lower in Norway than in many other European countries. Thanks to the strong economic fundamentals and some key economic sectors, such as oil and gas, the slowdown in economic growth was only temporary and the economy recovered relatively quickly. To some extent the level of unemployment increased but, thanks to the flexible labour market, it remained relatively low. The strength of public finances, in terms of low debt and budget deficits, allows the government to provide generous wage subsidies to support businesses and workers. Although the share of street homeless did not increase significantly, data show a rise in the number of sheltered homeless around 2008, when figures peaked. As with the economic indicators, the country quickly returned to pre-crisis levels along the downward trend.

The reduction over time may indicate effective homelessness policies and social programs in Norway. Since 2010, several national strategies have been launched to address homelessness with a focus on prevention and provision of stable housing solutions. According to Dyb (2017), a housing-led approach and significant investment in affordable housing has contributed to Norway's success in reducing homelessness in recent years. Like the Housing First Program (see Chapter 7), also the housing-led approach prioritizes the provision of stable housing. The difference is somewhat subtle since the priority of Housing First is to provide permanent housing without preconditions and to ensure tailored support services, while the housing-led approach offers a broader range of housing solutions and strategies.

As in Finland, Norway welfare state is based on strong social welfare policies combined with universal healthcare and plays a central role in supporting people experiencing homelessness. In addition, government agencies, community organizations and NGOs work closely together on an ongoing basis to implement interventions and ensure a comprehensive support for vulnerable populations. Also in this case, the key to success seems to be a comprehensive approach combined with a strong commitment to housing as a fundamental right for everyone.

In Denmark, the Danish Centre for Social Science Research (VIVE) has been collecting data on homelessness every two years since 2007. The only exception is 2021, when data collection was postponed to 2022 due to the Covid-19 pandemic. The data collection method mirrors the one used in Norway, involving the completion of a questionnaire for each homeless individual encountered or known to service providers during a specific week. Participating service providers include both public welfare services and civil society organizations, such as shelters, street outreach teams, or other social and health services that may be in contact with homeless individuals. Specific measures are taken to avoid double counting of service users.

The trends over time are depicted in **Figure 10**. The graph shows some fluctuations in the total reported homelessness over the years. There is a clear upward trend in both the reported total and the sheltered homeless from 2007 to 2017, and then a general trend reversal. Instead, the share of street homeless remained fairly stable until 2019, when it started to decrease. According to the latest data collection, nearly 5,800 individuals were homeless in Denmark in 2022 (corresponding to 15 people

4 Over-time trends in homelessness across European countries

Figure 10 **Over time trends in homelessness in Denmark**

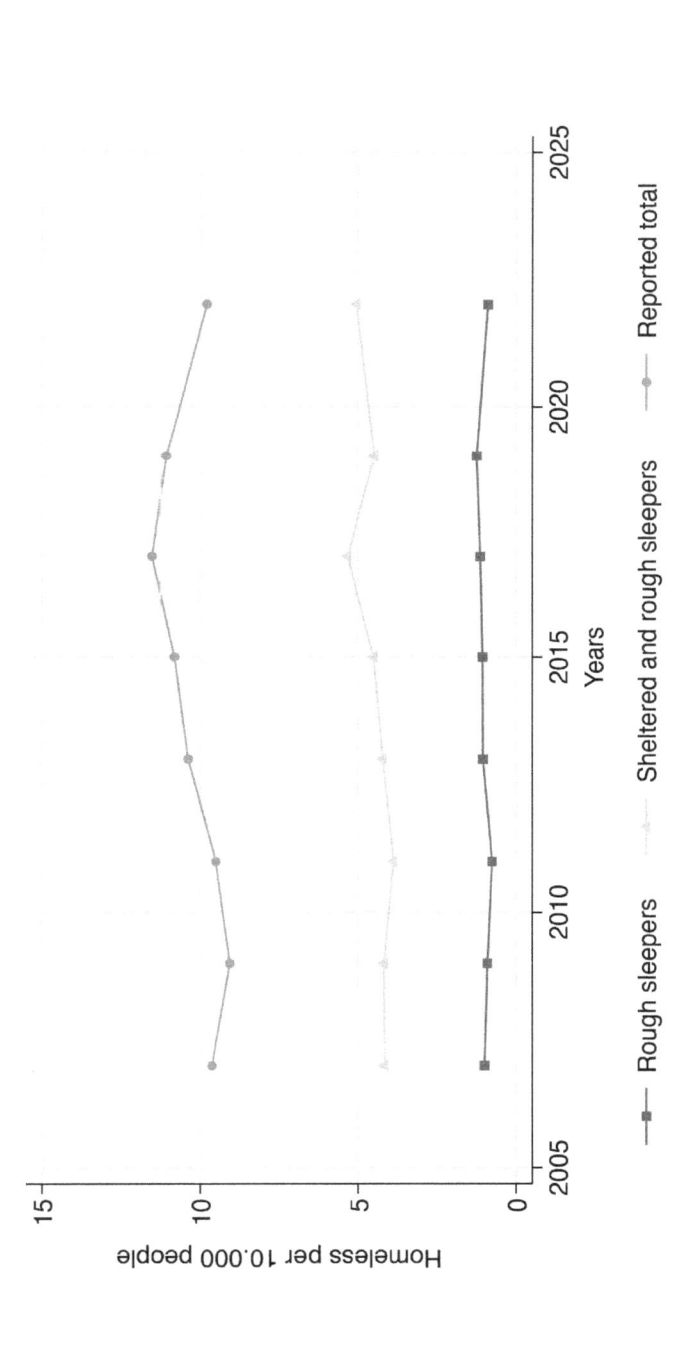

Note: Service-based administrative data, 1 week

per 10.000 inhabitants), marking a 10 percent decrease since 2019. Notably, there has also been a decline in the number of rough sleepers, from 732 to 535 individuals (from 1,3 to 0,9 people per 10.000 inhabitants).

Benjaminsen (2022) suggests that the observed reduction in homelessness may be tied to the interventions aimed at addressing the issue. Indeed, in recent years, there has been a deliberate emphasis on improving access to housing and support services, notably through the implementation of the Housing First approach. The country has also invested significant resources in expanding access to support services for homeless people, addressing mental health problems, drug and alcohol addiction, and barriers to employment. Another key element is the significant effort to improve coordination between public welfare services and private organizations to provide integrated support to people.

Preventive policies are also crucial in addressing the root economic causes of homelessness, such as unemployment, housing affordability, and poverty (O'Sullivan, 2022). Considering the labor market, Denmark provides income support to low-income individuals and families, invests in employment services and vocational training programs to help individuals to find secure employment and increase their financial independence. Furthermore, interventions in the housing sphere are significant and include subsidies for affordable housing construction, rent control measures, and incentives for private individuals to develop affordable units. Other programs provide financial assistance, mediation services and temporary housing solutions in case of eviction. All measures are aimed at reducing the risk of homelessness. Finally, in Denmark, outreach teams and social workers engage constantly and promptly with individuals and family at risk of homelessness. Their objective is to provide support and adequate resources in critical situations before they escalate into homelessness. These early intervention efforts address challenges and provide assistance well in advance, attempting to target individuals at *risk* of homelessness (OECD, Tax – benefit database, 2022).

On top of that, the country's decision-making process is primarily data-driven. Biennal surveys provide policymakers with insights into trends and patterns, allowing them to identify areas for intervention, and allocate resources effectively.

Overall, the country adopts a proactive approach and provides comprehensive support services.

In **Germany**, the Federal Statistical Office introduced a nationwide data collection system on homelessness in 2022, to be implemented every year on January 31. The data collection also involves biannual surveys in representative municipalities to gain an understanding of other forms of housing exclusion, one week after the main data collection (Feantsa, 2023). However, before 2022, there were no official statistics on homelessness at the federal level. National estimates have been released annually since 1999 by the National Federation for the Homeless in Germany (Bundesarbeitsgemeinschaft Wohnungslosenhilfe BAG W), the umbrella organization of non-profit service providers for homeless people. Aggregate figures were computed over a one-year period and included a variety of living situations. Separate estimates were only available for rough sleepers, as shown in **Figure 11**. Unfortunately, details on the

Figure 11   **Over time trends in homelessness in Germany**

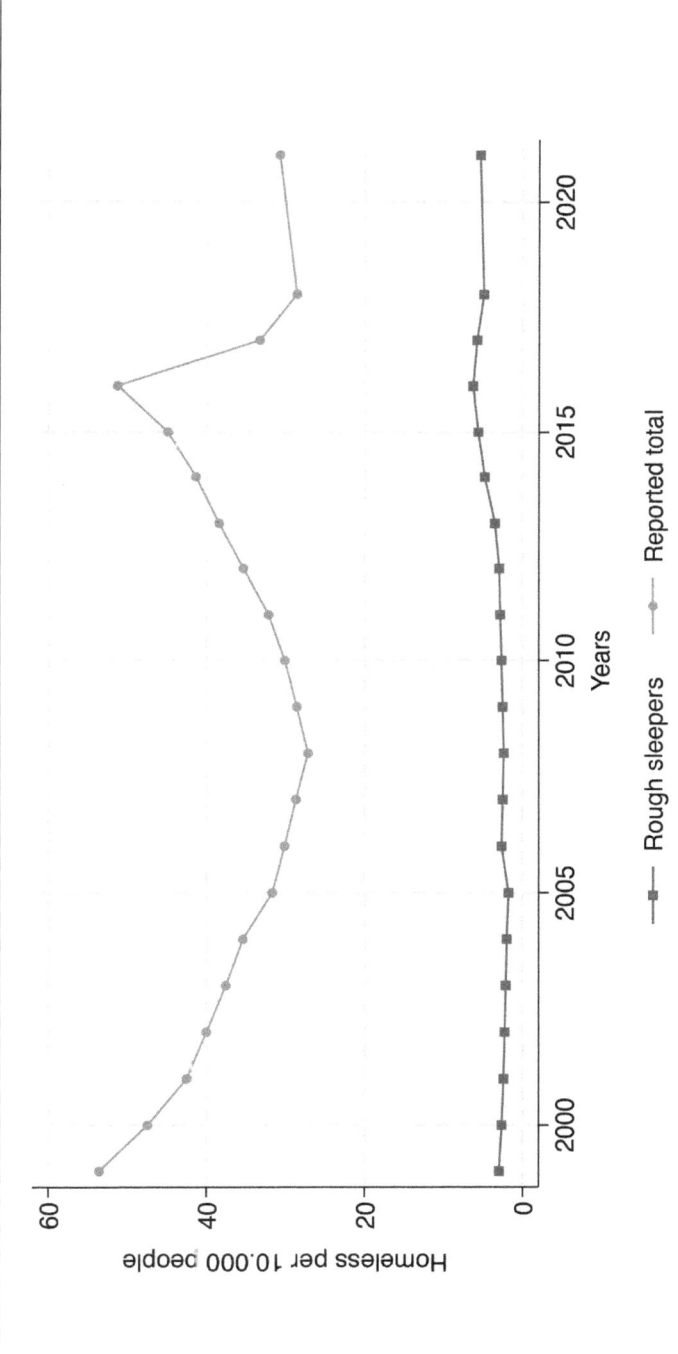

Note: Service-based estimates, 1 year

estimation method are not easily available². According to BAG W estimates, from the year 1999 to approximately 2010, there was a gradual decrease in the total number of homeless individuals. However, after 2010, a marked increase is observed, peaking around 2015 before starting to decline again. By 2020, there was a notable decrease in both the total number of homeless people and the number of rough sleepers compared to the peak around 2015. Unlike the previously discussed countries, where the number of rough sleepers was more or less stable, in Germany their incidence decreased slightly until 2005, when it started to increase, peaking in 2016, and then remained almost constant with a small decrease before the pandemic. By 2022, the numbers were rising again.

The upward trend seems to follow the evolution of the economic crisis in the euro area in the last decade. Germany experienced a significant slowdown in economic growth: GDP growth rate declined and the contraction in the economic activity was more pronounced in export-oriented industries. The unemployment rate increased, and job losses were significant, especially among low-skilled workers and young people in the early stages of their careers. The banking sector faced challenges and some banks required public intervention and bailout measures. The unavoidable credit crunch produced negative effects, especially on liquidity-constrained individuals. Different policies were implemented to mitigate the impact: expansionary fiscal policies, subsidies to industries, and investment in active labor market policies, such as short-time work programs. Despite the safety net provided by the social welfare system, both inequality and poverty rates increased. All these elements may have contributed to the rise in homelessness.

Germany has faced other significant challenges in the last decade. According to Eurostat data,³ housing costs in the main cities have skyrocketed, making it increasingly difficult for low-income individuals and families to find affordable solutions and exacerbating housing instability. Another critical aspect is the influx of migrants and refugees, which put pressure on the housing market, especially in urban areas where the demand was already high (Unal and Erol, 2024). Finally, as in many other developed countrties, the increase in mental illness, substance abuse, and family breakdowns, may have influenced the risk of homelessness among youth and the elderly (Busch-Geertsema, 2023).

Data collection and monitoring have been recognized as the first pillars to face the increase of the phenomenon. In this vein, the introduction of a nationwide data collection system is aimed at better understanding the nature of homelessness and the trajectories followed by individuals. Regular and comparable data are essential to inform policy decisions and to allocate resources in a rational way. In addition,

---

² BAG W publishes homeless statistics on a regular basis since 1999. Estimation methods, however, are not entirely clear. According to available sources, "annual nationwide estimations are based on its own monitoring system, taking into account developments in the housing market, labour market, migration, social security, and drawing on regional statistics and BAG W flash surveys" (Feantsa, 2014).

³ Updated figures can be found in the most recent intercative publication "Housing in Europe" freely available at this link https://ec.europa.eu/eurostat/web/interactive-publications/housing-2023

thanks to its strong financial stability, the country was able to expand social welfare programs to provide support in terms of financial resources, healthcare assistance, housing, and essential support services to those subjects at risk of homelessness, such as low-income and less educated individuals, people with a history of addiction or criminal proceedings. Following the example of other countries, like Denmark, significant effort was made to integrate services and interventions, improving the coordination between public and private organizations.

Another interesting case is **Hungary**, which since 1999 has conducted an annual survey on homelessness on February 3. The survey was initially limited to Budapest and then has gradually expanded to include more municipalities. The survey is organized by homeless service providers and includes both service users and rough sleepers. Participation is voluntary for both service providers and users, leading to counts that are more of a lower bound than a comprehensive census. Originally, service staff read the survey questions to users, but the questionnaire has since become self-administered, with assistance available. Although coverage has improved over time, the survey still has limitations, such as potential misinterpretation of questions and incomplete coverage. Notably, data on survey coverage are not available. Nonetheless, it remains Hungary's most reliable source of homelessness data (Fruzsina et al., 2019). **Figure 12** presents available comparable data from 2008 to 2020. Based on these data, the trend in sheltered homeless has been increasing until 2015, followed by a decline. In 2008, homeless people accounted for 3 individuals per 10,000 inhabitants, more than doubling by 2015 to approximately 7 per 10,000 inhabitants. The trend for rough sleepers follows a similar pattern, but began to reverse two years later in 2017.

The Great Recession seems to have exacerbated homelessness. The impact of the crisis on the Hungarian economy was significant. The national currency depreciated by around 23% against major currencies, which worsened the debt burden for agents with loans in foreign currencies. The public debt increased by approximately 4% compared to pre-crisis level (EEAG; 2012). Additionally, the effects of the crisis were long lasting. More than ten years after the crisis, based on OECD data, the country experienced low growth rates, low fertility rates, increased income inequality, and heightened migration. These shifts have long-term implications for the labour force and social cohesion.

In recent years, Hungary's approach to tackling homelessness has evolved significantly. Non-governmental organizations play a crucial role in addressing homelessness, as in many other countries (Fruzsina et al., 2019). In some municipalities, such as Budapest, significant efforts have been made to improve standards of quality in shelters, reject stigma, reintegrate people into society, and enhance the provision of affordable housing by renovating vacant municipal apartments. In 2022, for example, Budapest adopted the "Home, for Everyone" strategy, whose aim is to promote a more inclusive and preventive approach.

Available data do not allow studying the effect of the pandemic on the incidence of the phenomenon. However, during the health emergency, the country implemented

Figure 12   **Over-time trends in homelessness in Hungary**

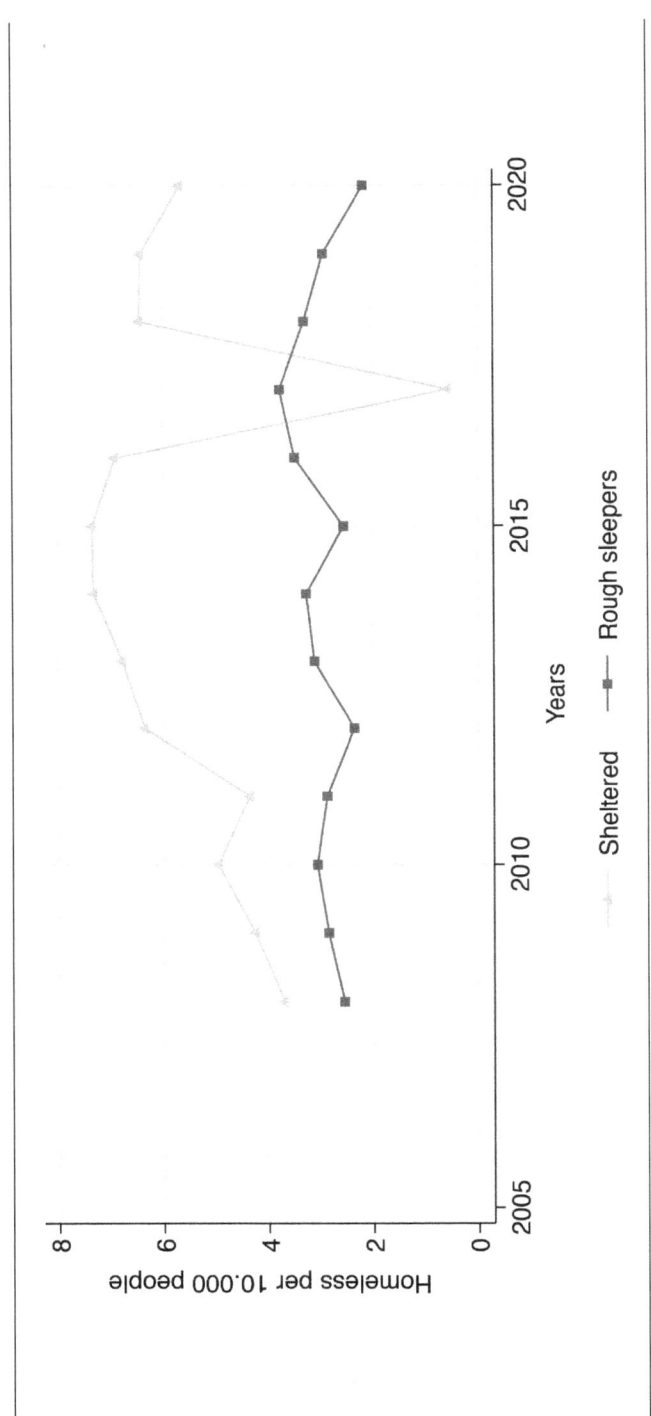

4   Over-time trends in homelessness across European countries   63

ad hoc additional measures to protect the homeless. Vacant properties were converted into shelters to reduce the risk of overcrowding in existing shelters, homeless people were included in the groups having right to early access to vaccinations, and fees for some services were suspended (Gray, 2022) .

Finally, **Figure 13** and **Figure 14** show other European countries where comparable data collections have been conducted over time. The frequency and methods of data collections, duration of observation periods, and target categories of homeless people vary significantly across these countries, as previously discussed in Chapter 3. Such variability makes it more difficult to make comparisons and draw inferences. **Figure 13** in particular focuses on data collections with short observation periods, such as one night or one week, facilitating more meaningful cross-country comparisons. Conversely, **Figure 14** includes national data collections characterized by longer observation periods, all of which are service-based.

To improve homelessness policies across Europe, member countries should adopt a fully standardized approach to data collection. This means harmoninizing both the frequency and the methodologies used, to ensure data comparability and reliability across different regions. Establishing a uniform data collection standard would help policymakers and researchers to accurately analyze trends, compare regional differences, and assess the effectiveness of existing policies.

A further important step would be to create a centralized database for homelessness statistics to facilitate analysis, better understand the phenomenon, anticipate changes, and formulate policy. These steps are crucial for gaining a comprehensive understanding of homelessness and to tackle it effectively at the European level.

4.1.2 Australia and the US

This section focuses on data collection strategies in both Australia and the United States, spotlighting trends in the homeless population over time.

The Australian Government has made significant investments in the collection of data on homeless people over the years. Enumerations of homeless people have been attempted every census since 2001, at five-year intervals. Administrative data on persons receiving homelessness services has been collected at the national level and, in more recent years, the Australian Government has invested in a national longitudinal surveys on persons vulnerable to homelessness, possibly the only one of its kind in the world, called Journeys Home.

In this section, we examine homelessness in Australia, drawing primarily from the Census of Population and Housing. In absolute terms, the homeless population in Australia grew from 105,304 individuals in 2001 to 122,490 in 2021. Yet, during the same period, Australia's total population consistently rose as well. Consequently, the proportion of homeless individuals relative to the total population actually declined, dropping from 54.6 homeless individuals per 10,000 people in 2001 to 47.7 in 2021.

Available data are displayed in **Figure 15**. More specifically, the figure outlines three specific categories of homeless individuals: the reported total in the top graph

Figure 13 Over-time trends in homelessness, European countries, short observation period

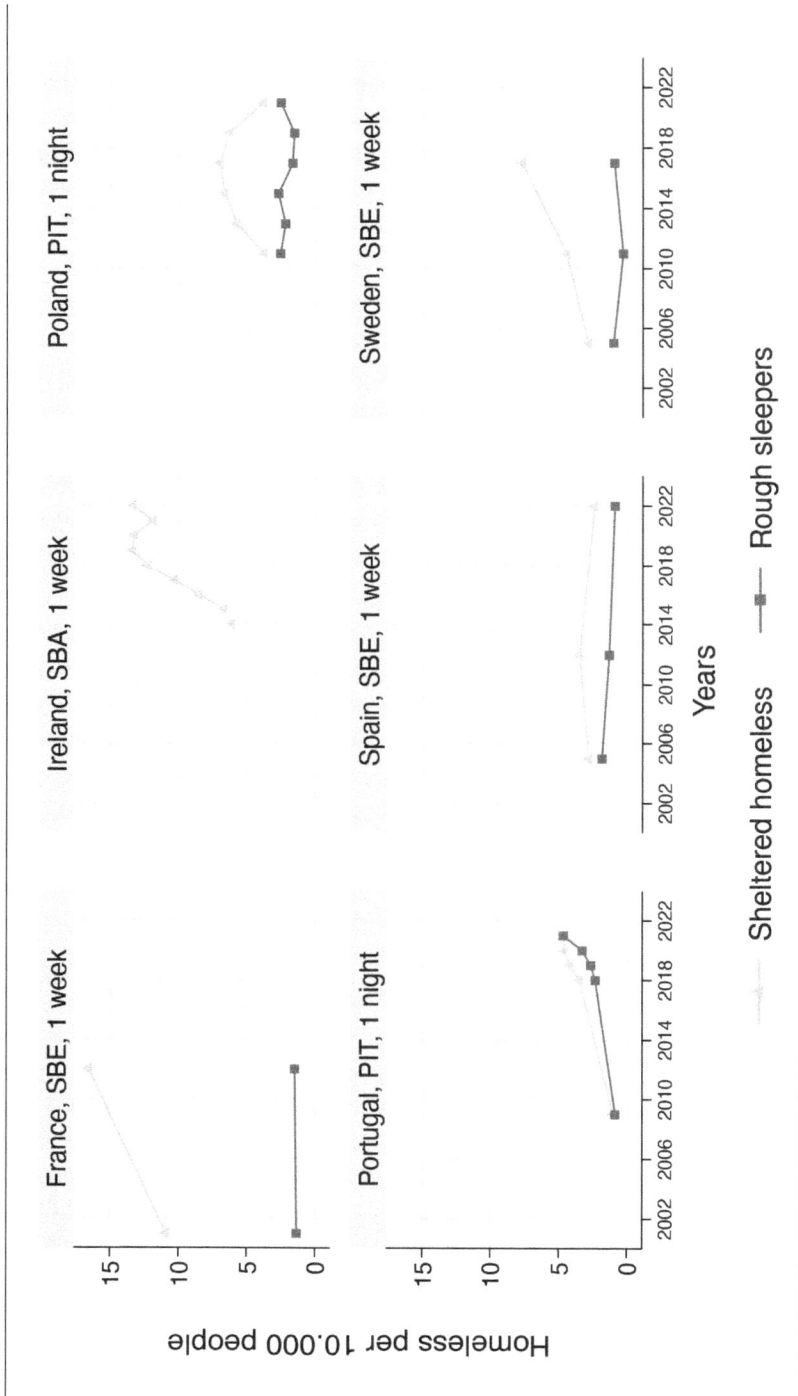

Graphs by country, method of data collection, and period

4 Over-time trends in homelessness across European countries

Figure 14 **Over-time trends in homelessness, European countries, long observation period**

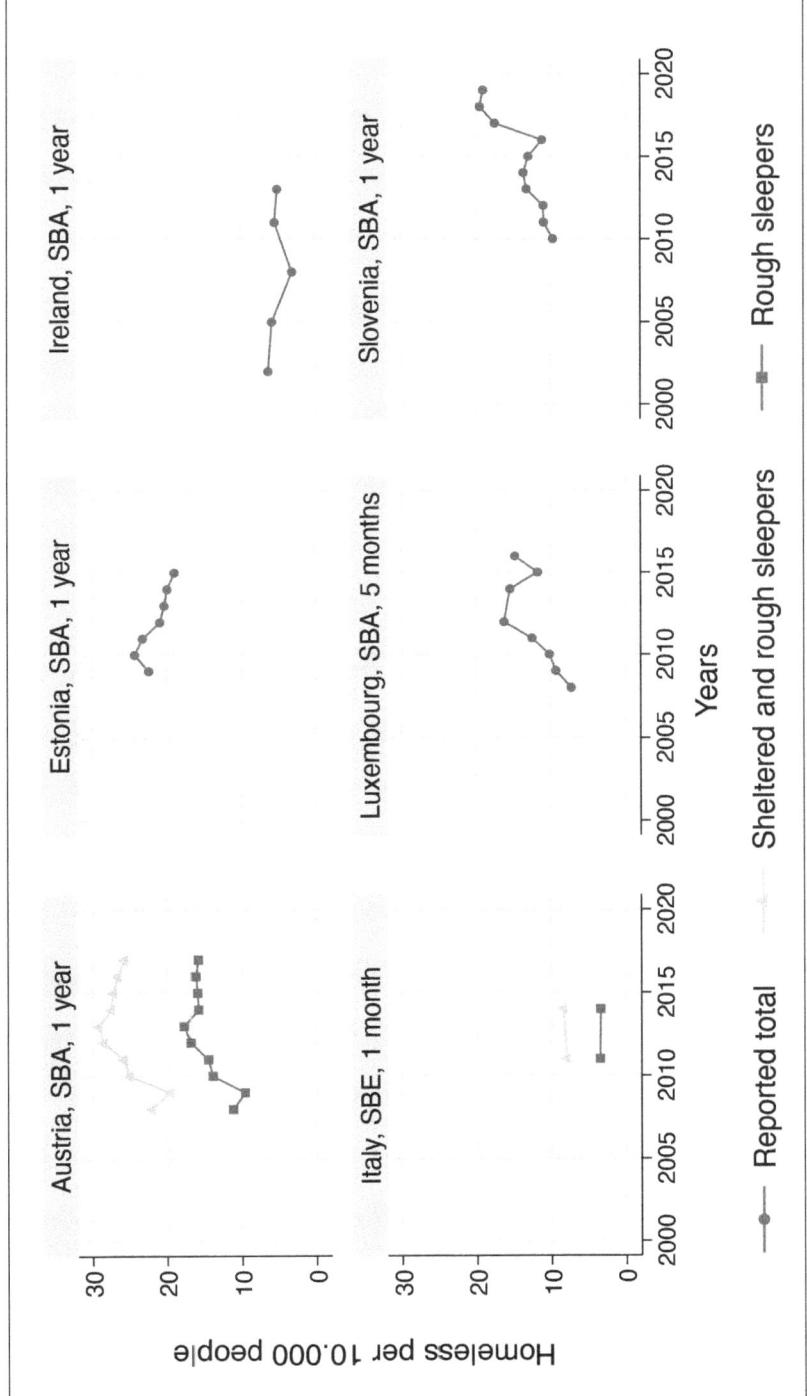

Graphs by country, method of data collection, and period

Figure 15 **Over time trends in homelessness in Australia**

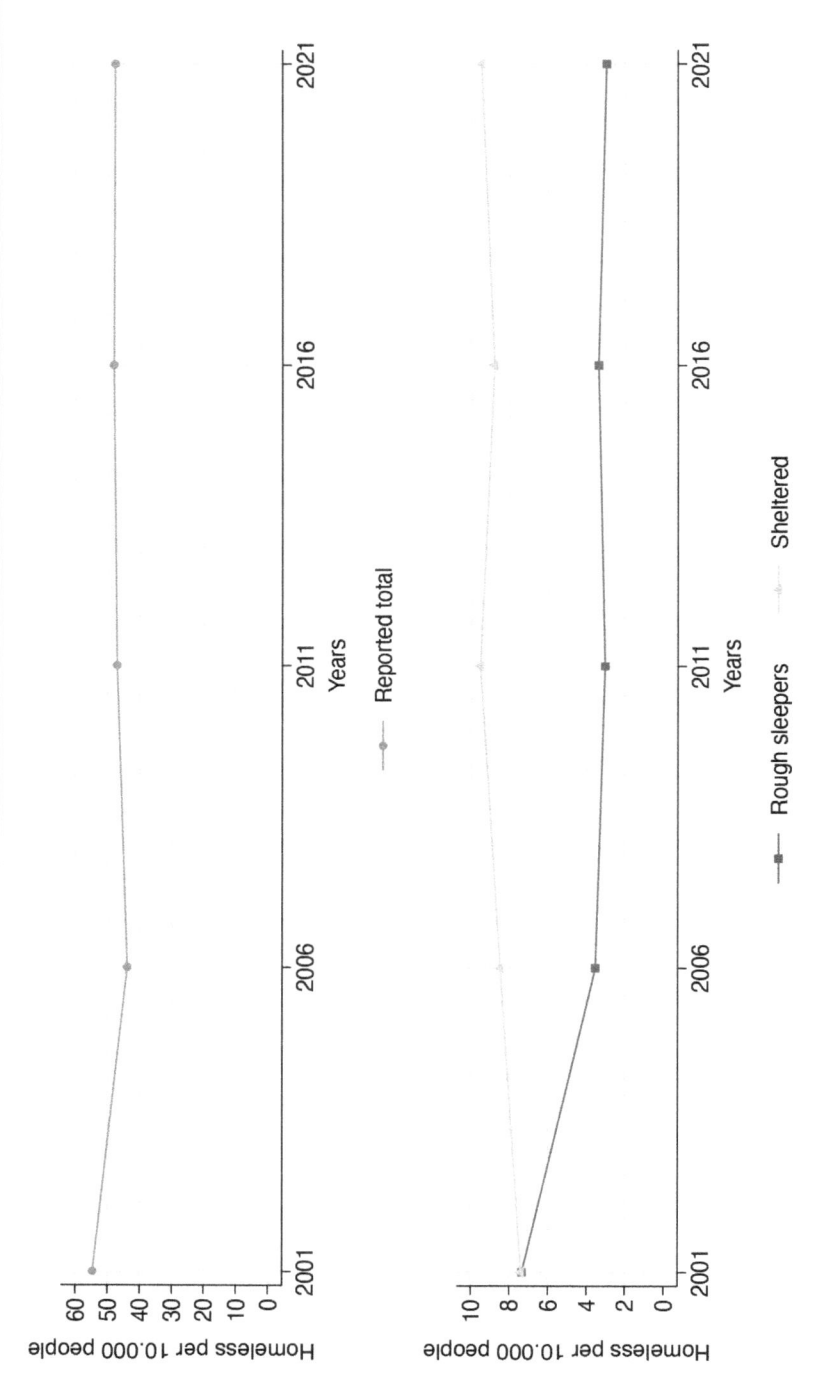

Note: Service-based estimates, 1 day

and those who are rough sleepers or sheltered in the lower graph. The line corresponding to the overall homelessness rate shows a decline from 2001 to 2006, followed by a slight increase and then a plateau from 2011 onward. Sheltered homeless and rough sleepers both show a relatively stable trend over the 20-year period.

Data for the US come from the Annual Homeless Assessment Report (AHAR) published regularly by the U.S. Department of Housing and Urban Development since 2005 (HUD, 2024). As discussed in Chapter 1, these data only focus on 'streets-and-shelters population,' and do not take into account precariously housed individuals. The most recent HUD survey, conducted in 2022, found that 582,462 people were homeless on a single night, which translates to 17.5 people per 10,000 inhabitants. Of these, 40% were located in unsheltered locations.

Figure 16 illustrates trends in both sheltered homeless individuals and rough sleepers over time. While sheltered homeless individuals exhibit a gradual decline throughout the period, rough sleepers demonstrate a more pronounced decrease from 2008 to approximately 2014, followed by a gradual increase. This indicates diverging trends between the two categories in recent years.

4.2 Trends at the city level

In **Figure 17** and **Figure 18**, we present the trends in homelessness across European cities where comparable data collections are available over time. **Figure 17** specifically highlights national capitals or large cities in Europe, while **Figure 18** includes medium-sized European cities. The focus remains on rough sleepers and sheltered homeless individuals, whenever information is accessible. Finally, in **Figure 19**, we illustrate the trends over time in seven US cities and Toronto, Canada. The evidence observed from the Figures highlights substantial heterogeneity across cities in terms of homelessness prevalence and dynamics. Additionally, there is notable variation in the proportion of people sleeping rough compared to the total number of sheltered and unsheltered homeless individuals (as already observed in Chapter 3), with this ratio fluctuating significantly over time. These differences across cities can be attributed to local conditions and policies, which appear to play a key role in shaping homelessness prevalence and dynamics at local level. Factors such as availability of affordable housing, access to support services, and implementation of targeted interventions likely contribute to the observed differences in homelessness trends among urban areas.

However, as from country level data, the share of rough sleepers is substantially more stable than the share of sheltered individuals. This could depend on the fact that the shelter supply is somehow elastic and varies a lot in response to external changes. When new shelters open or existing ones expand, more homeless individuals can be accommodated, leading to a temporary increase in the sheltered count. Conversely, when shelters face funding cuts or closures, the sheltered numbers drop. Seasonal and weather-related factors also impact these figures. In colder months, there may be a spike in sheltered individuals as people seek refuge from harsh conditions, whereas

Figure 16 Over time trends in homelessness in the US

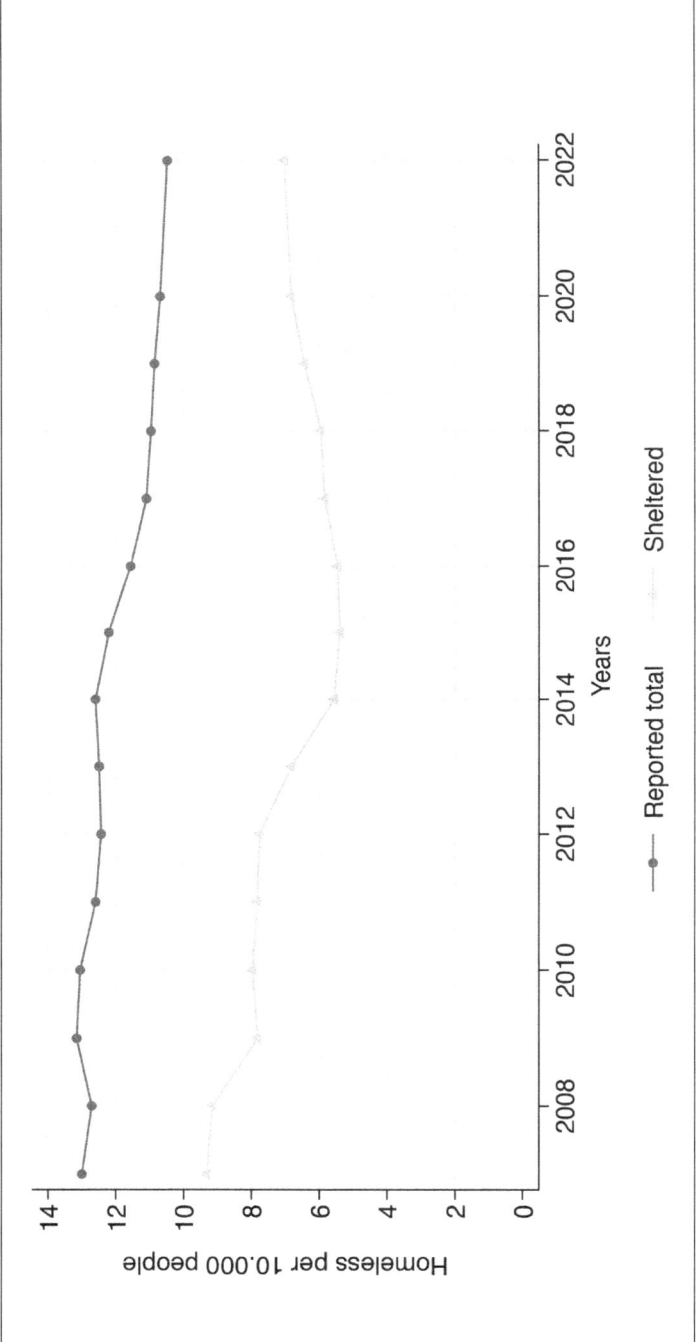

Note: Service-based estimates, 1 day

4   Over-time trends in homelessness across European countries   69

Figure 17   **Over time trends in homelessness in European cities, capitals and large cities**

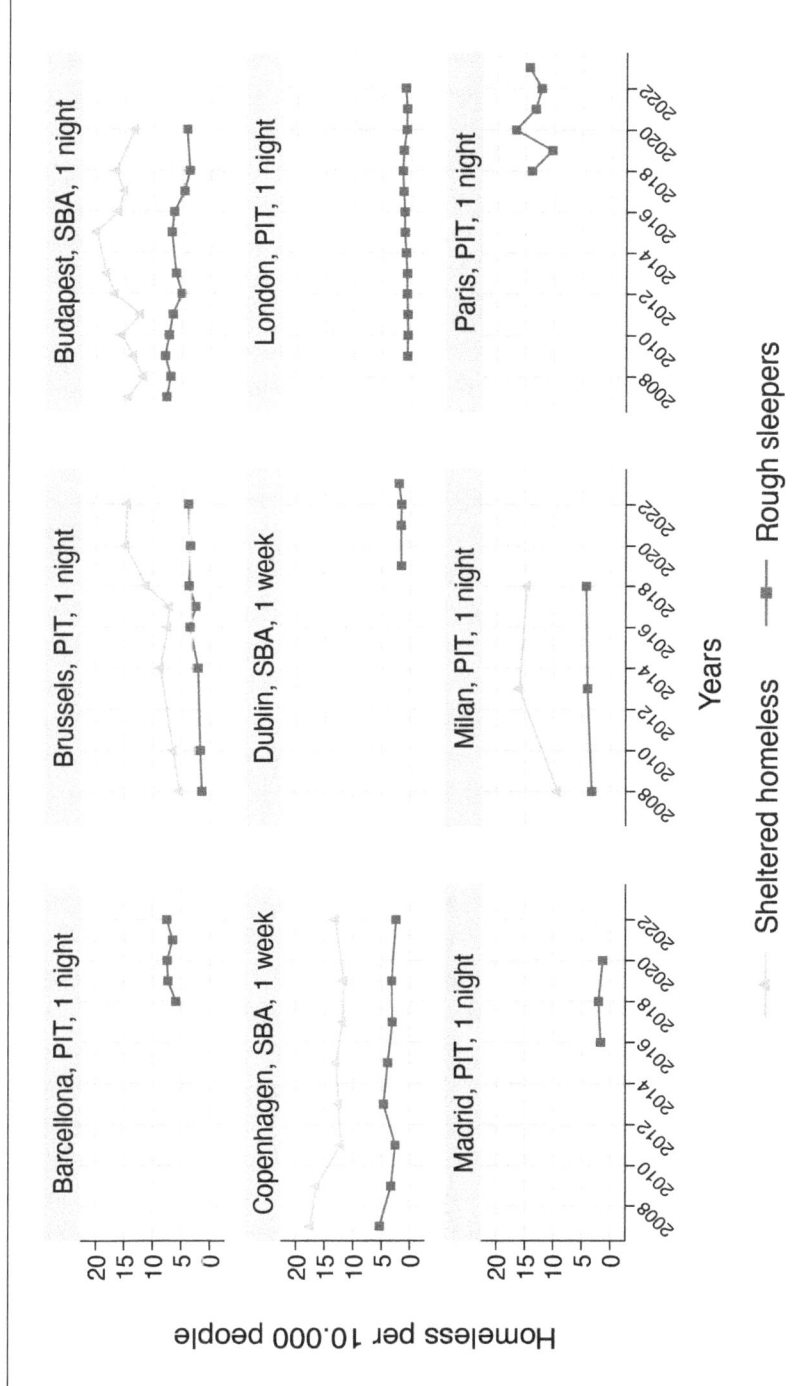

Graphs by city, method of data collection, and period

Figure 18 Over time trends in homelessness in European cities, medium-sized cities

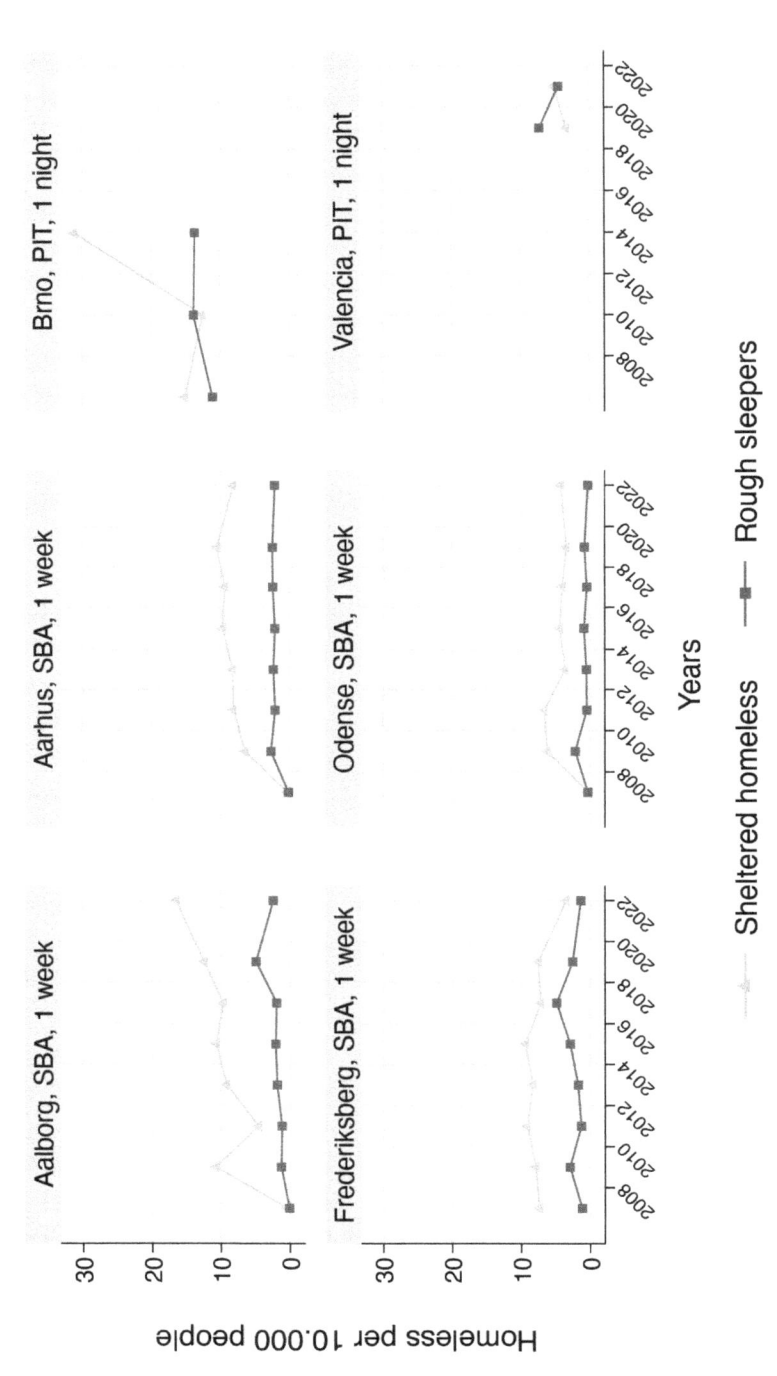

Graphs by city, method of data collection, and period

4 Over-time trends in homelessness across European countries

Figure 19 Over time trends in homelessness in seven US cities and Toronto, Canada

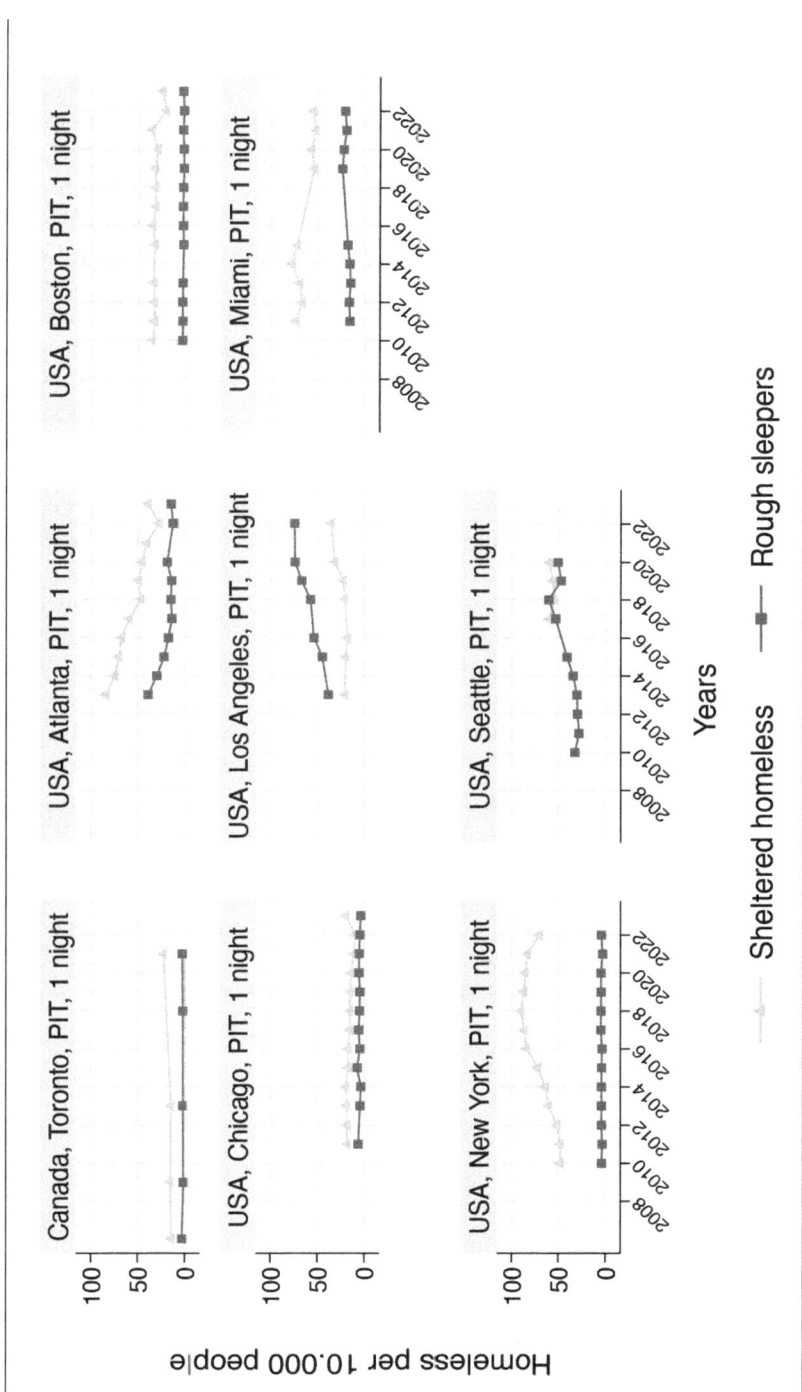

Graphs by city, method of data collection, and period

in milder weather the numbers may decrease as individuals choose or are forced to sleep outside. Although countries or cities generally conduct counts in the same period each year to ensure comparability, exogenous shocks could affect the economy from one year to the next. Local policies and their enforcement can also influence the number of sheltered homeless. When a country implements policies that increase enforcement against rough sleeping or that facilitate the transition of rough sleepers into shelters, changes in the incidence between the two groups emerge. It is also important to consider the consistency among data collection methodologies. Counting rough sleepers is often more straightforward and consistent since it relies on visual counts based on objective characteristics and surveys. Instead, tracking sheltered individuals requires access to various data sources collected by different service providers. Data collection and reporting practices may vary a lot and may be less accurate and biased. Also rules to access shelters may affect data. In many cases, people are eligible for shelters only if they meet certain conditions, in terms of substance use, health conditions, and adherence to rules. These rules can change a lot from one year to the next or from a service provider to another. As a result, the population of rough sleepers who either do not qualify for or choose not to use shelters could be more stable over time.

The data presented in this chapter clearly highlight the importance of having longitudinal data collected with consistent methodologies. From a policy perspective, they allow policymakers to assess the effectiveness of their interventions: by looking at trends and changes in homelessness rates over the years, authorities can adjust policies and allocate resources more efficiently where they are most needed. From a research perspective, having comparable data allows for more accurate and sophisticated analyses that lead to the development of more targeted and effective interventions. This kind of data is also essential for comparative studies across regions and cities to identify best practices and learn from new approaches. From a public perspective, transparent and accessible data can increase public awareness and lead to greater support for all initiatives to tackle the phenomenon. In addition, if data collection follows internationally recognized standard, it may be simpler to share knowledge and facilitate collaboration among different actors.

5 What does contribute to homelessness?

Homelessness is a complex and multidimensional phenomenon that has long been studied by social scientists, such as sociologists, anthropologists, psychologists and, so far, few economists. The sociological and psychological literature has underlined different reasons for homelessness, which can be roughly divided into two categories: personal reasons and structural/institutional reasons (Shelter, 2008). Personal factors include drug and alcohol abuse, criminal activity, debt (mortgage or rent arrears), poor physical and mental health conditions, breakdown in social and family relationships, lack of qualifications or social support. In particular, the family background seems to play a crucial role in explaining homelessness, especially when it is characterized by disputes, divorce, sexual and physical abuse, domestic violence, death of family members, parents with drug or alcohol related problems. The structural/institutional causes of homelessness are related to the socio-economic context in which an individual lives and include, among others, unemployment and poverty rates, lack of affordable housing, housing policies and the welfare system. In most cases, individual and institutional factors are highly correlated and interact creating undesirable vicious cycles. For example, in periods of low economic growth and high unemployment, vulnerable individuals may lose their jobs, their income situation deteriorates and, if not adequately supported, they may begin to experience financial distress, leading to stress and psychological problems or alcohol consumption, which in extreme cases may lead to the loss of their homes.

Some previous work has also looked at the determinants of the duration of spells of homelessness (Piliavin, Wright, Mare and Westerfelt, 1996). Homelessness spells are generally longer for those with a history of drug or alcohol abuse, while having received government benefits in the past seems to have a controversial effect on the average length of a spell of homelessness (Allgood and Warren, 2003).

The goal of this chapter is to investigate how country-specific features affect homelessness, using our newly constructed dataset on the number of homeless individuals. We will attempt to shed some light on existing correlations between the incidence of homelessness and the socio-economic features of a particular geographical area. We will investigate whether any variation in the prevalence of homelessness over time can be explained by institutional, cultural, or structural factors. Namely, we explore to what extent i) socio-economic conditions, ii) regulations in the labor market and in the welfare regime, iii) political orientations and iv) housing market features can explain different patterns in the incidence of homelessness.

5.1 Data on a country's institutional characteristics

In economic theory, starting with the seminal work of Hall and Jones (1999), the role of institutions in economic development has been widely documented. In particular, there is evidence that institutions affect cross-country differences in the level of per capita income, economic growth and its volatility (Acemoglu, Johnson and Robinson 2010). Institutions define the 'rules of the game' of society (North, 1990): they include norms, regulations and laws that influence and shape individuals' and groups' behaviour. They are both formal (laws or contracts) and informal (conventions, habits, traditions or social norms), and they change and evolve over time within a given society. From an economic point of view, institutions are important because they shape the incentives of economic actors in society. Institutions are exogenous to individuals, but since they are determined as a collective choice by members of the community according to the effect they expect to produce, they are typically formed endogenously over time.

In order to explore how the share of homeless is driven by socio-economic dynamics, changes in the housing market, and policy reforms, we assembled several indicators from different data sources. We focus on five structural dimensions of the institutional framework that could potentially affect the number of homeless in a given economy: (i) the socio-economic context, (ii) the welfare state, (iii) the labor market, (iv) the political context, and (v) the housing market.

As indicators for socio-economic conditions, we consider standard measures of a country's economic well-being: the GDP per capita and the Gini coefficient. In addition, since some available evidence suggests that homelessness disproportionately affects minority populations, we also take into account the share of immigrants over the total population, the percentage of the population living at the national poverty line or at $1.90 a day, in a given country. To account for the dynamics of the housing market, we consider the OECD house price index.

Depending on the adopted welfare state, national governments play different roles in protecting and promoting the economic and social well-being of their citizens and could also influence the number of homeless people. Indeed, different welfare state systems have different capacities to assess and address the needs of the population. In order to test whether alternative welfare systems affect homelessness prevalence, we use different indicators commonly used to classify welfare regimes. The simplest are based on public spending on specific welfare programs. Internationally comparable statistics are available in the OECD Social Expenditure Database (SOCX), which provides data on overall social expenditure, social expenditure on active labor market policies, and social expenditure on housing policies. All three measures are calculated relative to GDP. However, the relative quality of the welfare state can also be measured by considering many other aspects, such as the replacement rates of key social benefits, the duration of social benefits, the types of requirement people have to meet in order to qualify for a benefit, the number of waiting days included in the rules or the number of people covered by the social scheme. Based on these aspects, welfare states are more or less 'generous' and potentially moderate the risk of material deprivation and income poverty. Hence, from the Comparative Welfare Entitlements Dataset, we recover the welfare state generosity index, available for almost all countries since the early 1970s. This index was constructed by taking into account pensions and income received in case of sickness, unemployment or disability insurance, and by using the replacement ratio, coverage, eligibility, and timing of different schemes. The higher the score on this index, the more generous the systems are. The index overcomes the limitations of traditional spending measures since it takes into account the size of the beneficiaries.

To capture the effect of labor market conditions, we consider the unemployment rate and labor market policies. Active Labour Market Policy statistics provide information on labor market interventions explicitly targeting people facing difficulties in the labour market: the unemployed, persons employed but at risk of involuntary job loss, and inactive persons wishing to enter the labor market. The OECD indicators on employment protection legislation measure the procedures and the costs involved in dismissing individuals or groups of workers and the procedures involved in hiring workers on fixed-term or temporary job contracts.

Data on *political orientation* are taken from the Parliament and Government Composition Database (Döring and Manow, 2010), which includes observations on all parties, electoral rules, and cabinets in the postwar period for all the EU and most OECD countries. Starting from this information, Döring and Manow (2010) classify each party elected to Parliament on a 0-10 scale, ranging from the most left-wing (0) to the most right-wing (10). The seat-weighted average of the parties elected in a legislature or supporting a cabinet is the final measure of the political orientation of policy makers. In addition, since typically men and women have different preferences and act very differently, we collect data on the share of women in parliament.

5.2 Correlation between the volume of homeless and socio-economic factors Europe

We combine this set of data on socio-economic conditions and policies at the country level with the available data on homelessness. The link between homelessness data and institutional data is made by taking the lagged value of each explanatory variable measuring the institutional context. Given that homelessness is the result of a process, the very basic idea is that the institutional setting prevailing in a given period can be used as a predictor of the future probability of homelessness in the same geographical area. A sensitivity analysis was conducted using different lags to test the robustness of the results. It should be noted that, as already mentioned above, the data collection methodology on the number of homeless varies somewhat between countries and, in some cases, between years within the same country. This implies that homelessness figures are only comparable within countries and only in cases in which the data were collected according to the same methodology at different points in time. Given these limitations, we restrict our analysis to the subset of fully comparable data and we exploit determinants of time variation.

In the three panels of **Figure 20**, we report the correlation between the socio-economic dimensions of the institutional setting and the number of homeless by country, distinguishing between street and shelter. The illustrative evidence suggests that the countries with the higher rates of homelessness are those that have experienced a higher increase in inequality, as measured by the Gini Index and the share of migrants. Homelessness is also higher in richer countries, as measured by the GDP per capita, and in countries where the share of the population living on $1.90 a day is higher. The same evidence emerges also when distinguishing between sheltered and street homeless. Some exceptions are found for the street homeless but it is important to highlight that for them, the lower availability of data might translate into less variability, generating less stable results. On the other hand, the strictness of national immigration laws is not correlated with homelessness.

As expected, the housing market also plays a role. In particular, homelessness is higher as the share of housing expenditure in total consumption increases. Instead, the Housing Price Index (HPI) is not (or negatively) correlated with homelessness. The index measures changes in the market prices of all household dwellings (apartments, single-family houses, terraced houses, and others), both new and existing, regardless of whether they are purchased for owner-occupancy or as an investment. The index covers transactions of dwellings within the household sector and transactions of the household sector with other institutional sectors. The figures are based on final market prices paid by households and include the price of land. The assumption is that the higher cost of living creates economic hardship for more vulnerable individuals and increases the incidence of sheltered homelessness, as individuals seek alternatives when experiencing housing shocks. However, the data suggest the opposite relationship. The negative relationship may arise because a high house price index can attract investment in affordable housing and new construction, increasing the supply of housing and providing more options for the population. This may lead to less competition for housing, lower vacancy rates, greater housing stability, and thus less homelessness.

Finally, as expected, an increase in the share of households with housing affordability problems in terms of overburdened costs is associated with a higher incidence of homelessness. Symmetrically, as the share of owners in the country increases, the share of homeless people decreases.

5.3 Correlation between homelessness and welfare generosity in Europe

Another potential institutional feature that could predict changes in homelessness is the structure of the welfare state. Modern welfare states compensate individuals for life-course risks providing by financial buffers – through benefits, transfers or specific entitlements – against the adverse consequences of events such as unemployment, illnesses or old age. In principle, welfare states help to reduce income fluc-

5 What does contribute to homelessness?

Figure 20 Homelessness and socio-economic conditions

Panel a) Total Homeless share

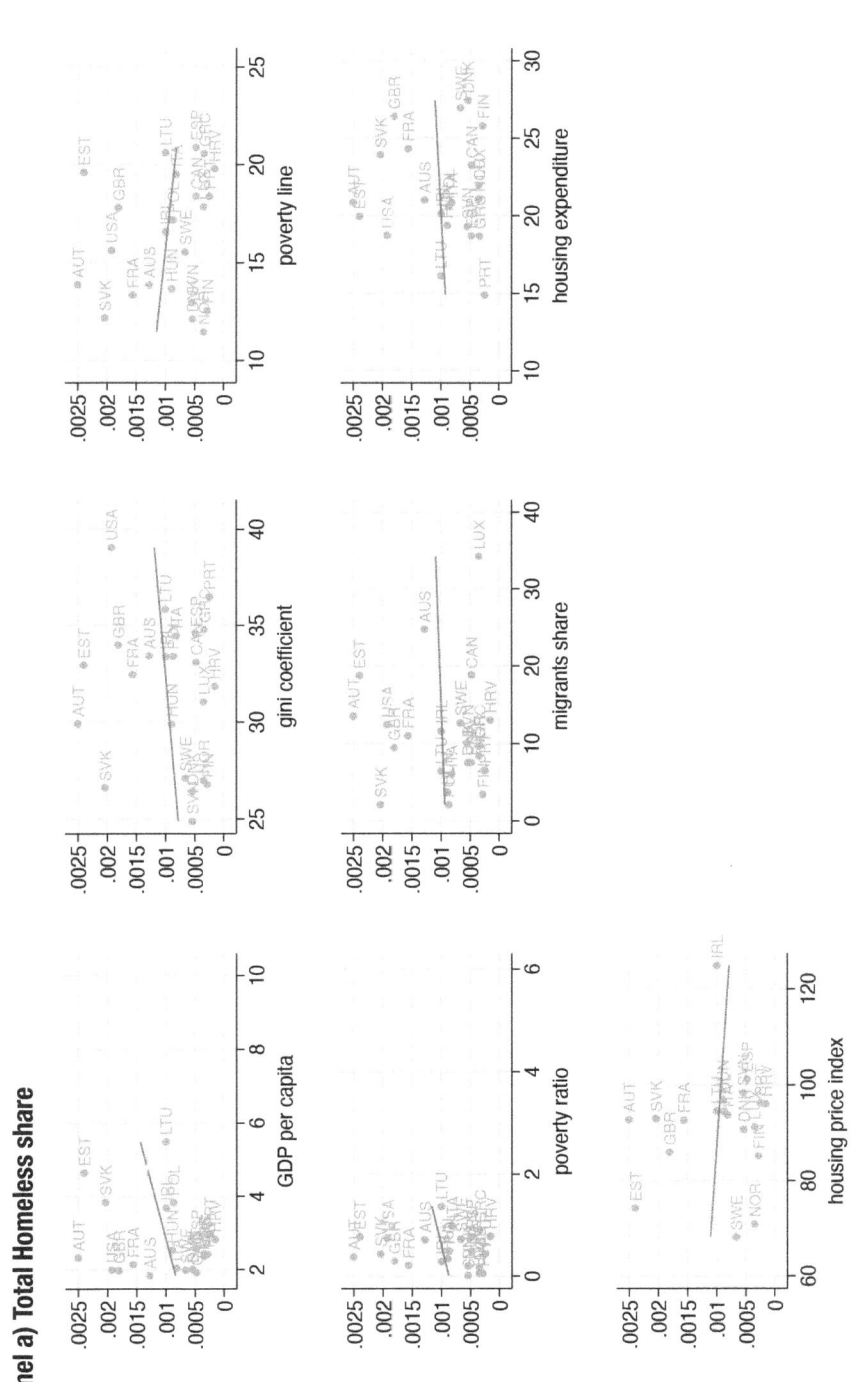

Figure 20 Homelessness and socio-economic conditions (continued)

Panel b) Street

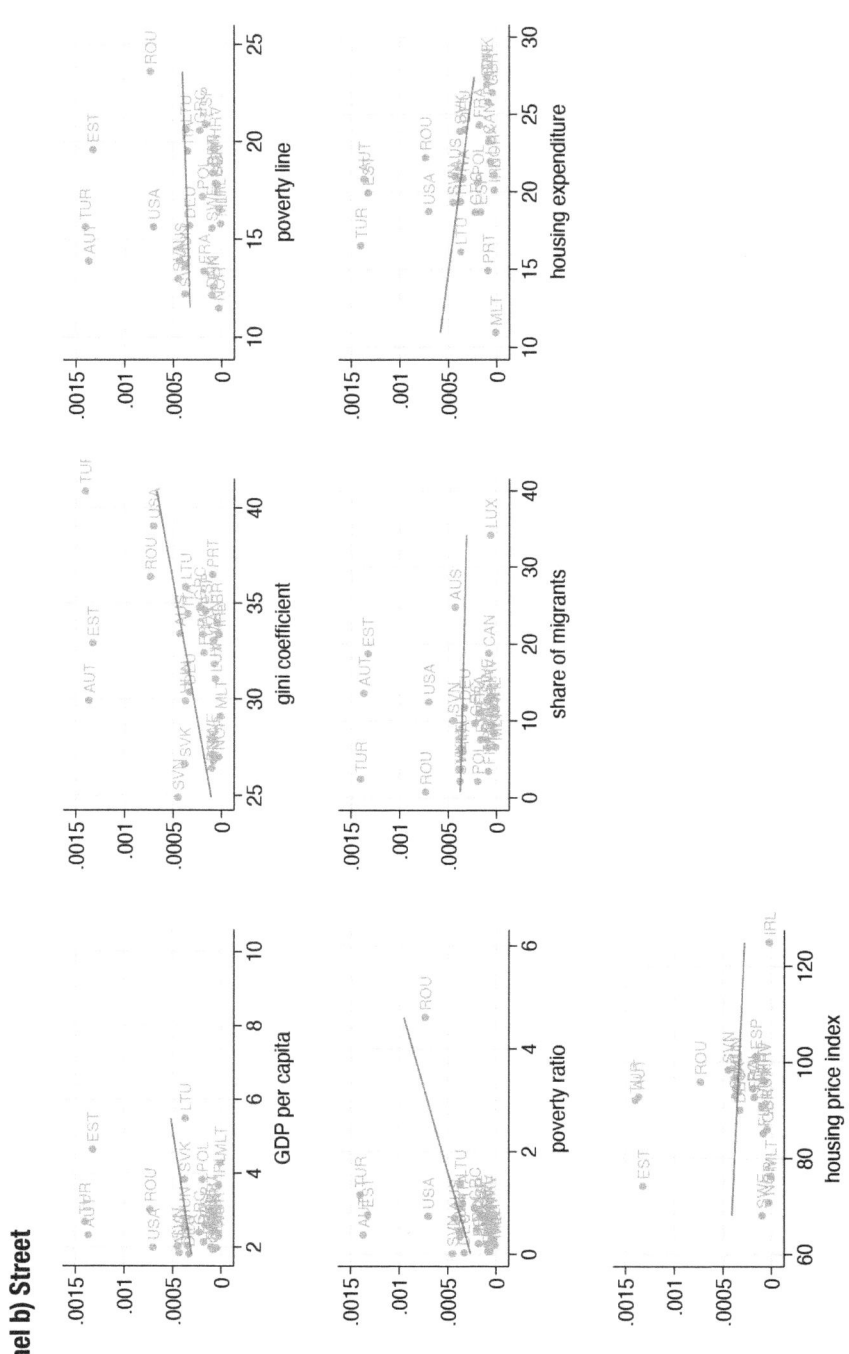

5 What does contribute to homelessness?

Figure 20 Homelessness and socio-economic conditions (continued)

Panel c) Shelter

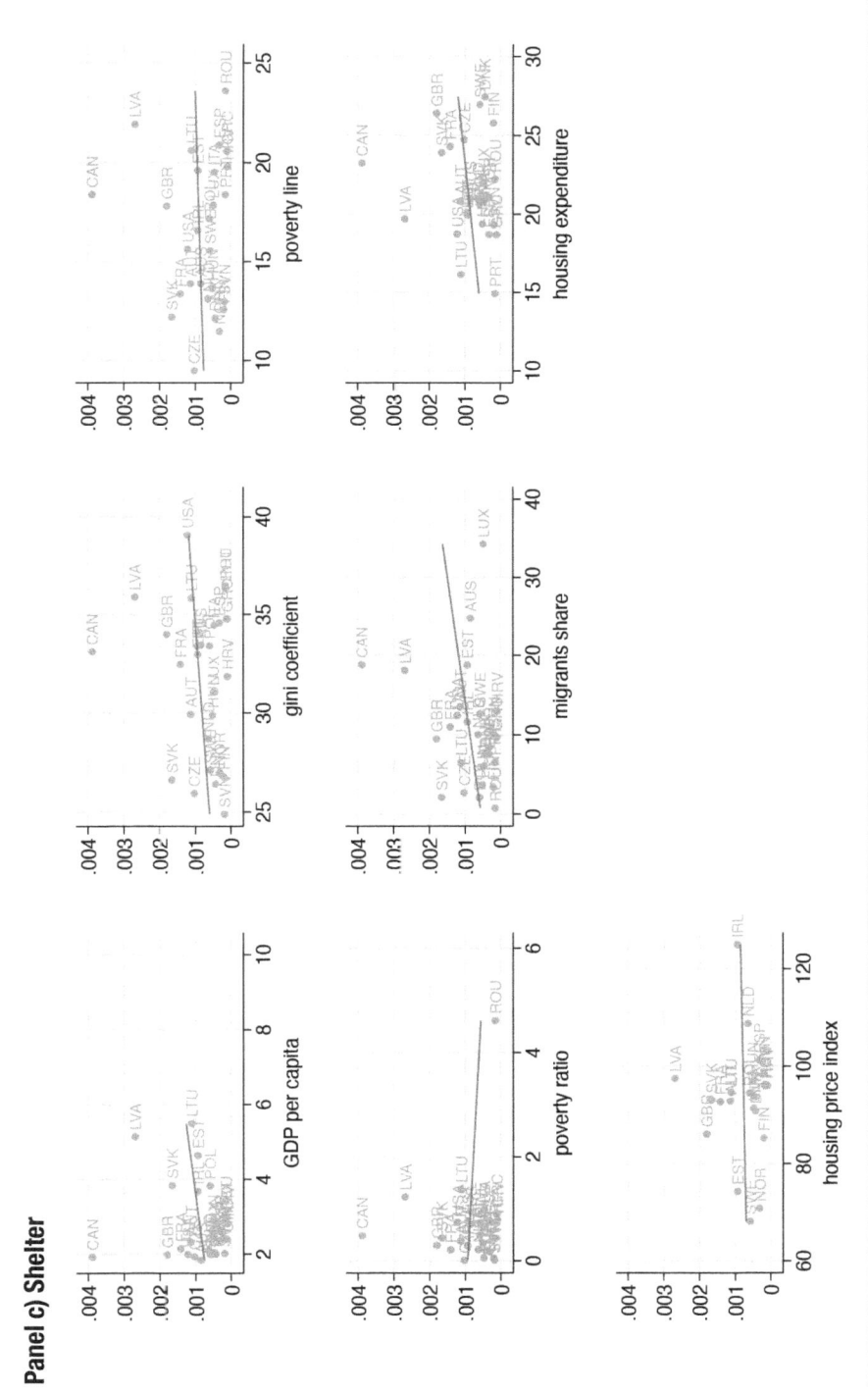

tuations and economic inequalities in modern societies. In **Figure 21**, we report the correlation between the generosity of the welfare state, as measured by various social expenditures as a percentage of GDP, and the incidence of homelessness. As expected, inspection of the data reveals a strong negative correlation between the generosity of the welfare state and the number of homeless people in a given country. Welfare generosity refers to the level of financial assistance and support provided to individuals through social welfare programs, such as housing assistance, health insurance, unemployment benefits, pensions or social services in general. Our analysis suggests that when the public sector invests more in fighting poverty and social exclusion, in a broad sense, homelessness is lower. The overall social expenditure over GDP is negatively correlated with the share of homelessness. Social spending allows for the implementation of programs that help people at risk of homelessness to access stable and affordable housing, financial support, or appropriate services. An even stronger effect is found when public spending on social housing as a percentage of GDP is negatively correlated with overall homelessness, sheltered homelessness and street homelessness, and the effect is higher when street homelessness is considered. Social housing can play a crucial role in both preventing and ending homelessness since it offers more affordable and secure places to live. People are much less likely to become homeless again if they move into social housing rather than private rented housing. Certainly, public infrastructure investment in housing could help bridge the looming housing investment gap while reducing homelessness and housing stress. However, it is important to stress that the effect on the sheltered rate may be spurious, as countries with higher government investment in housing are also those with higher public services for the homeless.

Instead, the expenditure on unemployment benefit generosity is slightly positively correlated with overall homelessness, suggesting that if not well calibrated, these policies could trap individuals in poverty and that this social safety net could have negative effects, reducing incentives to be active in the labor market. Finally, the generosity of pension systems is negatively correlated with homelessness in a statistically significant way. The same negative correlation emerges when focusing on the generosity of health insurance.

The link between welfare generosity and homelessness highlights the importance of providing adequate support to prevent and effectively address homelessness.

5.4 Correlation between homelessness and the labor market

The impact of labor market institutions on economic outcomes has been extensively studied in many OECD countries. Since unemployment has been shown to be one of the main causes of homelessness (Braga and Corno, 2011), we examine the relationship between labor market characteristics and homelessness rates in our sample. Data suggest that labor markets with higher employment rates and lower unemployment rates are associated with higher homelessness incidence. This apparently surprising and counterintuitive result can be explained in different ways. First, many ur-

5 What does contribute to homelessness?

Figure 21 Homelessness and the welfare state

Panel a) Total Homeless share

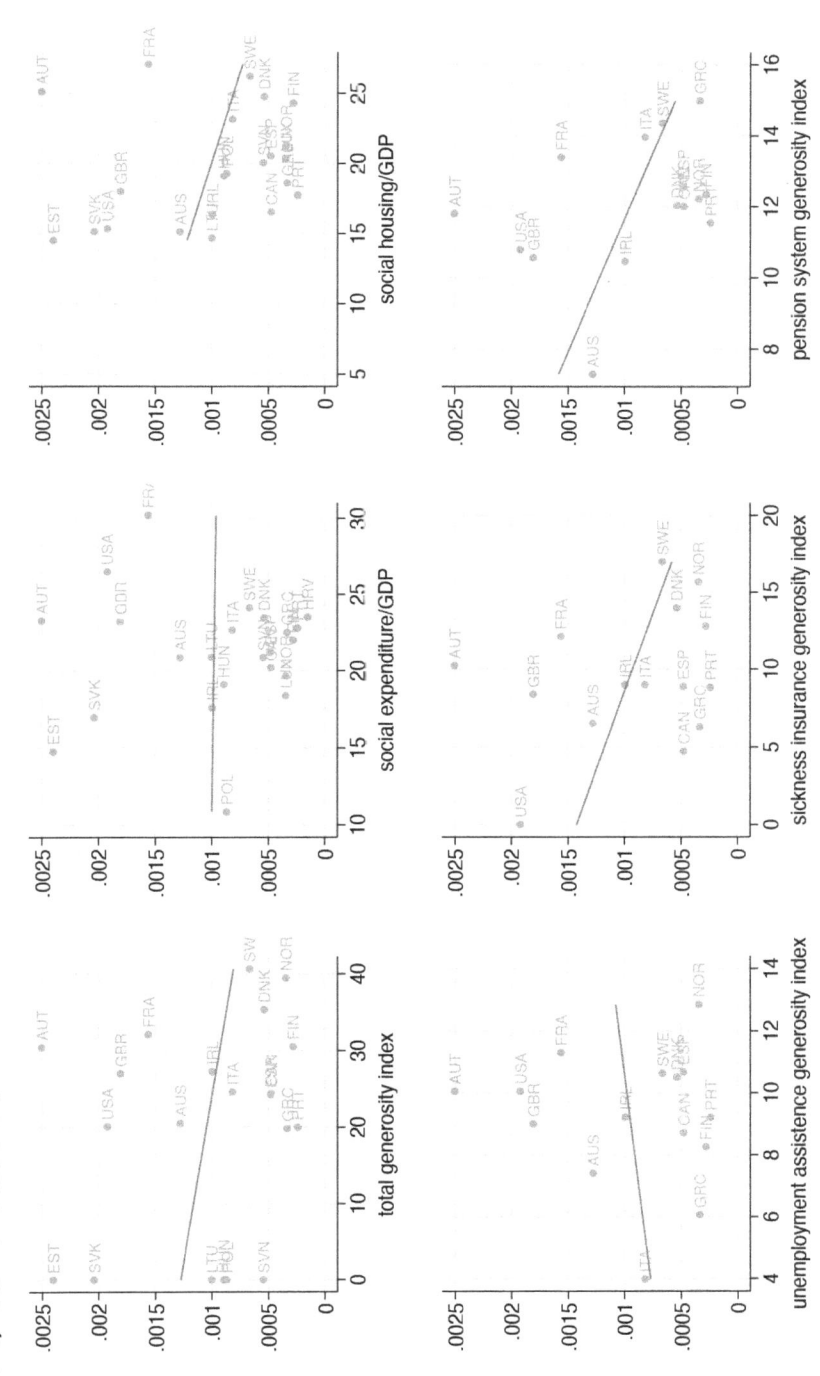

Figure 21   Homelessness and the welfare state (continued)

Panel b) Street

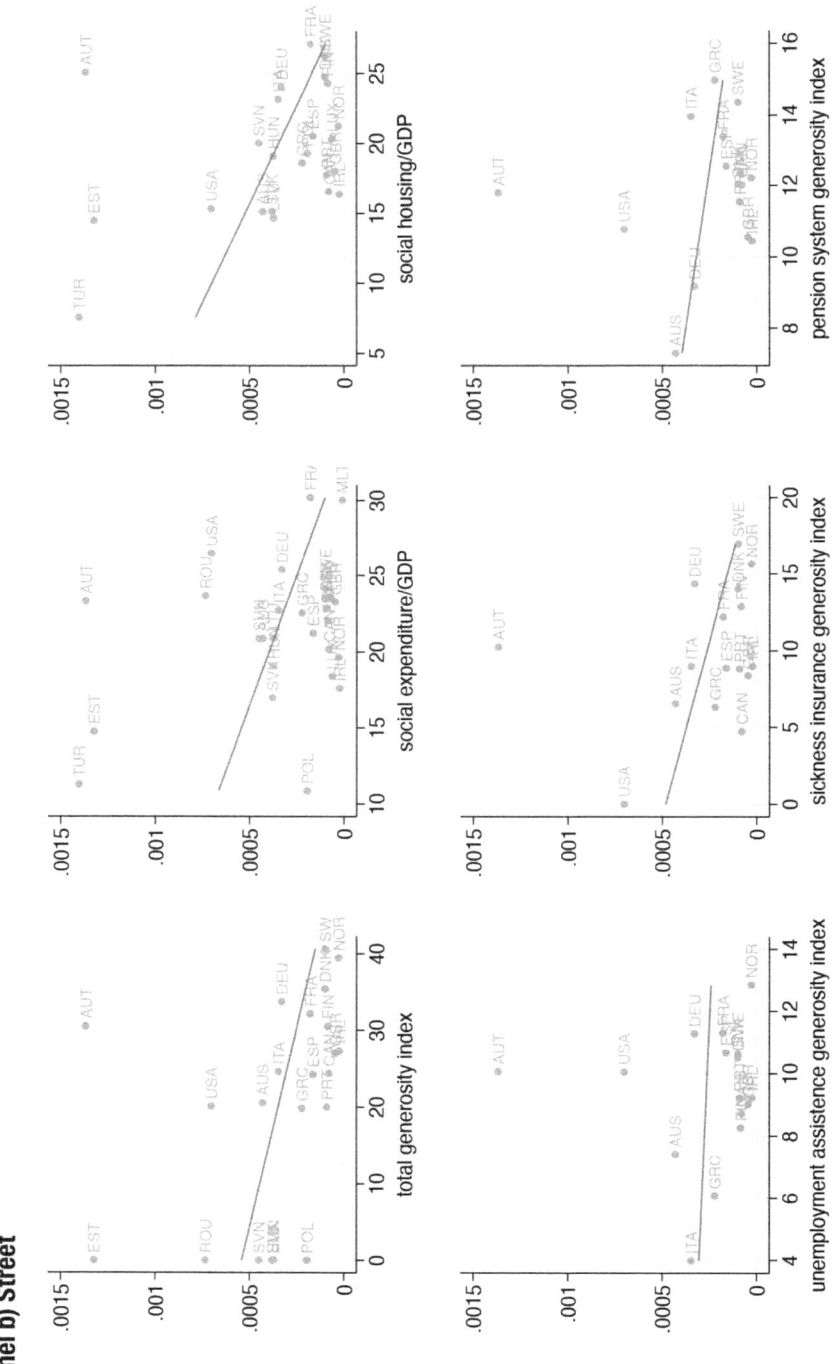

5 What does contribute to homelessness?

Figure 21 Homelessness and the welfare state (continued)

Panel c) Shelter

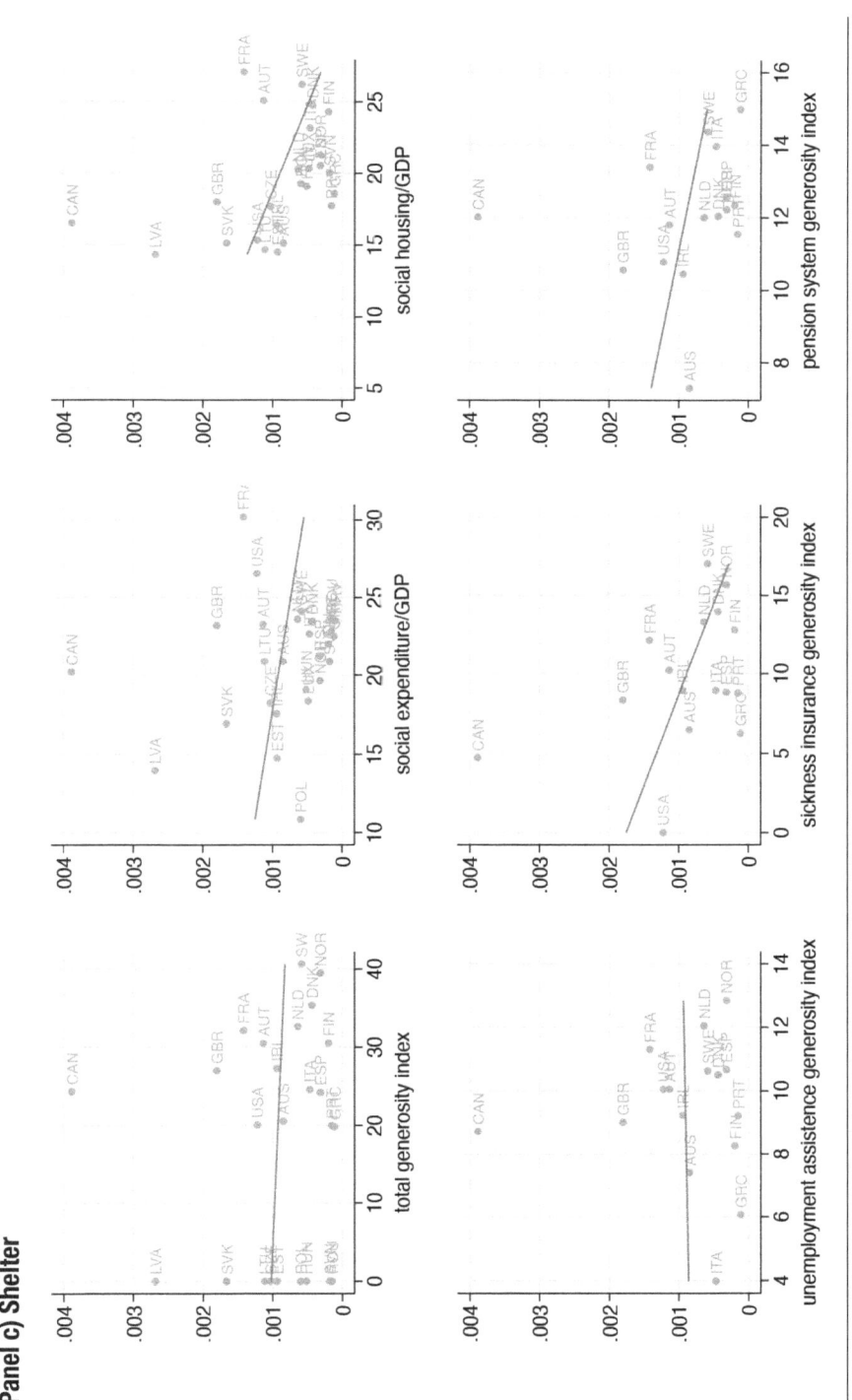

ban areas with higher employment opportunities are also characterized by extremely high housing costs that make it difficult for the working poor to afford stable housing. Second, some individuals experiencing homelessness may be employed in temporary, part-time or low-wage jobs.

Labor market trends are mainly driven by the business cycle, but labor market institutions are critical to the well-functioning of the labor market, influencing the patterns of job creation, job destruction, and working conditions. Labor market institutions refer to formal laws and government policies as well as informal rules and practices. In our analysis we focus on two main dimensions: active labor market policies and employment protection legislation.

Figure 22 shows a strong negative correlation between active labor market policies and homelessness rates. Increased investment in active labour market policies should increase labour market participation, reduce inactivity and the risk of poverty. The provision of vocational training programmes, job placement services and subsidized employment initiatives is an effective way of helping individuals to access better paid job opportunities in order to obtain a secure and sustainable income. In this way, people are more likely to maintain stable housing and reduce their risk of homelessness.

In addition, employment protection legislation is associated with less homelessness in the overall population, and the negative correlation is somewhat stronger when employment protection legislation for temporary workers is considered. Since temporary workers are by definition less secure and have lower wages on average, *ceteris paribus*, higher protection for them may reduce the risk of extreme poverty, social exclusion and homelessness.

5.5   Correlation between homelessness and political orientation

The next dimension we analyze is the political setting. In general, left- and right-leaning political parties prioritize different policies in their political agenda. For example, they may place different weights on reducing poverty and income inequality. Depending on the partisan orientation, we expect alternative institutions to be active. Traditionally, left-leaning political parties have been strong supporters of generous interventions and more inclined towards inclusive policies. Indeed, their supporters are largely overrepresented in the lower tail of the income distribution. As expected, a first inspection of the data shows a positive correlation between the homelessness rate and right-wing parliaments/cabinets (**Figure 23**). Instead, having more women in parliament significantly reduces the number of homeless people both on the streets and in shelters. Women are underrepresented in political offices almost everywhere and this underrepresentation affects policy choices. Our evidence suggests that women in deliberative bodies could have substantive effects and since major policy changes typically require legislative approval women presence could makes a significant difference also in terms of homelessness reduction.

Moreover, we examine the correlation between the World Bank Legal Rights In-

5 What does contribute to homelessness?

Figure 22 Homelessness and labor market policies

Panel a) Total Homeless share

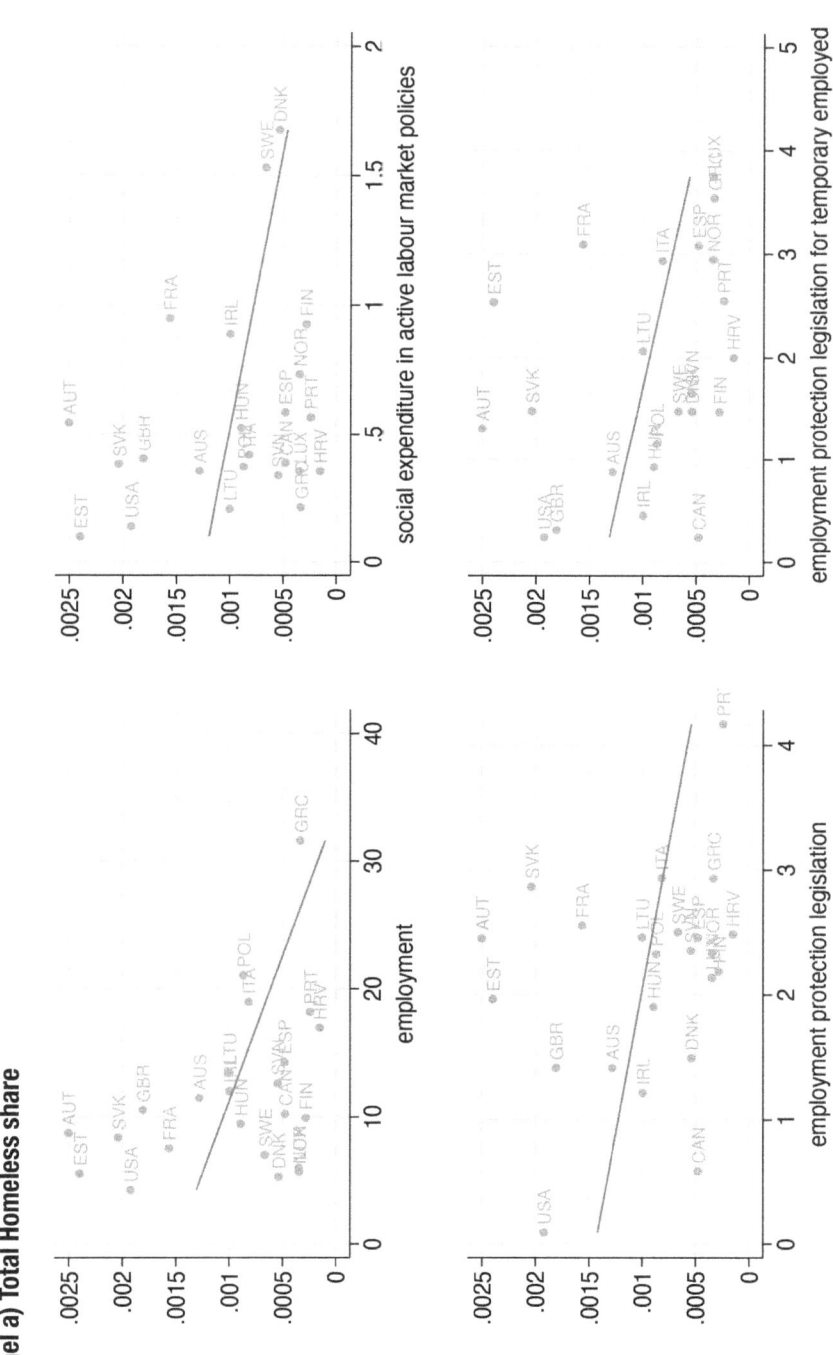

Figure 22 Homelessness and labor market policies (continued)

Panel b) Street

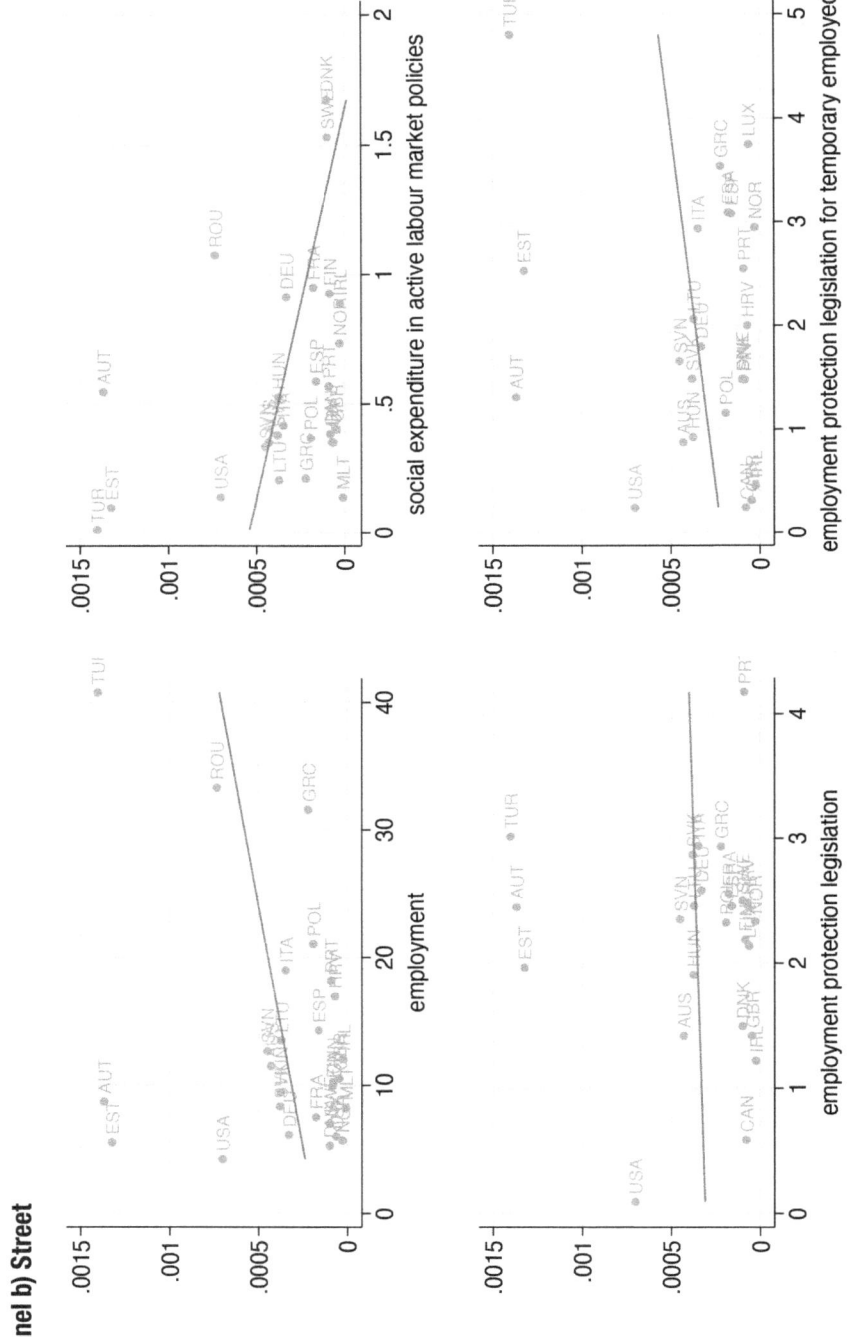

Figure 22 Homelessness and labor market policies (continued)

Panel c) Shelter

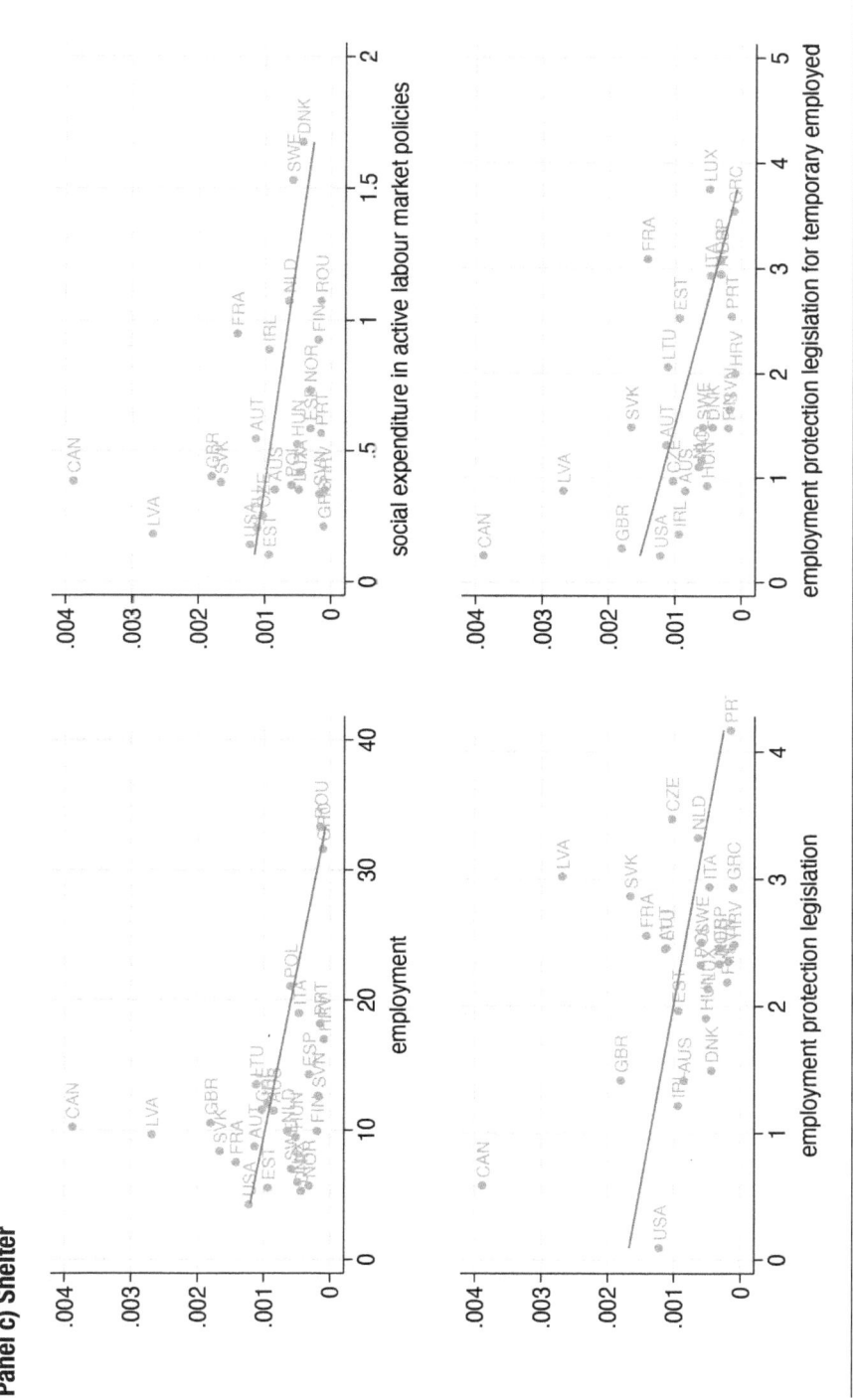

dex and the prevalence of homelessness. The relationship between the two variables is positive. A higher score on the index is generally considered beneficial for promoting economic development through easier access to credit. However, countries with strong legal rights protection may have higher housing prices leading to gentrification, greater inequality, and limited social safety nets, and these factors may increase the risk of homelessness. Finally, strong legal rights protections can go hand in hand with limited tenant protections, making it easier to evict tenants with shorter (or no) notice and to raise rents.

The key message of this descriptive evidence is that homelessness is not an inevitable condition; it can be shaped and reduced through effective policy. In addition, it clearly emerges that homelessness is not solely determined by GDP growth and other standard macroeconomic variables: in fact, most economic fluctuations have minimal impact on homelessness. Instead, institutional factors play a more significant role. However, since different institutional features can have opposing effects, it is essential from a policy standpoint to carefully calibrate interventions for maximum effectiveness.

5.6 Homelessness and social housing

Different indicators can be used to characterised a county's housing market. If we take the number of dwellings per 1000 inhabitants as a crude measure of housing availability, it is around 495 in Europe, above the OECD average of around 470 (OECD Affordable Housing Database, 2024). It is higher in continental (around 450) and especially Southern European countries and it is lower in some Eastern European countries (between 300 and 350). In most countries, the number of dwellings per thousand inhabitants has increased over the last decade. The exceptions are Croatia, Ireland, the Czech Republic, Iceland and Luxembourg. These figures give an immediate snapshot, but do not provide information on housing shortages, as they do not take into account the actual number of households or household formation patterns, which would give a better indication of supply compared to demand. For years, in many countries, the response to increased demand for housing has been to increase investment in housing, so that the housing stock per inhabitant has grown. In the presence of an economic crisis (i.e. the 2008 economic crisis), housing investment suddenly collapsed. Using the construction production index as a proxy for residential investment, during the Great Recession (in 2008, 2010, and 2012), there was a significant negative downturn, especially in the construction of new buildings. As a result, the shortage of housing pushes up house prices and affects housing affordability.

To better understand how the housing market affects homelessness, it is important to consider the role of the public sector through the provision of social housing and how it has changed over time. Over the last fifteen years, the Great Financial Crisis, the European sovereign debt crisis, the Covid pandemic crisis and the energy crisis have put increasing pressure on the budgets of European households, and housing af-

Figure 23 **Homelessness and political orientation**

Panel a) Total Homeless share

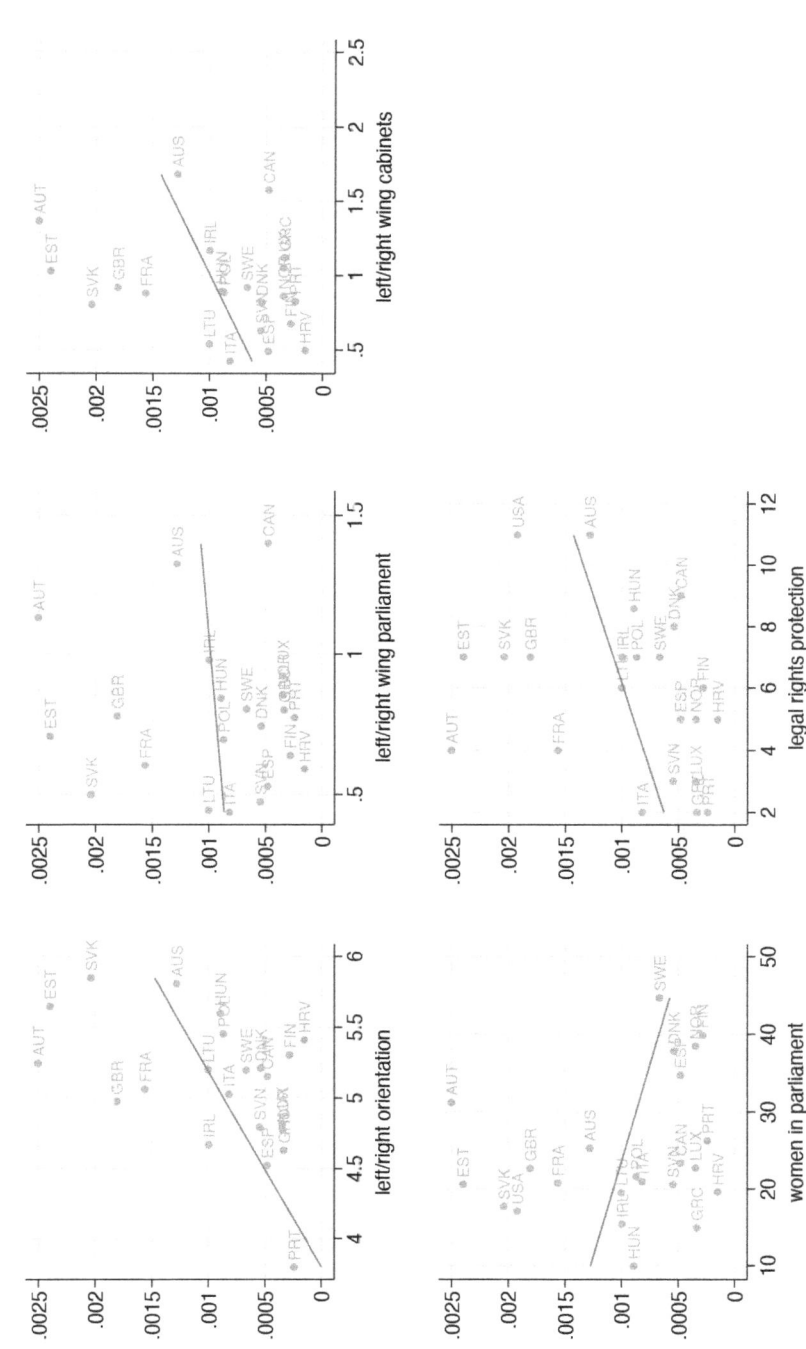

Figure 23 Homelessness and political orientation (continued)

Panel b) Street

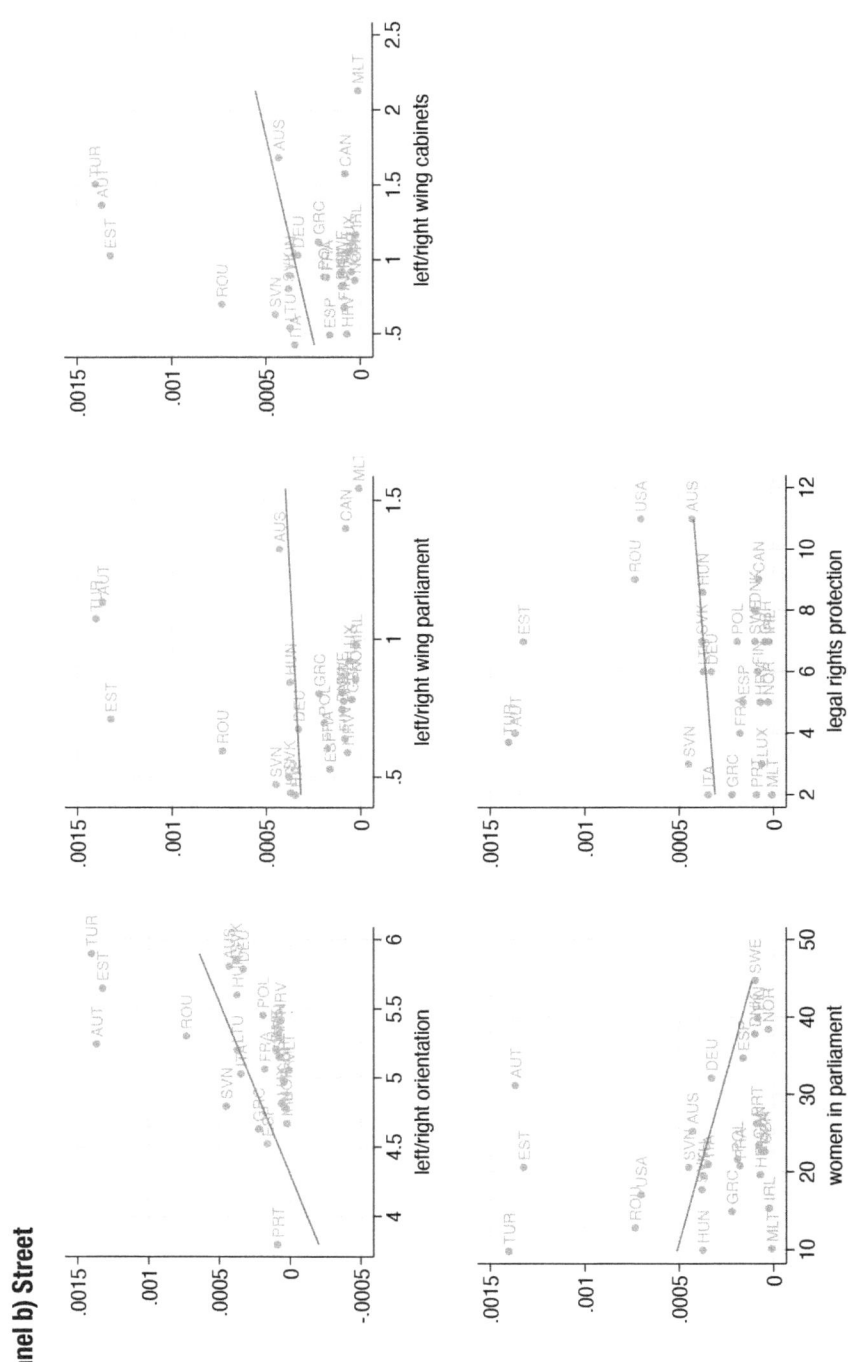

Figure 23 Homelessness and political orientation (continued)

Panel c) Shelter

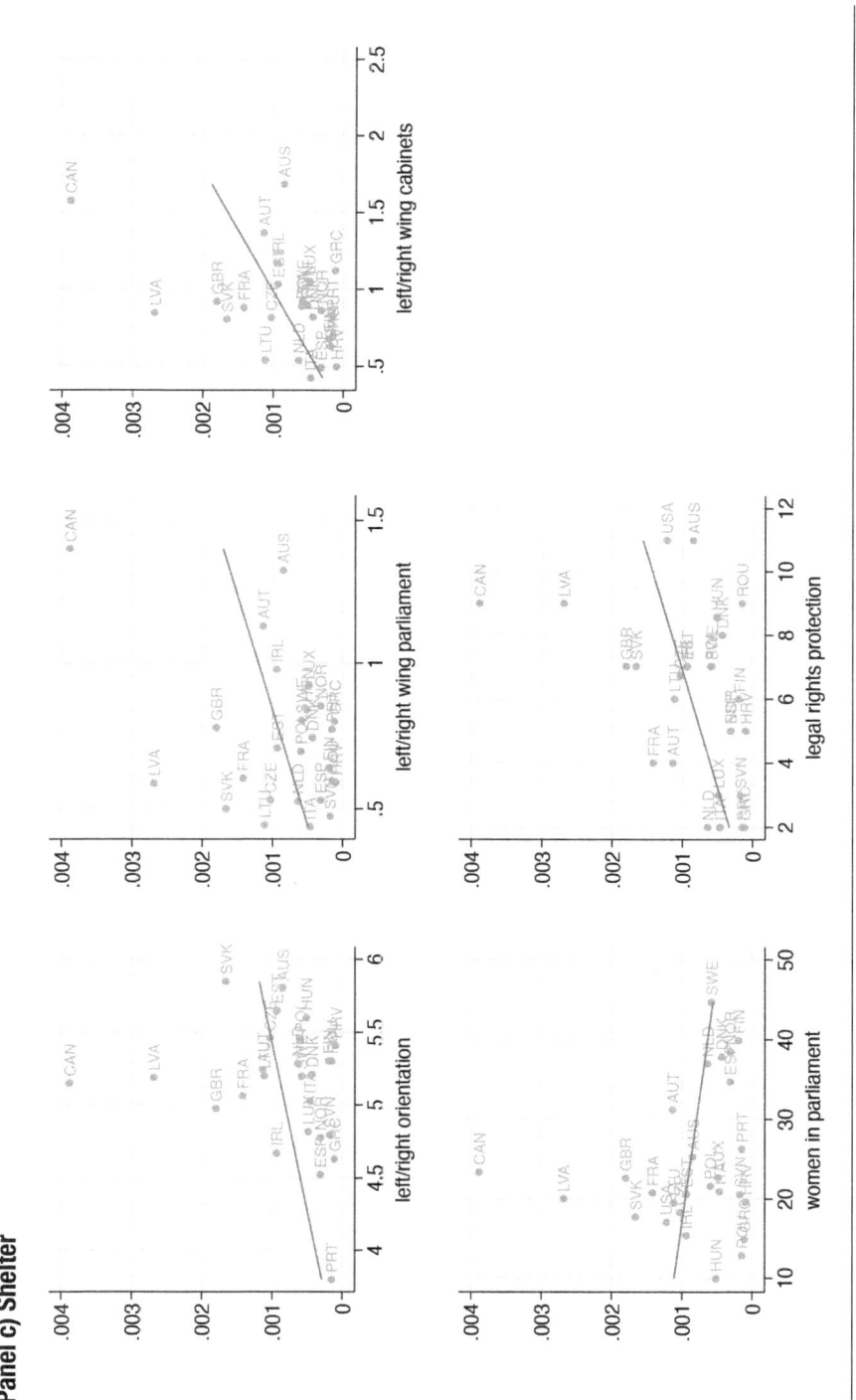

fordability has become a growing concern at the European level. Access to affordable housing was one of the priorities identified in the 2014 EU Annual Growth Survey. The survey highlighted that policies to combat poverty and provide broad access to affordable housing are essential to ensure social protection, support social change and reduce inequalities and poverty over time. Similarly, according to the progress report of the Europe 2020 Strategy *'the cost and quality of housing are a key determinant of living standards and wellbeing, especially for the most vulnerable people.'*

Social housing is one of the possible tools to enhance affordability. The term social housing has two alternative connotations. The first refers to all types of housing that receive some form of public subsidy or social assistance, either directly or indirectly, which can include tax relief on mortgage interest, tax incentives for home ownership, subsidies to builders, depreciation allowances for investments in residential property, or the provision of collective public services (roads, electricity, water or sewerage) for housing below cost. This definition is very inclusive, namely whenever the private housing stock receives some public subsidies, it should be included in the social housing sector. The second definition largely refers to traditional public housing, namely government-subsidized housing and social rental housing, but also includes new forms of publicly supported and non-market housing, such as cooperatives, income-based rentals, limited-dividend and non-profit housing provided by social agencies, community groups, non-profit private firms and political organisations other than governments. The common distinction of these new forms is that they are collectively managed on a not-for-profit basis, with their rents set (at least partially) according to the ability to pay. Public subsidies are used to reduce initial capital costs or operating costs, with a wider target than traditional policies. There are three common elements in the definition of social housing across EU Member States: the mission, the objectives and the target. Social housing aims to increase the supply of affordable housing through construction, management or purchase. The target population for social housing is identified according to socio-economic status or the presence of vulnerabilities. Beyond these similarities, there is no common official definition of social housing across Europe, and not all 27 EU Member States even use the term.1 The size of the social housing market varies considerably across the EU. Using the share of the social rental stock in the total housing stock as a crude indicator, the Netherlands, Austria and Denmark have the highest shares (32%, 23% and 19% respectively) compared to the EU average (8.3%), while the Eastern and Mediterranean countries have less than 5% of the total social housing stock and Greece and Latvia have none (**Figure 24**).

Four dimensions characterize and differentiate social housing models and policies: tenure, service providers, beneficiaries, and financing arrangements.

In terms of tenure, social housing is rented in most countries, but in many countries it is also available for sale. In addition, some countries provide for intermediate tenure, a shared ownership solution where tenants buy a share of the dwelling and pay rent for the remainder, as is increasingly the case in the UK. Others, including some Mediterranean countries (such as Cyprus, Greece and Spain), have provided social housing as low-cost housing for sale. Social rental is present in all Member

Figure 24 Social housing share

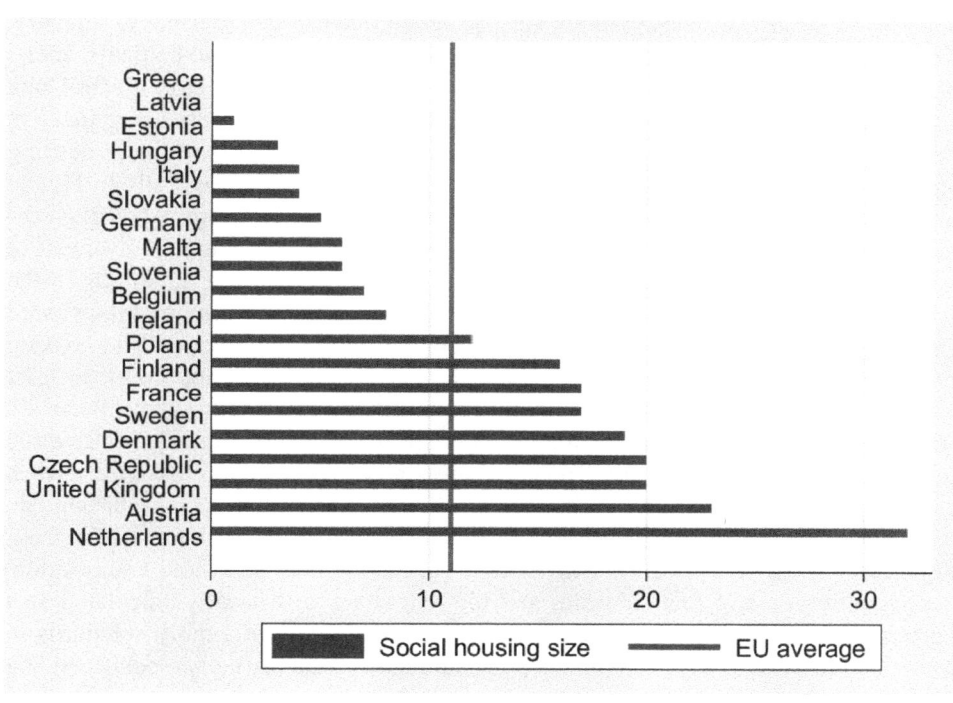

Source: CECODHAS

States apart from Greece, whereas home ownership is not present in Northern Europe and in most Eastern countries. Moreover, shared ownership is present in some countries, without a particular geographical pattern. The provision of social housing involves a variety of stakeholders: local authorities, public companies, non-profit or limited-profit associations and companies, cooperatives, and in some cases even private for-profit developers and investors. Historically, social housing was created by the private sector, both charitable institutions and private companies, in the early 20th century when industrialization and urbanization increased housing needs. Faced with the pressing housing needs of the post-war period, many States took over those private initiatives in the 1950s to offer a more general and wide-scale service. In the 1990s, the progressive decentralization of responsibilities to the regional and local levels gradually reduced the responsibility of public actors in the provision of housing. Finally, in the last decade, private and non-profit organizations have become more involved in the provision of housing services, thanks to large government subsidies and financial assistance, while the public sector regulates and programs housing provision. The most recent trend in the sector indicates an ever-growing involvement of many stakeholders, yet with the private and the public sectors having well-defined roles: local authorities manage the existing social housing stock while the private sector is responsible for developing new social housing. Cooperatives also play a crucial role in some countries, namely Austria, Belgium, Estonia, Germany, Hungary, Italy, Poland, Portugal, Spain and Sweden. In Denmark and the Netherlands, social housing provision is the prerogative of the private non-profit sector. Central and Eastern European countries have followed a divergent trend, experiencing massive housing privatization since 1990, leaving public authorities with a minimal housing stock, which is the only form of social housing currently available. Only in Poland and Slovenia has there been a marginal growth of a small non-profit housing sector. Recent years have also seen an increase in the participation and involvement of non-specialized actors such as commercial developers and private landlords in the social housing sector. In Germany, for example, non-profit institutions disappeared from the sector in 1989, followed by the system of allocating public funds to housing providers in exchange for the right to use the housing for social purposes, at least temporarily. Similarly, in Italy, private providers are allowed to participate in certain social housing schemes after signing an agreement with local municipalities, while in Spain, preferential loans are available to potential providers and developers when such dwellings are qualified as protected dwellings. Other countries have also begun to use such provision schemes. In the Czech Republic, municipalities or non-profit organizations provide social housing based on income and household composition. Tenants often receive rent subsidies and the rent charged is usually calculated as a percentage of their income. Social housing units meet certain quality standards in terms of building safety, maintenance and amenities. Interestingly, social housing programs offer additional support services to help tenants with various needs, such as employment assistance, counseling or access to healthcare.

In England, a significant proportion of social housing is managed by local authorities, but not-for-profit organizations and for-profit companies are also entitled to develop, manage and own social housing. Secure tenancies are usually granted, providing long-term stability and protection against eviction. Tenants have the right to remain in their homes as long as they meet the terms of their agreement. Rents are lower than market rents and are set at an affordable level based on household income and local housing market conditions. They may be all low-cost rents, below-market affordable rents, or subsidized rents. People with the greatest need, such as the homeless, those living in unsuitable conditions or those at risk of homelessness. The historic *Right to Buy* scheme allows tenants to purchase their homes at a discounted price: this certainly increases equity, but at the cost of significantly reducing the stock of social housing available. As in other countries, some providers offer additional services such as employment support, social assistance or participation in social inclusion schemes.

Significant geographical variation has also emerged in terms of potential beneficiaries. Social or public housing is a universal service potentially directed to all citizens in some countries, with the public sector only playing a market regulating role and enhancing social mix in accordance with local policies. On the other hand, social housing in other countries is a targeted service, with the sector operating separately from the private rental market, and only households for which the market is deemed unable to provide housing can benefit. In particular, in some countries eligibility is based on means-tested income thresholds, while in others the target population is specifically the most vulnerable households. Income thresholds are the most common criteria used to define eligibility for social housing. In countries such as Austria, France and Germany, the maximum income threshold is set at a sufficiently high level to ensure a mix of incomes among beneficiaries, while in other countries (such as Italy) such thresholds are set at very low levels. Other criteria used to allocate housing are household needs based on observable individual characteristics such as housing conditions, homelessness, unhealthy housing, overcrowding and forced cohabitation. In some cases, it is possible to identify target groups with priority applications, generally including youth, elderly, disabled, large families, mentally disabled, homeless, ethnic minorities or refugees. It should be stressed that in some countries (Denmark, Sweden and the United Kingdom), registration on social housing waiting lists is open to all in order to avoid social segregation and to ensure that public housing is accessible to all sections of society. In practice, however, applications are largely needs-based and, despite the absence of an income ceiling, there is a strong correlation with income conditions.

The energy supply crisis with the unprecedented increase in energy prices, the geopolitical tensions, together with the economic and social consequences of the Covid-19 pandemic, have exacerbated the problem of affordable housing in many countries. The socio-economic conditions of a growing proportion of the population have deteriorated, leading to increased demand for affordable housing and social assistance in most European countries. At the same time, the social housing sector faced significant budgetary constraints in almost all Member States due to the decreasing trend in the resources used to finance the sector. European countries have applied differing strategies to deal with the economic crisis, with each country choosing to finance a specific type (or group) of social expenditure that could provide a 'safety net' for an increasing share of the population experiencing severe economic conditions. Eurostat data show that EU housing markets are characterized by high levels of home ownership, with the most recent data showing home ownership rates ranging from 40% (Germany) to over 90% (in some Eastern European countries - i.e. Estonia, Romania and Bulgaria). On average, homeownership rates are higher in Southern Europe than in Northern Europe. Symmetrically, the size of the rental sector varies widely, being small in Eastern and Southern Europe and large in Northern Europe. The relative weight of private or social renting varies considerably between countries. Following the deep economic crisis, European countries have experienced a significant increase in poverty rates and housing exclusion.

In response to the growing need for housing that is not being met by the market, social housing has faced significant budgetary constraints due to the declining trend in the resources used to finance the sector. This has limited the ability to build new social housing units or maintain existing ones. Priorities have also changed, shifting the political agenda away from social housing and towards more urging needs. In addition, in many areas it has become extremely difficult to find suitable land for social housing developments at an affordable price. Finally, in some cases, changes in regulatory requirements and bureaucratic processes have slowed the development of new social housing projects, making it difficult to meet increasing demand within a reasonable timeframe.

Thus, the sustainability of social housing provision has been severely affected by unexpected shocks to both the demand and supply sides of the market in many countries over the last decade. It is difficult to summarize the main trends in the social housing sector across Europe in recent years. The lack of unique definition of social housing, the disparity of available indicators, the non-homogeneous time span and the variety of data collection methods used by national institutions make comparisons between countries and over time very difficult. Nevertheless, the rough data show some common trends and features for most countries in recent years. In particular, the key elements of the social housing sector in Europe in the last decade are: an increasing delegation to local government, a special focus on fragile populations, a downward trend in the share of social housing over the total housing stock. Starting from this observation, we subsequently present a summary of the trends in social housing provisions across European countries.

During the crisis, the increasing share of the population at risk of housing exclusion translates into a growing demand for social housing, as confirmed by the upward trend in the number of people registered on social housing waiting lists in recent years or in the aftermath of the 2008 financial crisis. Indeed, the economic crisis is worsening the socio-economic conditions of the majority of the population, and a growing proportion of households are experiencing difficulties in accessing and maintaining adequate housing, with rent and mortgage arrears increasing. In addition, the increase in repossessions and evictions is forcing people to rely on more affordable housing provided by housing associations. These two phenomena have led to increased demand for affordable housing and social benefits. Middle-class households and workers with temporary or atypical contracts make up a large proportion of the potential beneficiaries. The former, on average, experience an increase in unemployment rate and a decrease in the perceived social benefits. The latter have limited access to stable tenancy or home ownership.

The latest figures from Housing Europe (2023) indicate that, since 2020, over 12 million households have been on waiting lists for social housing. The situation is extremely problematic in some countries where the excess demand appears to be significant (UK, France or the Netherlands). In the UK, for example, more than 1.1 million people are on social housing waiting lists, while in France the figure is more than 1.5 million. According to the German Institute for Economic Research, there are more than 4 million households on waiting lists in Germany, and the problem is particularly acute in large cities (Berlin, Munich and Hamburg). In both Spain and Italy, more than 550,000 households are looking for affordable housing and the main causes are the population growth due to immigration and the energy crisis. A similar pattern emerged during the 2008 crisis when, for example, the number of people in need of social housing increased by 75% in Ireland and by 200% in England. Faced

5 What does contribute to homelessness?

with such a huge increase in demand, most countries responded with public spending on social housing.

A key difference in recent years is that in many countries significant resources have been made available through the EU Resilience and Recovery Funds. Some housing providers are experiencing unprecedented funding opportunities in a context of high uncertainty, but at the same time the rising costs of new construction and renovation in recent years are becoming unsustainable in some cases. The share of GDP spent on social housing varies between countries, reflecting their specific housing policies, economic conditions and social welfare systems. On average, it accounts for about 2% of GDP in 2020, compared to less than 1% in the last decade.

BOX Case study on the 2008 crisis

Social housing expenditure as a percentage of GDP experienced a sharp increase between 2007 and 2008, followed by a less rapid but still positive growth in 2008 and 2009, as shown in **Figure 25**, where data are averaged across Europe. On average, social housing expenditure represented 0.1% of GDP in the EU-27 area. A different trend emerges for rent benefits as a percentage of GDP, which decreased between 2006 and 2007, before experiencing positive growth in both 2008 and 2009. However, the broad European averages hide important differences across groups of countries. Interesting trends emerge when countries are grouped by GDP level (**Figure 26**). Social housing expenditure as a percentage of GDP increases on average in countries belonging to the two highest GDP quartiles, rising from 0.17% to 0.21% in the fourth quartile group and from 0.02% to 0.05% in the third GDP quartile group. On the other hand, there are no patterns in the countries with the two lowest GDPs: social housing expenditure as a percentage of

Figure 25 Social housing expenditure as % of GDP by GDP quartiles

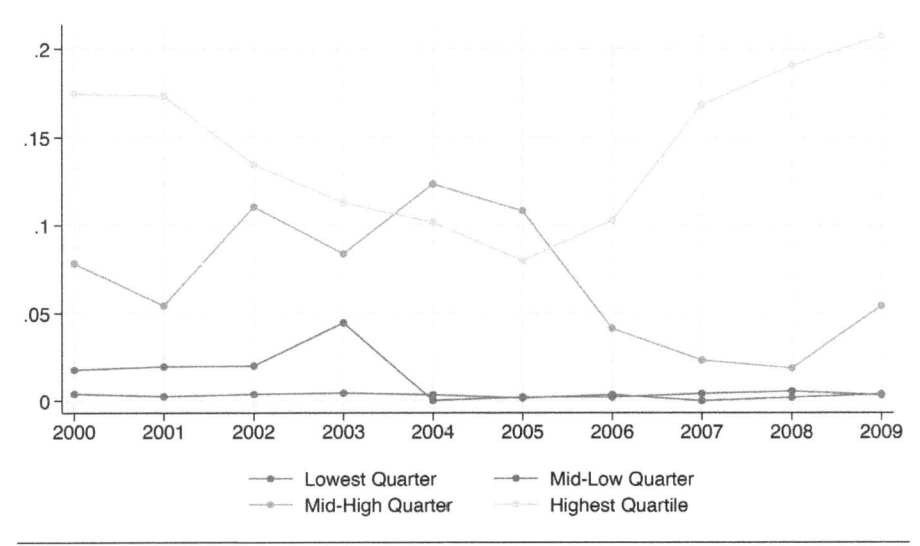

Source: Eurostat.

Figure 26   Rent benefits as % of GDP by GDP quartiles

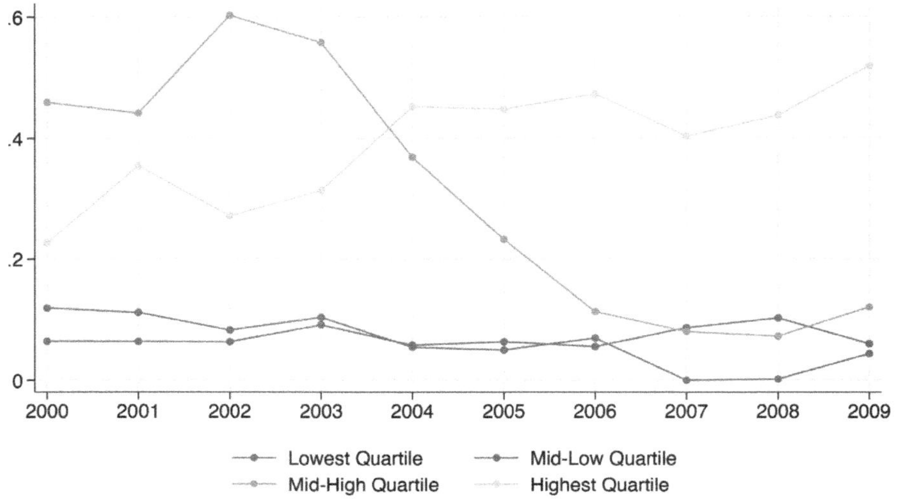

[Line chart showing rent benefits as % of GDP from 2000 to 2009 for four GDP quartiles: Lowest Quartile, Mid-Low Quartile, Mid-High Quartile, Highest Quartile]

Source: Eurostat.

GDP remains stable at values slightly above than 0.05%. Symmetrically, as can be seen in Figure 14, the dynamics of rental payments increase on average in all GDP country groups except for the middle-low quartile, where they decrease from 2003 onwards. All quartiles except the middle-low quartile reacted to the 2008 crisis with an increase in rent payments.

Previous patterns have highlighted that European countries are applying differing strategies to deal with the economic crisis, with each country choosing to finance a specific type (or group) of social expenditure that could provide a 'safety net' for an increasing share of the population experiencing severe economic conditions. In addition, it is clear that the economic crisis has had a different impact on various indicators within the social housing sector. The case of Ireland is emblematic as it provides an example of a winning strategy followed by governments in adjusting public expenditure in the social housing sector. Due to the impact of the financial crisis on the Irish economy and government revenues, government funding to housing associations for the provision of social housing for rent has been suspended or withdrawn, with the exception of some special needs schemes. As a result, the previous model of 100% government funding to housing associations for the provision of social housing for vulnerable households has been discontinued. Government funding to housing associations was only maintained for some special needs schemes, namely for pensioners or people with disabilities. As the economic crisis has created a double challenge for European countries, increasing the housing needs not met by the market and limiting the availability of public resources, one possible way of handling this trade-off was a significant rationalization of the social housing sector. This could be achieved, as in the case of Ireland, by reallocating public resources to those segments of the population in greater need. Although the previous discussion based on relevant country groups could be useful in identifying common patterns across European countries, it is worth noting that the extent to which European countries have been affected by the economic crisis and how the socio-economic downturn has affected their social housing sectors varies considerably. Accordingly, **Figure 27** and **Figure 28** report the trends in social housing expenditure as a percentage of GDP and rent benefits as a percentage of GDP for each European country where data are available.

5 What does contribute to homelessness?

Figure 27 Social housing expenditure as % of GDP by country

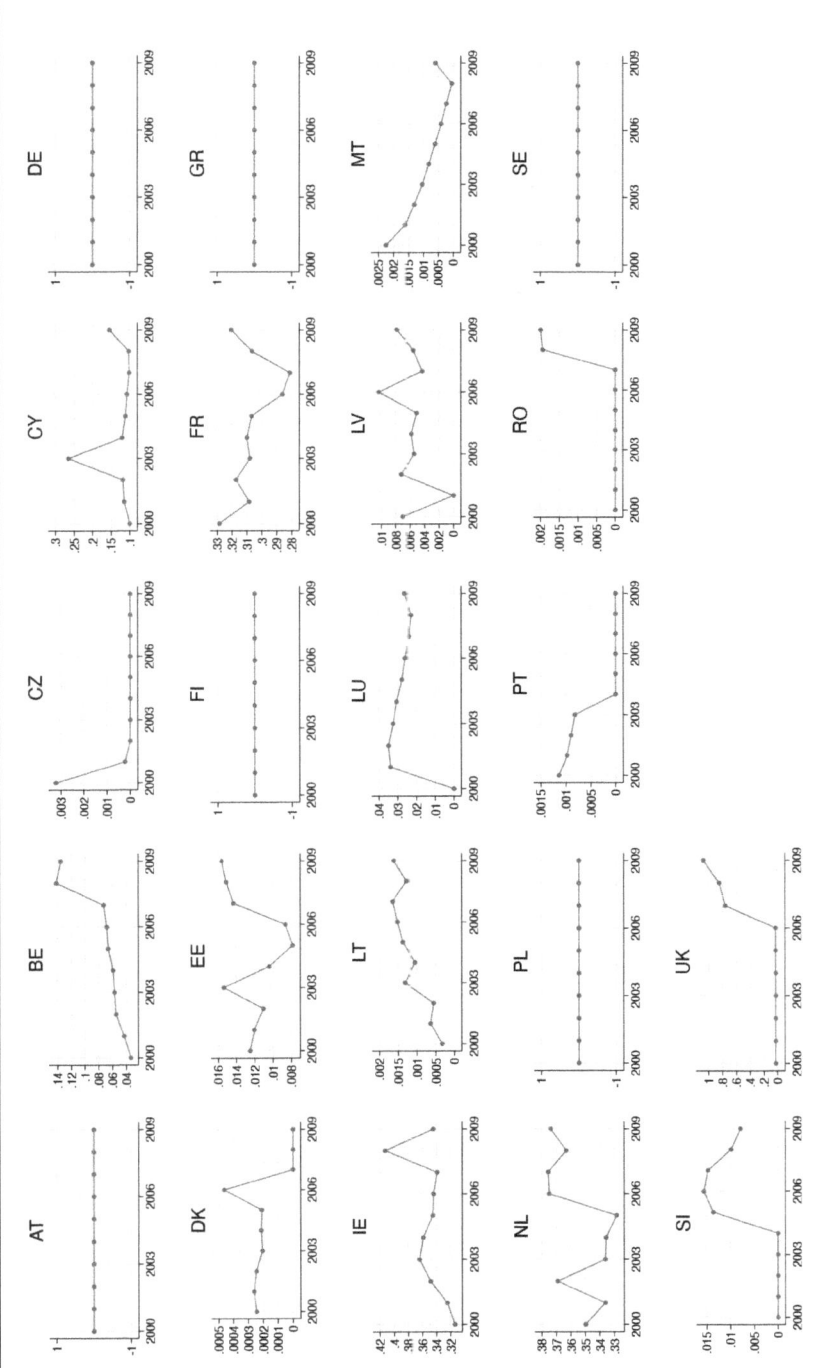

Source: Eurostat.
Notes: Data not available for Hungary, Italy, Slovakia and Spain. Bulgaria is omitted from the analysis because only a short time-series is available.

Figure 28   Rent benefits as % of GDP by country

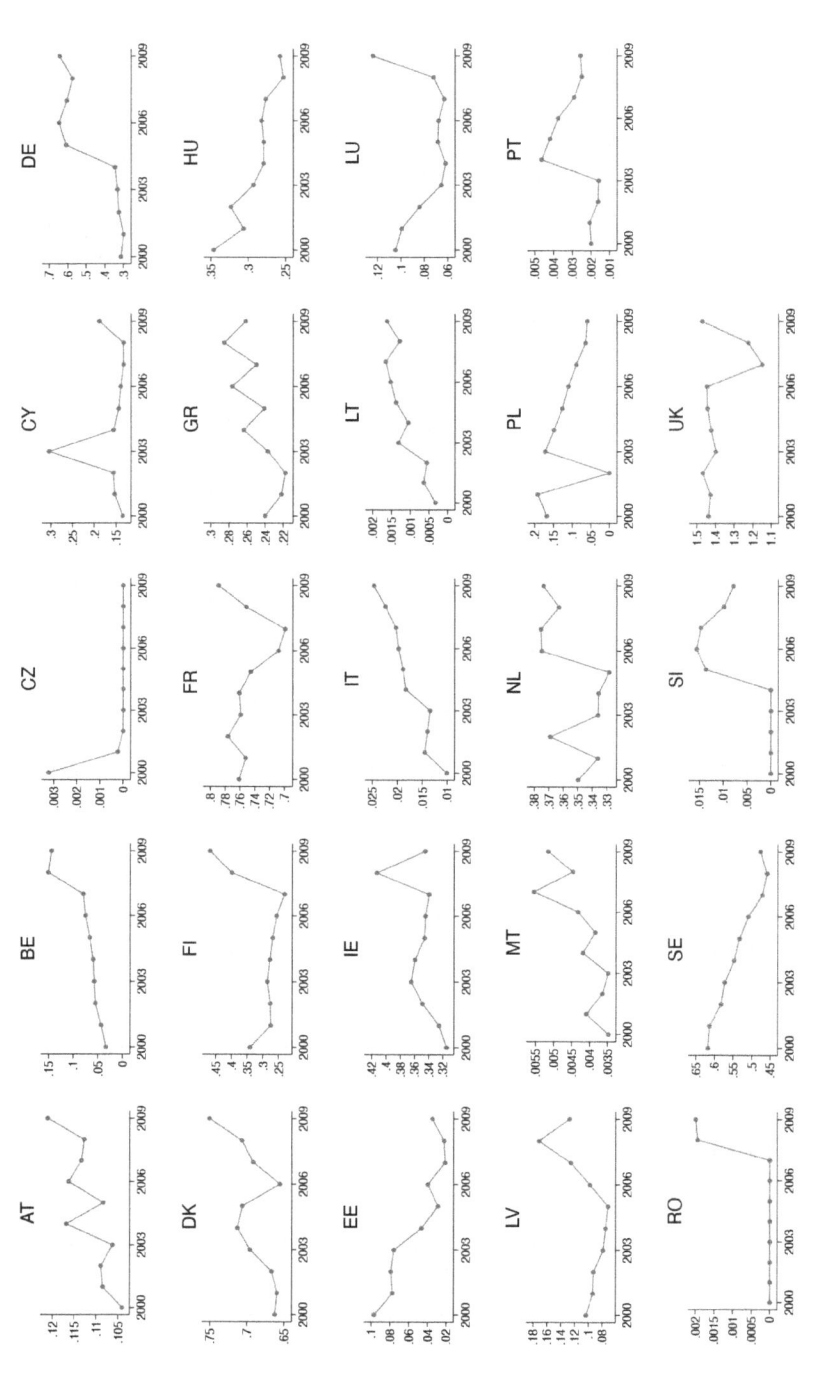

Source: Eurostat.
Notes: Data not available for Spain. Bulgaria and Slovakia are omitted from the analysis because only few observations are available.

5 What does contribute to homelessness?

Between 2008 and 2009, social housing expenditure showed a negative variation in Belgium, Ireland and Slovenia, while rental payments decreased in Greece, Ireland, Latvia, Poland, Portugal and Slovenia. This underlines that some countries increased their investment in social housing after the economic crisis in order to support the large proportion of the population facing the socio-economic consequences of the crisis. In other countries, especially those most affected by the crisis, expenditure on social housing decreased in the immediate aftermath of the crisis.

Data on the population distribution by tenure status over the same period appears to suggest two main patterns (Figure 29). Firstly, between 2007 and 2010 the percentage of the population living in an accommodation rented at a reduced rate or provided free of charge decreased in the majority of European countries. Secondly, in most European countries this percentage decreased among the population below 60% of the average income, while it increased among the population above 60% of the average income. According to the Eurostat definition, reduced-rate renters would include those who: (a) renting social housing; (b) renting at a reduced rate from an employer; or (c) living in accommodation where the actual rent is fixed by law. Based on the literature, this variable may be interpreted as a proxy for the size of the social housing sector.

Figure 29 Percentage of households living in an accommodation rented at a reduced rate or provided for free

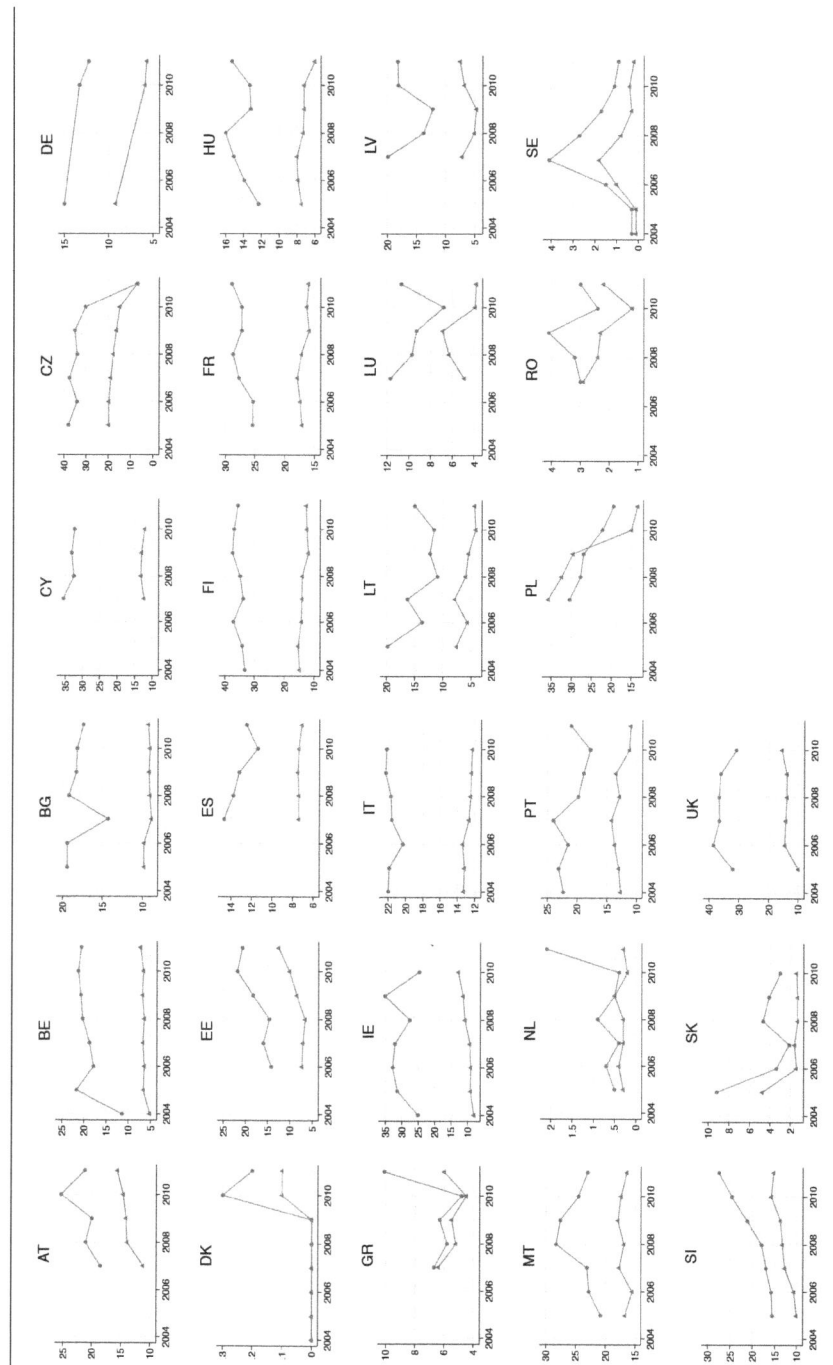

Source: Eurostat.
Notes: Blue lines refer to households below 60% of average income; red lines to households above 60% of average income.

6 Who are the homeless and those at risk of homelessness?

After a detailed comparison of the number of homeless people and their correlates across countries and over time, we now move to the analysis of homeless people's characteristics. In particular, in this chapter we attempt to understand who are homeless individuals using information from available survey data.

6.1 The characteristics of homeless individuals: Evidence from an original point in time survey in Italy

We launched one of the few rigorous and representative surveys in Europe among homeless people in Italy in Milan in 2008. The survey was then organized in subsequent years and other major Italian cities – in Milan, in 2013 and 2018, in Turin in 2010 and in Rome in 2014 – for a total of 5 rounds of data collection. Data have been collected at the individual level for people in shelters, eliciting information not only related to their socio-demographic characteristics, but also to the labor market, their family background, their expectations, etc.

Conducting a survey among homeless people involves many challenges. First, it is difficult to clearly define the target population. Second, it is very challenging to provide reliable estimates of the homeless population within a city, since the risk of counting and interviewing the same person twice is extremely high. The **Italian Homeless Survey 2008-2018 (IHS, 2008-2018)** targeted all persons who reside in (i) places not meant for human habitation, such as cars, parks, sidewalks, abandoned buildings (unsheltered homeless) and (ii) emergency shelters (sheltered homeless). In the definition of a homeless person, the housing component is dominant: not having a home is the common feature of all surveyed individuals and does not necessarily imply a lack of social relationships. In order to obtain the most rigorous estimate, the IHS used the so-called S-night approach (see Chapter 1 for a detailed description), which consists of two major phases: a point-in-time count and a comprehensive qualitative assessment via trained interviews. The point-in-time count aims at identifying all the homeless sleeping in the street and in shelters on a single night. This approach also allows the enumerators to assess whether observed individuals meet the study's definition of homelessness and ensures minimal variation in identification criteria. The S-Night approach shows only a snapshot of the homeless population, but if the count is repeated at regular intervals, it will provide insight into the trend over time.

The reference nights for the count were January 14th, 2008, March 3rd, 2013 and February 19th, 2018 in Milan; January 18th, 2010 in Turin and March 17th, 2014 in Rome.

The main drawback of the point-in-time method is the risk of missing homeless people who are hidden from public view during late-night hours. We applied some efforts to overcome this criticism and get the most reliable estimate. We divided each city into smaller areas, following the main streets, so that a team of 3-4 enumerators could reasonably cover them during the night of the count. Enumerators were asked to walk every street and other public places in their assigned area. To reduce the risk of skipping some streets, researchers provided them with enlarged maps of their target area. There were some criteria for the count: closed tents and closed cardboard dwellings were counted as one homeless person, while for abandoned cars/caravans enumerators tried to understand how many persons were sleeping there. To be sure all enumerators started the count at the same time, they met one hour before the kick-off in few strategic locations in each city. There, they also collected useful materials for the night (e.g., flashlights, food, beverages, and notebooks). Besides counting, volunteers have two additional tasks: (i) to report a homeless person's location as precisely as possible by describing the street, the closest house number, and the exact sleeping place (e.g. under a bench); (ii) to detect some observable characteristics, such as ethnicity, gender, and estimated age, which are a key information to test for a potential sample selection. Volunteers paired these statistical activities with hot beverages and food distribution. In the meantime, other teams of enumerators collected information on the number, names, gender, age and nationality of the homeless people living in the city's emergency shelters. The average duration of the count was about 3 hours, from 10 p.m. to 1 a.m.

The count was necessary to have a precise idea of the phenomenon's dimension and to construct a census from which randomly select a sample of respondents. Questionnaires to the unsheltered homeless were performed on the following 2/3 nights, depending on the number of homeless counted in each city. All data collection was then completed in a single week to minimize sample attrition. The survey involved approximately 350 volunteers in each city. On the street, researchers attempted to obtain a complete count of the homeless by sending enumerators back to the locations identified during the count. Sheltered homeless were randomly sampled from the population based on the shelter size, oversampling small shelters and under-sampling large shelters.

A potential drawback of conducting the count and the interviews on two different days (even if in very close proximity) is the attrition rate, since people counted could have moved the day after. To control for the fact that the homeless people counted were the same as those interviewed, the first question on the survey was "Did you sleep here last night?" and, if not, "Where did you sleep?" Researchers cross-checked this information against the locations of homeless people recorded during the count.

Self-reported answers can be biased for many reasons. This might be particularly true in surveys of the homeless: they can be under the influence of alcohol or drugs during the survey, and they are more likely to suffer from mental illness compared to

6 Who are the homeless and those at risk of homelessness?

the general population. To address this drawback, the enumerators fill out a one-page questionnaire describing respondent's condition at the end of the survey. The survey did not include questionnaires administered to homeless persons with intoxication or mental illness. As an incentive, enumerators distributed grocery vouchers to the respondents who fully completed the questionnaire. The questionnaire was written in Italian and translated into other languages (i.e. Romanian and French). The average interview time was about 30 minutes.

The count and the interviews were not conducted on the same day for two main reasons. First, it is difficult to interview people during an overnight count. During the count, enumerators meticulously checked for the presence of homeless people by walking every street in the city, and there would not be remaining time to also select and interview them. Second, while it is optimal to conduct a late-night count (from around midnight to 3 a.m.) to maximize the probability of observing more visible people sleeping outside, the ideal time for interviews is around 9 p.m., when they have settled down but are still awake and able to talk. The survey took place in winter, when the average daily temperature in Italy is at its lowest and shelters are likely to be at peak capacity: it is easier to count people in shelters than on the street, and conducting the count on a night when the shelters are at their busiest is likely to yield the most accurate count. Counting and interviewing people sleeping in open locations during the winter months may also lead to a more realistic picture of the chronically unsheltered homeless. Furthermore, to facilitate the identification of homeless people and to reduce the likelihood of the surveyors being overwhelmed by potential respondents, the count was conducted on Mondays, a day with less pedestrian traffic.

As reported in **Table 10**, the results of the Italian Homeless Survey show that the street and shelter homeless population accounts for 1560 homeless in Milan in 2008, 765 in Turin in 2010, 2637 in Milan in 2013, 3276 in Rome in 2014 and 2608 in Milan again in 2018. This corresponds approximately to 0.12 percent, 0.08 percent, 0.20 percent, 0.11 percent and 0.19 percent of the total population in the respective city in the reference year.

Table 10   **Number of homeless counted and interviewed by year and city**

	Milan 2008	Turin 2010	Milan 2013	Rome 2014	Milan 2018
General population	1,298,972	907,563	1,324,169	2,863,322	1,378,689
N. of homeless counted	1560	765	2637	3276	2608
% of the general population	0.12	0.08	0.20	0.11	0.19
N. of homeless interviewed	561	428	968	1184	993

Notes: Population in each city come from ISTAT (Italy). The data on the number of homeless in Milan, Turin and Rome come from the Milan Homeless Survey (MHS, 2008, 2013 and 2018), Turin Homeless Survey (2013) and Rome Homeless Survey (2014), respectively.

Table 11   Descriptive statistics

	All sample	Milan 2008	Turin 2010	Milan 2013	Rome 2014	Milan 2018
Average age	43.61	44.68	39.98	41.51	45.32	44.90
% of female	16.95	14.26	20.10	15.83	18.41	16.45
% of immigrants	66.49	55.61	61.01	75.74	65.39	72.63
% of with criminal convictions	23.37	29.62	31.19	18.44	23.30	20.72
Average duration (years)	4.70	5.19	4.00	3.42	5.43	5.10

Notes: For "criminal convictions," we included both individuals who have been in prison at least once and individuals who have been convicted. Questions used: "Have you ever been to prison? / Have you ever been in jail?"; "Have you ever been convicted/have you ever been convicted of a crime?" Source: Sample of homeless interviewed in Milan (2008, 2013 and 2018), Turin (2010) and Rome (2014).

The first part of the survey investigates the socio-demographic characteristics of the homeless (see **Table 11**). The average age of the sample is very similar across cities and approximately equal to 43.5 years, ranging from 17 to 88 years. Women represent only 16.9 percent of the total sample, but the gender composition varies slightly across cities, with the highest proportion of female homeless in Turin (20.1 percent). The vast majority of homeless people are immigrants: 61 percent in Turin in 2010, 55.6 percent in Milan in 2008, 74.7 percent in Milan in 2013, 72.6 percent in Milan in 2018 and 65.4 percent in Rome in 2014. **Table 11** also shows a strong relationship between homelessness and criminal behavior: more than 20 percent of the respondents reported a criminal record, peaking in Turin where the proportion of people with at least one prison sentence is 31 percent. This figure has relevant implications from a policy perspective. So programs targeting rehabilitation in prison and housing assistance upon release might have positive spillover effects on reducing homelessness. One limitation of the survey is that it does not differentiate among different types of criminal offenses: the researchers felt that it was too sensitive and subjective to ask questions about the type of crime committed. However, in order to gain some insight into the type of crime generally committed by homeless people, they assembled administrative data from the prison statistical offices on the type of crime committed by inmates in Milan who declared "missing residence" at the time of arrest. Typically, crimes committed by the homeless are linked to drug trafficking and violation of immigration law, followed by burglary, robbery and prostitution. The average duration of homelessness – calculated from the first day on the street to the date of the survey – is about 4 years.

A first relevant question to answer is: what are the main reasons driving people to live on the street? Some of them, such as unemployment and poverty, can be predictable, but others are less intuitive. **Figure 30** shows the main reason for the homeless interviewed in Italy. The main reason for homelessness is lack of work. For the Ital-

6 Who are the homeless and those at risk of homelessness?

Figure 30 Reason for homelessness

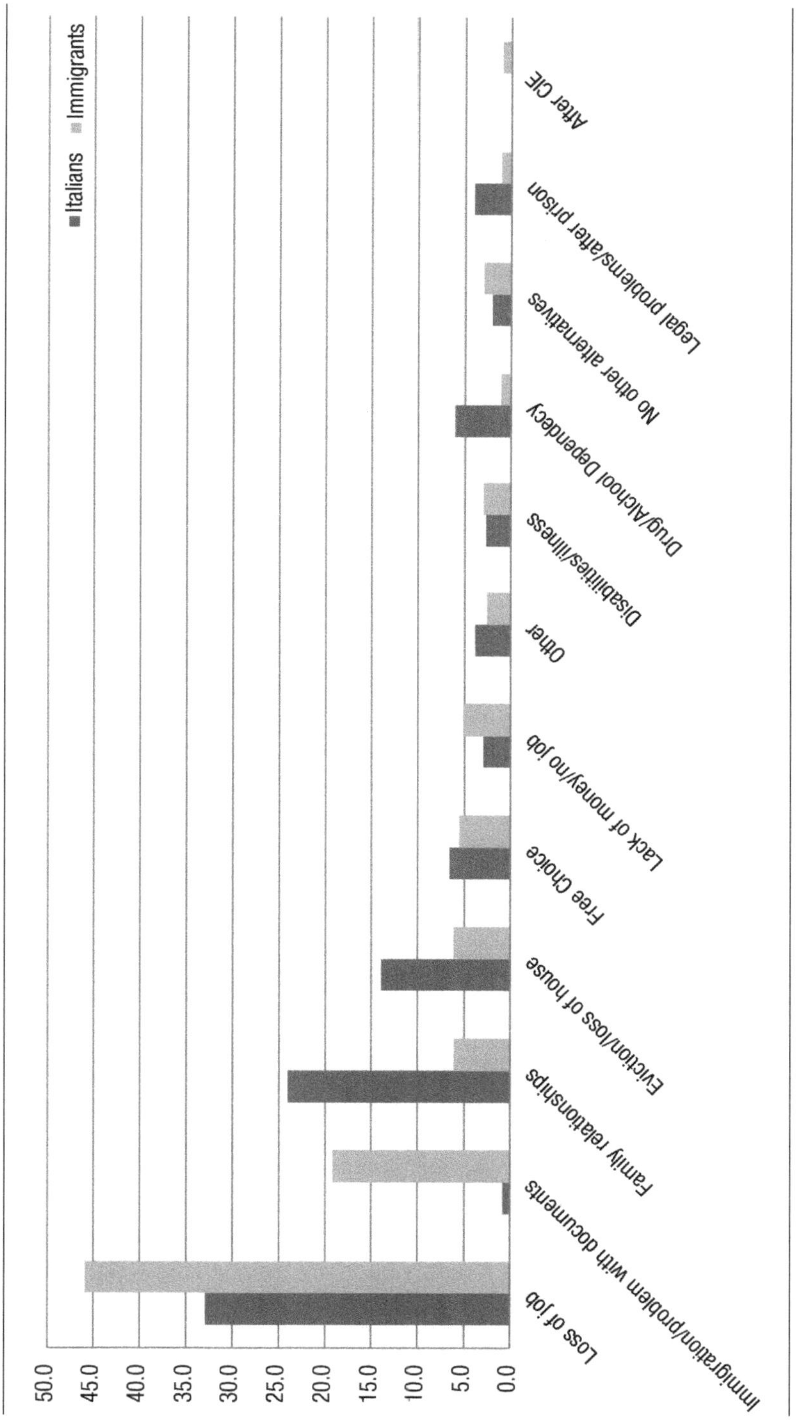

ian homeless, the second most common reason is the breakdown of family relationships, suggesting that the family might be an important source of insurance against economic and psychological shocks. For foreign respondents, immigration is another important cause: at the beginning of their stay in the host country, immigrants face problems related to their limited language proficiency, their scarce knowledge of the Italian welfare system, the labor and the housing markets and the lack of a legal residence permit. 7.3 percent of the sample reported eviction as the first reason for homelessness and 5.3 percent declared that homelessness was a choice. The other most common reasons were drug and alcohol addiction and a criminal record.

Figure 31 reports the nationality of the homeless by place of interview. Among the homeless people interviewed in Italy, 66.5 percent are immigrants. Romanians are the prevalent group in the sample (about 14,6 percent), followed by homeless people from North Africa – mainly Moroccans and Algerians – and Indians. If we cross-check information on age and nationality, we note that Italians are much older than immigrants: the average age of Italians is over 50, while the average age of immigrants is 39. Not surprisingly, immigrants are younger since they generally migrate to find a job and tend to reside in shelters, where it is easier to create a social network or to be supported by peers. The test for the equality of the respondents' average age between Italians and immigrants rejects the null with a p-value of 0.000.

Table 12 reports the educational level of the homeless interviewed. Column 1 shows that the average level of schooling is around 9 years and, surprisingly, homeless educational distribution is in line with that of the Italian population, except for the proportion of people without any formal education, which is more than double in our sample (ISTAT, 2005). Specifically, 14 percent of the sample have completed primary school, about 30.5 percent secondary school, and 9.9 percent have a university degree. By splitting the sample between Italians and immigrants, the statistics show that immigrants have a higher level of education compared to the Italian homeless (9.7 years compared to 8.6 years, respectively). Another interesting result shows that, on average, illegal immigrants have a slightly higher number of years of education compared to legal immigrants. The t-test for statistical significance of the difference between the two coefficients rejects the null with a p-value of 0.000. Looking at the level of education across cities, we find that homeless people living in Turin are, on average, more educated than those living in Milan or Rome.

The data showing that family breakdown is a major cause of homelessness (see **Table 13**) is confirmed by the data on marital status. **Table 13**, Panel A shows that nearly 40 percent of respondents who live on the street are single, 22.9 percent are divorced, 10 percent are widows/ers, only about 19 percent are currently married and about 5 percent have a partner (column 1). These figures are very different from the statistics on the marital status in the general population, where the fraction of divorced individuals is extremely lower and equal to 1.7 percent (ISTAT, 2008). These findings seem to be in line with the literature arguing that the family represents a natural source of insurance for its members. For example, Bentolila and Ichino (2007) study how countries with different family ties (namely Italy and Spain with strong family ties versus the US and the UK with less strong ties) cope with unem-

6 Who are the homeless and those at risk of homelessness?

Figure 31   Nationality and average age

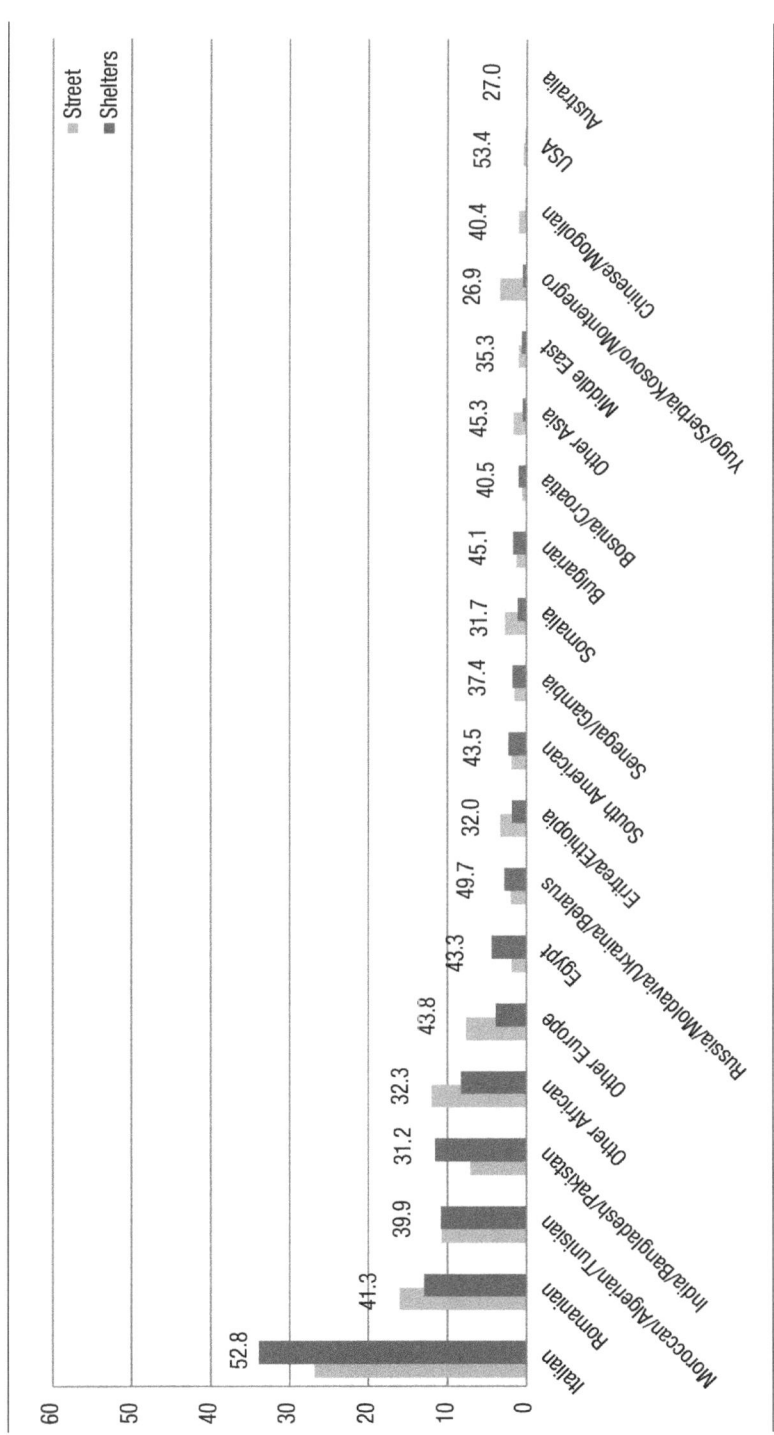

Table 12 Highest educational level

	All sample	Italians	Immigrants	Milan 2008	Turin 2010	Milan 2013	Rome 2014	Milan 2018
None/Never attended school	7.98	4.43	9.49	5.53	2.81	6.58	11.64	9.25
Elementary school	14.00	19.70	11.17	18.00	3.32	12.71	17.20	13.94
Middle school	30.45	39.90	24.08	34.76	17.90	32.58	28.84	33.05
Professional Diploma	17.19	17.14	18.83	14.80	43.22	12.71	16.27	12.38
High school	17.46	13.00	20.46	17.29	11.51	21.00	18.43	15.50
University and higher degree	9.87	4.33	12.76	8.02	20.97	9.65	7.62	8.77
Other	2.26	0.89	2.30	0.00	0.00	4.77	0.00	4.81
Don't answer/Don't know	0.80	0.59	0.92	1.60	0.26	0.00	0.00	2.28
Total	100.0	100.0	100.0	100.0	100.0	100.0	100.0	100.0
Average years of education	9.30	8.63	9.74	9.08	11.61	9.47	8.67	8.87

Notes: Author's calculations on the sample of homeless interviewed in Milan (2008, 2013 and 2018), Turin (2010) and Rome (2014).

Table 13 Marital status and family background

	All sample	Italians	Immigrants	Milan 2008	Turin 2010	Milan 2013	Rome 2014	Milan 2018
Panel A: Marital Status								
Widow/er	10.12	12.77	10.61	4.28	54.99	5.36	5.07	4.21
Married	19.78	7.93	25.86	18.36	18.93	25.00	16.32	19.71
Separated/Divorced	22.88	35.20	16.10	29.06	24.30	18.53	24.38	20.91
Single	39.78	37.52	40.14	40.64	1.78	44.42	45.57	45.07
With a partner	5.21	3.97	4.78	0.00	0.00	6.69	5.97	8.65
Other	0.98	1.55	1.01	6.42	0.00	0.00	0.00	0.00
Don't answer	1.25	1.06	1.50	1.25	0.00	0.00	2.69	1.45
Panel B: Children								
Children	49.93	47.08	51.11	48.48	49.61	51.38	50.79	48.56
At least one children death	7.92	7.18	8.33	5.68	7.69	7.32	9.93	.
Panel C: Parents								
Mother dead[1]	29.38	42.63	25.56	30.43	28.42	30.66	28.57	30.74
Father dead[1]	49.13	55.13	47.28	45.91	46.92	49.69	53.49	46.91
Panel D: Talk with relatives								
Last 3 months	66.01	55.73	70.21	64.17	64.55	68.92	64.66	66.98

Notes: Question used in Panel A: "What is your current marital status", in Panel B: "Do you have any children?" and "Are all your children still alive?", in Panel C: "Is your mother/father still alive?", in Panel D: "Have you spoken to any relatives in the last three months?". 1: Sample of homeless younger than 51 years. Source: Sample of homeless interviewed in Milan (2008, 2013 and 2018), Turin (2010) and Rome (2014).

ployment shocks. They find that consumption losses after the termination of a job are much lower in Mediterranean Europe, due to strong family ties. When looking at the statistics on marital status separately by natives and immigrants (columns 2-3), we note a higher proportion of divorced/separated among Italians. Homeless marital status is similar across cities of interview. Panel B reports the proportion of the respondents with children. About half of the respondents have at least one child. It is interesting to note the very high rate of child deaths among the unsheltered homeless: about 8 percent reported having experienced the death of at least one child, again suggesting that family-related shocks may be an important determinant of homelessness. In Panel C of **Table 13**, we report the proportion of individuals younger than 51 years old without parents. About 30 percent of the unsheltered homeless have lost their mother and about 50 percent have lost their father. One section of the questionnaire investigates the current relationship of homeless people to their relatives, by asking whether they have spoken to any of their relatives in the past three months and in the past year (Panel D). Looking at the full sample, only 66 percent of the sample report having spoken to relatives in the last three months.

The conventional wisdom is that homeless people are not active in the labor market. The Italian Homeless Survey tells us a different story. Panel A of **Table 14** reports labor market characteristics for the sample of homeless people interviewed. About 75 percent of the population was working before ending up on the street, and the highest proportion of people employed before homelessness is among those interviewed in Milan in 2018. An analysis of the type of job shows that before becoming homeless, people were mainly employed in low-skilled sectors. In particular, homeless people were employed as factory workers, carpenters and bricklayers, and domestic workers. This is a common feature among Italians and immigrants. The average monthly wage was around 950 euros and was higher in the Italian homeless sample. The survey also investigates the current situation of the homeless in the labor market. **Table 14**, Panel B reports the proportion of the homeless currently employed or who were employed in the previous month. It is very interesting and surprising to note that about 15.5 percent of the respondents were employed at the time of the survey, with a peak of almost 29 percent among the homeless interviewed in Milan in 2008. People who reported having a job at the time of the survey or in the previous month worked mainly in the unskilled sector as manual workers or in the service sector as domestic workers, cleaners, cooks or waiters.

The lack of adequate housing, combined with a lack of a regular source of income, makes it very difficult for the homeless to satisfy their daily needs. Therefore, homeless people have to rely on formal and informal sources of help to survive. One section of the survey elicits information about the homeless' of financial help. **Table 15** reports the proportion of individuals who received financial help in the last month (39.19% among Italians and 9.89% among immigrants) by income source. Among those declaring to receive in-cash help, only about 19 percent receive government subsidies (welfare check, disability/unemployment insurance, pensions), signaling that the take up rate of government programs is fairly low. This percentage increases to 39.2 percent if we consider only the subsample of Italian homeless. Indeed, to

6 Who are the homeless and those at risk of homelessness?

Table 14 Occupation

	All sample	Italians	Immigrants	Milan 2008	Turin 2010	Milan 2013	Rome 2014	Milan 2018
Panel A: Labor market characteristics before homelessness								
Percentage of employed before becoming homeless	75.84	70.93	73.98	55.61	21.11	93.05	87.92	90.50
Type of Job								
Factory worker	18.84	21.16	18.83	31.90	30.64	15.16	12.27	15.57
Brickery/carpenter/Electrician/Plumber	12.07	7.67	14.90	9.00	12.12	12.70	13.39	12.01
Domestic worker/Nanny/cleaner	10.80	6.16	13.00	10.84	10.10	10.79	11.14	10.66
Cook/Waitress/Waiter	8.87	12.21	7.42	10.22	9.43	7.65	9.51	8.12
Administration/white collar	2.75	3.49	1.71	--	5.72	1.78	2.88	4.57
Gardener	2.27	2.33	2.22	1.84	2.02	2.60	2.38	2.20
Vendor/flyering/peddler/parking attendant	1.69	1.63	1.65	2.25	6.73	0.14	0.75	1.86
Socially useful	0.96	1.28	0.89	--	3.70	0.82	1.00	0.51
Other	40.58	43.14	38.11	31.50	19.54	48.36	44.93	43.15
Do not answer	1.17	0.93	1.27	2.45	--	--	1.75	1.35
Average monthly wage (euro)	950.4	1.048.50	867.00	951.71	853.40	999.00	866.40	1.072.00
obs.	2908	860	1577	489	297	732	799	591

Table 14   Occupation (continued)

	All sample	Italians	Immigrants	Milan 2008	Turin 2010	Milan 2013	Rome 2014	Milan 2018
Panel B: Labor market characteristics during homelessness								
Percentage of current employed	15.45	17.15	12.56	28.76	15.56	11.68	10.55	19.53
Type of Job								
Factory worker	16.31	18.34	17.20	36.45	13.11	12.04	8.94	12.58
Brickery/carpenter/Electrician/Plumber	4.66	0.59	6.80	4.67	--	6.48	3.25	6.29
Domestic worker/Nanny/cleaner	10.04	5.92	11.60	9.35	--	12.04	12.20	11.32
Cook/Waitress/Waiter	5.56	7.10	2.40	5.61	1.64	2.78	6.50	8.18
Administration/white collar	1.79	1.18	2.40	--	--	4.63	1.63	1.89
Gardener	3.05	7.10	1.60	4.67	9.84	1.85	2.44	0.63
Vendor/flyering/peddler/parking attendant	3.58	1.18	2.80	2.80	--	0.93	2.44	8.18
Socially useful	1.43	1.78	1.20	--	--	3.70	1.63	1.26
Other	47.85	50.30	46.40	36.45	57.38	55.55	45.53	48.43
Do not answer	5.73	6.51	7.60	--	18.03	--	15.44	1.24
Average monthly wage (euro)	577.2	558.45	540.26	--	481.00	660.77	498.00	652.20
obs.	558	169	250	107	61	108	123	159

Notes: Questions used: "Are you currently working?; "What is your job?"; "Did you have a job before ending up on the street (in the shelter)?" (2008), "Did you have a job the first time you slept on the street?" (2010); "Have you ever had a job during your life/have you ever had a paid job?" (2013, 2014 & 2018); "What was the last job you held?" (2008-2018). Source: Sample of homeless interviewed in Milan (2008, 2013 and 2018), Turin (2010) and Rome (2014). Note 1: For years 2013-2018 it is to be interpreted as individuals who have worked at least once in their life. 2008 and 2010 waves asked directly whether the individual had a job when ended up on the street/shelter. Obs refers to the number of observations available for job type. No value is reported for average monthly wage in 2008 because of the extremely low number of observations.

6 Who are the homeless and those at risk of homelessness?

Table 15 Main source of income

Sources of income	All sample	Italians	Immigrants	age>59	age<60	Milan 2008	Turin 2010	Milan 2013	Rome 2014	Rome 2015
Gov. Subsidie[1]	19.16	39.19	9.89	46.35	13.80	20.14	17.18	16.57	29.11	14.41
pension	6.55	14.70	1.62	23.96	2.51	5.88	2.09	5.79	10.43	8.41
unemployment benefit	3.36	4.72	2.31	5.85	2.94	0.53	2.31	5.25	3.32	4.69
Perman/occas work	21.69	21.60	21.74	12.46	23.16	30.84	22.32	21.63	16.20	--
Saving[2]	16.30	19.48	14.07	17.87	15.98	24.06	16.31	13.41	14.30	16.35
Friends	12.70	6.39	12.19	10.76	13.18	5.53	10.29	18.12	6.58	21.48
Family/relatives	8.34	5.60	7.76	6.16	8.79	5.53	8.31	10.54	4.65	12.81
Illegal activities	1.93	2.13	1.35	1.00	2.11	1.07	0.86	1.30	1.03	4.65
Handout/charity	10.51	10.89	9.84	9.94	10.52	2.32	10.83	10.83	7.64	19.35

Notes: 1) in "government subsidies" we report only the most common ones (e.g. welfare check/unemployment benefit/disabilities insurance/pension); 2) "savings" is the percentage of individuals that affirm to have savings at the time of the interview for the years 2008, 2013 and 2014; 2010 is the percentage of individuals who managed to accumulate savings in the previous year, whereas for 2018 is the percentage of individuals who managed to accumulate savings in the previous month.
Source: sample of homeless interviewed in Milan (2008, 2013 and 2018), Turin (2010) and Rome (2014).

be eligible for welfare checks it is required to be Italian and to have a residence in Italy. Regular immigrants can benefit from disability/unemployment insurance and pensions if they meet the eligibility criteria based on age and disability quotas. The most common types of subsidies are pensions and unemployment benefits. On average, beneficiaries of local public income transfers (municipal welfare checks) receive about 54 euros per week, while the average amount obtained through national public assistance (disability/unemployment benefits) is about 83 euros per week. About 21.7 percent of the sample declare that their main source of income is wages, either from permanent or temporary jobs and 16.3 percent of the homeless have savings. The other sources of income are informal sources, such as friends (12.7%), family/relatives (8.34%) and illegal activities (1.93%).

According to these basic statistics, it emerges that homeless people rely mainly on the private sector for assistance and there is room to improve and standardize the assistance provided by the public sector. The analysis also shows that some groups of people are more disadvantaged in accessing social services, such as immigrants. For example, although immigrants and natives face similar types of economic difficulties, their ability to cope with them is quite different since the two groups have different linguistic proficiency or do not have the same information about the local supply of social services. Moreover, undocumented immigrants typically face barriers to accessing services and opportunities in the labor market. Therefore, it would be appropriate to design specific initiatives, targeting the most disadvantaged groups of the population, who are typically excluded from official social assistance programs.

As a final step, we examine whether homeless people generally have realistic expectations about the time they will spend on the street. In this respect, we included two questions in the survey regarding expectations. Namely, we asked "How much longer do you expect to sleep on the street?" and "How long did you expect to stay on the street when you first arrived?" Based on these questions, we construct an ex-ante and ex-post measure of expectations about the duration of homelessness. The results reported in **Table 16** indicate that when they first arrived on the streets, 23.2 percent of the respondents thought they would stay less than a month, while this percentage dropped to 15 percent when we asked how long they expected to stay at the time of the survey. These findings show how homeless people revised their expectations of length of stay upward over time. The interpretation of the above findings is more comprehensive once we merge these figures with the length of each homelessness window. In other words, to investigate whether periods of homelessness are expected or not, past expectations – how long homeless people thought they would stay on the streets when they first arrived – should be compared with the sum of the number of months from their first appearance on the streets to the date of the survey and future expectations – how long they still expect to stay on the streets. Whenever the first is different from the second, we can conclude that the duration of the homeless status would not have been forecasted correctly. Only for 29 percent of the sample were correct in their initial prediction, and this percentage is slightly higher for immigrants (33 percent), showing that homelessness is a totally unexpected shock for which individuals are completely unprepared.

Table 16 Expectations

	All sample	Italian	Foreign	Milan 2008	Turin 2010	Milan 2013	Rome 2014	Milan 2018
Past expectations[1]								
Less than one month	23.20	23.45	26.01	29.41	26.60	25.71	21.89	14.90
1-3 months	14.43	13.99	13.86	17.11	14.89	13.95	11.54	16.90
4-6 months	7.48	7.78	6.36	13.37	2.66	5.68	5.57	10.29
6 months/one year	5.88	6.73	4.71	6.24	6.38	5.30	4.68	7.83
More than one year	4.99	6.94	2.95	5.88	6.91	3.75	3.18	7.37
Forever	4.60	6.41	3.52	4.46	2.93	4.01	5.57	4.92
Don't know/Don't answer	39.41	34.70	42.59	23.53	39.63	41.60	47.56	37.79
Obs.	2.631	951	1.761	561	376	774	1005	651
Future expectations[2]								
Less than one month	14.98	13.50	15.89	29.41	26.60	25.71	21.89	14.90
1-3 months	13.88	13.30	14.31	17.11	14.89	13.95	11.54	16.90
4-6 months	6.81	5.42	7.54	13.37	2.66	5.68	5.57	10.29
6 months/one year	6.21	6.90	5.86	6.24	6.38	5.30	4.68	7.83
More than one year	5.27	8.28	3.62	5.88	6.91	3.75	3.18	7.37
Forever	6.24	9.66	4.48	4.46	2.93	4.01	5.57	4.92
Don't know/Don't answer	46.61	42.96	48.32	23.53	39.63	41.60	47.56	37.79
Obs.	2.997	1015	1.964	561	376	774	1005	651

Notes: 1) expectations to stay on the street/shelter when they arrived for the first time. 2) expectations to stay on the street/shelter in the future at the time of the survey. Source: Sample of homeless interviewed in Milan (2008, 2013 and 2018), Turin (2010) and Rome (2014).

BOX: Case study on Australia

An interesting case is represented by Australia. Wood et al. (2014) and Johnson, Scutella, Tseng and Wood (2015) show that the Australian economic and structural factors are particularly important in explaining the spatial variation in homelessness. Such kind of studies are extremely limited in the international panorama due to the lack of disaggregated data with sufficient variability. The Australian Journeys Home project, on the other hand, has the advantage of following individuals over time, which makes it possible to understand how the risks of homelessness vary according to the housing and labor market characteristics of different areas. The Australian context also provides sufficient geographic variability in the labor and housing markets to produce robust and interesting results. Housing market conditions are captured by the median private rental price in an area, a measure commonly used as an indicator of rental market tightness, using area-level data from the latest available Census of Population and Housing. The indicator of local labor market conditions is the monthly regional unemployment rate from the Regional Labor Force Statistics. The results suggest that the likelihood of experiencing homelessness in the six months after being housed, conditional on being housed, is higher for vulnerable men than women (confirming the findings of Wood et al. 2014), and lower for those with children, while age and country of birth are not associated with homelessness. There is also evidence that those with relatively low levels (years) of schooling are more likely to exit formal housing, as are those who did not have a primary caregiver at age 14. Regular drug use increases the likelihood of homelessness, alcohol use has a weaker effect, while irregular drug use and smoking have insignificant effects. The impact of poor health on homelessness is mixed. While having a long-term health condition does not appear to affect the likelihood of becoming homeless, being diagnosed with bipolar disorder or schizophrenia reduces the likelihood of falling out of stable housing and into homelessness. Although people with mental illness are considered to be particularly vulnerable to homelessness, it is also true that they are special targets for treatment and care (including institutionalization). Because people with diagnosed mental health problems are prioritized by service providers, they are less likely to experience homelessness than undiagnosed people who may also be vulnerable to homelessness due to other risk factors. Social support is important in reducing the risk of homelessness. However, those housed in any wave are more likely to become homeless in the next 6 months if they have a previous experience of primary homelessness. This finding has a particular policy resonance because it supports an emphasis on interventions that sustain exits from homelessness.

Both housing and labor markets have a significant impact on individual risk of homelessness. Median market rents are positively and significantly associated with entry into homelessness: a $100 increase in median market rents (a 30% increase in the national median weekly rent) increases the risk of entry by 1.6 percentage points, from a sample mean of 8% to 9.6%, which is a 20% increase in risk. The effect is both statistically significant and large. Local labor market conditions are critical to entry into homelessness, with a one percentage point increase (decrease) in the unemployment rate increasing (decreasing) the probability of entry into homelessness by one percentage point, or 12.5% at the sample mean entry probability. Since the average unemployment rate across regions is 5.6%, an increase to 6.6% would represent an 18% increase in the average unemployment rate. The effect on pathways to homelessness is therefore roughly equivalent to the effect of market rents in local housing markets.

What determines instead the probability of exiting homelessness, conditional on initial homelessness? Males or older individuals are less likely to exit homelessness, and the marginal effect estimates remain statistically significant also after controlling for other observables and for prior episodes of primary homelessness. Although individuals who are married or in a de facto relationship are less likely to enter homelessness, conditional on entering homelessness they are significantly less likely to escape homelessness than single individuals, which may reflect the increased difficulty of finding housing that meets the additional needs of a couple relative to a single person. On the other hand, individuals with children (whether in a relationship or not) are substantially more likely to find a way out of homelessness (by 24.3 percentage points), which may reflect service support that is targeted at families. Once homeless, higher educational attainment does not appear to accelerate exit from homelessness. However, current employment status appears to be better associated with exits with some labor market attachment than with none. However, this effect is only weakly significant and only relative to those who are not in the labor force. Although recent job loss was a significant antecedent of homelessness entries, it is now curious that persons who lost their job between 6 months and 2 years before were more likely to exit homelessness than others. This may have something to do with the way employment services target support.

Instead, the local housing and labor market conditions do not appear to significantly affect transitions out of homelessness.

7 The costs of homelessness and potential policies

People rarely think about the substantial amount of economic resources that go into addressing homelessness. These resources encompass both the direct expenses associated with service provision and the indirect costs related to the negative externalities imposed on society. The quantification of resources and expenditures associated with homelessness is particularly relevant given the prevalence of homelessness illustrated in previous chapters. Moreover, it is crucial to acknowledge that in recent years, many states have devoted significant resources to assisting the homeless, in light of their heightened vulnerability due to the Covid-19 pandemic.

In this final chapter of the book, we will attempt to assess the societal costs of homelessness and discuss policies aimed to reduce, mitigate, and prevent this problem.

7.1 The costs of homelessness

The monetary costs of homelessness can be broadly divided into direct and indirect costs, as well as in social and private costs.

The main direct costs are those associated with the provision of services such as temporary housing, canteen services or showers, food distribution, street services and social assistance. A significant share of direct costs are also those related to health care and social services, which on a per capita basis, are higher than the same costs for a typical representative citizen with a permanent and stable residence. In fact, homeless people use health and social services more often and more intensively than the general population with regular housing because of the rapid deterioration of their health and psychological status while living on the streets, as well as inadequate nutrition and low investment in preventive care. They are also more likely to use emergency health care and psychiatric services. The overall costs of health care must be added to the cost of the justice system since, as there is, on average, a higher incidence of criminal behavior among the homeless related to theft, drug or alcohol use, illegal immigration or lack of documents (Corno, 2017).

Indirect costs are those associated with the depletion of individual human capital and the reduction in the marginal productivity of labor, resulting from long-term unemployment, which is reflected either in lower productivity or in the exit from the labor market. Indirect costs are both private and social. The first are incurred directly by the subject who experiences the condition of absence of dwelling and stem from the fact that the lower marginal productivity of labor results in a consequent lower marginal return of the work or in a lower wage. The latter are borne by society as a whole and result from the fact that, at the macro level, the depreciation of human capital leads to an under-utilization of the productive potential of each individual and thus to a lower aggregate production.

Finally, additional costs are those associated with negative externalities. These are related to the management and maintenance of public urban spaces used as "homes" by the homeless, but also include non-monetary costs related to social cohesion in the area where homeless are settled. On the one hand, the management of urban spaces where homeless the people stay may requires additional resources for maintenance, sanitation or security. On the other hand, homelessness can affect social cohesion and well-being in urban areas by creating tensions and divisions within communities, by perpetuating stereotypes and barriers to social inclusion or by reducing trust as homeless people are perceived as a threat by residents. These negative externalities may extend well beyond the direct financial costs and have profound implications for society as a whole.

Although it is extremely difficult to precisely quantify the costs related to the absence of housing, from an economic point of view they typically have two main features. First, marginal costs increase with the incidence of the phenomenon in the population, since it becomes more costly to deal with the phenomenon as the number of homeless people increases. Second, total costs positively depend on the duration of homelessness: the more protracted homelessness becomes, the greater the likelihood that a temporary condition will become chronic and the greater the costs to be sustained.

Estimating the cost of homelessness is crucial not only to quantify the phenomenon, but also to understand how to allocate limited private and public resources effectively. In light of recent changes in the global economy, accurately quantifying these costs has become more important than ever. After a decade of fiscal austerity measures in many countries, which often led to reduced public spending and investment in social services, the socio-economic repercussions of the Covid-19 pandemic have brought new challenges. The health crisis increased the demand for public services and exacerbated the conditions of extreme poverty, highlighting the urgent need for effective resource allocation. Additionally, the current global geopolitical tensions and energy crises have introduced new complexities to the economic landscape, further straining public finances and necessitating a reassessment of resource distribution to effectively address these multiple challenges.

In the light of the above, a real quantification of costs appears more necessary than ever, given the dynamics of the phenomenon in recent years and the global macroeconomic context in which fiscal austerity measures are being implemented in many countries.

The worsening of socio-economic conditions resulting from the Covid-19 pandemic crisis, coupled with a subsequent surge in demand for public services posed a critical challenge to public finances.

Some studies have attempted to estimate the cost of official homelessness assistance for specific groups of the population. Although official statistics are not available, these studies uses data from the public budget or collect original data through surveys of a sample of service providers. For example, according to the U.S. National Alliance to End Homelessness (2017), a chronically homeless person (an individual with chronic and complex health conditions, including mental illness, substance use disorders, and medical conditions, who experiences long-term homelessness and sleeps on the streets or in shelters) costs taxpayers an average of $35,578 per year. Flaming et al. (2015) show that the average cost of direct public services alone is $83,000 per homeless person per year. A study conducted by the French government in 2017 estimated the annual cost of homelessness at €2 billion. In Spain, a similar study conducted by the Spanish Federation of Municipalities and Provinces, estimated the annual cost of homelessness in the country at around €3.8 billion. In Australia, the cost of homelessness varies from state to state and region to region, but in 2018 it was around $7 billion. Although there is considerable variation over time and across countries, these estimates highlight the significant financial burden that homelessness places on public services and society. It is worth noting that these estimates represent a lower bound, as they do not capture the full range of costs, such as impacts on mental health, criminal justice system involvement or lost productivity.

Available studies also show that the resources allocated are however unevenly distributed among the homeless population, with about 50% being absorbed by the 15% of the population who experience chronic and prolonged homelessness.

Another crucial element that is missing from previous estimates is the value of all voluntary activities for the homeless. Indeed, more than in other cases, voluntary organizations play a crucial role in dealing with homelessness. They provide services (emergency accommodation, meals, clothing, hygiene facilities or healthcare services) that fill gaps in the existing social services; they raise awareness about homelessness issues within communities and among policymakers; they develop and implement prevention programs by working with government agencies; and they foster collaboration within local communities to gather resources and promote involvement.

Volunteer estimates can be obtained by considering the value of volunteer time and the market prices of goods and services consumed by a typical homeless person. The value of volunteer time is the monetary value of the work a volunteer provides to local services. According to ILO standards (2011), volunteer work refers to "a service or activity provided without remuneration for the benefit of the community, the environment, and persons other than close relatives or those within the household." It can be calculated using the hourly earnings of different types of workers from official labor force statistics, depending on the activity we are interested in. All production and nonsupervisory workers in the private sector represent the baseline and the lower bound for these costs. Of course, it is also possible to determine also the value of more specialized skills. It is worth noting that volunteers also provide many intangibles to the homeless that are not immediately quantifiable. Symmetrically, it is also possible to value the goods or services provided by volunteer associations.

While these estimates do not focus specifically on volunteering, they provide a useful benchmark for understanding the economic contribution of volunteers to address homelessness. These figures can be used to complement information collected by many national and local surveys on volunteers that include questions about the types of activities volunteers engage in and the time they allocate to various causes.

7.2 What types of interventions might help to reduce homelessness?

7.2.1 Theoretical considerations

In many countries, operators have begun to evaluate interventions for homeless people on a cost-benefit basis. Indeed, in recent years there has been a growing call to rationalize these interventions, weighing their effectiveness against their efficiency to ensure a prudent allocation of resources.

There has been a clear trade-off in addressing the problem, as in many cases the drastic reduction in available resources has been accompanied by a significant and unexpected increase in people's needs. In a simple supply and demand model, this translates into an almost rigid supply function of services combined with an upward-sloping, increasingly right-sloping demand. As a result, there is no (or very limited) effect on quantity in the market for homeless services, only on prices. If prices are sticky, the market will only have excess demand, with homeless people competing for the limited services available.

Historically, the response to homelessness has been primarily an emergency one: when homelessness began to emerge as a problem in a country, the first response was to expand emergency services such as emergency shelters, day programs, and canteens for vulnerable populations. Behind this choice, there was (and still there is) the idea that homelessness is a temporary phenomenon almost unexpected and unpredictable. However, considering the analysis in the previous chapters, today, not only the volume of needs is changing, but also the nature of the needs to be met. While the number of homeless people has increased in most countries since 2007, the profile of the *typical* homeless person has also changed. In all countries, the traditional homeless – single, middle-aged men – has been joined by a growing number of women, young people, immigrants and families. If the profile has changed over the years, then the responses that are implemented need to be adapted and different. Different problems require different solutions: non-standardized and more flexible interventions capable of adapting to needs as they manifest and change. In particular, it is crucial to understand that each specific target requires different interventions, so that an integrated system should include essential services that provide answers to basic needs and more sophisticated interventions such as time-varying income support programs or training programs to upgrade skills and adapt to demand, as well as interventions for empowerment and achieving full autonomy.

In some contexts, efforts have been made in this direction, but in many cases a review of the organizational models of service delivery seems necessary. In recent years, the majority of Western countries have increased the total amount of resources invested in anti-poverty measures but in some cases, the framework of the service system has not been rethought.

On average in Europe, one third of per-capita expenditure on social services is allocated to poverty and economic hardship, but there are large regional differences and the interventions implemented vary widely depending on the specific target. In the absence of a national minimum level of basic social services, the services provided are extremely heterogeneous and their fluctuations are difficult to predict.

In general, the effectiveness of policies to promote social inclusion and combat homelessness is greater the greater their ability to prevent entry into the phenomenon and to avoid chronicity. Therefore, an ideal intervention should, on the one hand, offer social assistance to people at-risk of homelessness and, on the other hand, include short and ad hoc interventions that provide means of protection to those who are just falling into extreme poverty and social exclusion.

To prevent and reduce homelessness and social exclusion many levers are potentially available. The formal education system can provide people with the adequate skills needed to enter and progress in the labor market. Similarly, policies to increase intergenerational mobility or to ensure access to high quality health care and other social services can enhance social inclusion. In addition, when offering income support it is important to avoid long-term unemployment and inactivity: inclusive and active labor market policies make the matching process between vacancies and workers more efficient and keep the unemployed in contact with the labor market. Finally, wage-setting policies, fiscal policies, and the pension system, if well designed, can also provide a system of incentives to be fully engaged in the economic activity. Together with such policies, when specific exogenous unexpected shocks occur and people are in need, emergency services should provide the right answer, but only for the strictly necessary period of time and immediately afterwards should lead to full autonomy.

If this is true from a theoretical point of view, the reality is far from perfect. Broad preventive measures are mainly aimed at providing a solid framework to sustain people in a "normal" context, but it is difficult to identify specific preventive measure against homelessness. Symmetrically, homelessness is tackled mainly with emergency measures, rarely with specific preventive interventions and it seems extremely difficult to properly design programs leading to autonomy in a reasonable short period of time.

Although basic assistance interventions do not per se enhance inclusion and empowerment, in a context of emergency they represent the first and fundamental element of the service network. Unfortunately, emergency interventions are necessary but not sufficient to improve social inclusion and reduce homelessness in the long run.

In this sense, an alternative to the prevailing paradigm is to design policies for homelessness that vary over time, using an approach similar to unemployment benefits and active labor market policies. The basic idea is to provide people with the necessary support and incentives to move out of homelessness. We can imagine a system in which the base is represented by shelters and emergency assistance to meet basic needs, such as shelter, food, hygiene, and medical care. The second level of the system may include the provision of temporary housing along with counseling, life skills training, and employment assistance. This phase may also include financial assistance for rehousing. The final step is to implement a progressive support model where assistance is gradually reduced over time as individuals make progress, become employed, and increase their income. In such an approach, it will also be important to define an incentive system (including bonuses or rewards) in order to engage individuals in services and increase their participation in programs.

7.2.2 Available evidence on effective programs

When thinking about past policies designed to mitigate homelessness, the actual knowledge about what works and what doesn't is very limited. As we mentioned earlier, the main reason for this lack of progress has been the lack of good data on the number of homeless people at different times and in different places. You can't see how a policy affects homelessness if you can't measure homelessness. Still, some things have been learned, at least tentatively.

A first group of *correlational studies* has examined the contextual and demographic factors that lead to a higher homelessness in the US. Using data provided by HUD, these studies found that the variation in homelessness in the US during the 1980s could be explained mainly by changes in the housing market and, only marginally, by changes in the income distribution. Raphael (2010), based on counts of homeless people in various US cities and metropolitan areas, found that tighter housing market regulation in a metropolitan area is correlated with higher homelessness. Regulation is indeed highly correlated with housing prices and therefore negatively correlated with the number of people who can afford them. Consistently, Lee et al. (2003) and Byrne et al. (2013) identified the median rent level to be the dominant predictor of homelessness rates. Instead, Early and Olsen (2002) found that more subsidized housing units were not correlated with lower homelessness, but that better targeting of these subsidies to poor households did reduce homelessness.

Variation in the generosity of income maintenance programs has been tested in various cross-sectional regressions using data provided by HUD in the US, and the effects were found to be small or nonexistent (Honig and Filer 1993, Burt 1992).

Some labor market characteristics have also been found to be correlated with homelessness. Cebula and Saunoris (2021) found that US states with higher levels of entrepreneurship and greater overall labor market freedom have a smaller homeless populations, probably because of greater job opportunities available to them. Not surprisingly, previous studies on the community-level determinants of homelessness have found a positive and significant association between poor economic conditions, as measured by poverty and unemployment rates, less generous social safety net programs and homelessness rates (Honing and Filer, 1993; Burt, 1992; Early and Olsen, 2002; Quigley et al., 2001; Quigley and Raphael, 2002).[1]

Regarding demographic characteristics, the likelihood of homelessness is lower

---

[1] Climate conditions can also significantly affect homelessness. In this regard, some studies found that the higher the temperatures and the lower the precipitation, the higher is the homelessness rates

for female-headed households (Early, 2004) and those with secondary and postsecondary education (Cebula and Saunoris, 2021; Jarvis, 2015), but higher for African Americans (Burt, 2001; Culhane and Metraux, 1999) and those with parents with criminal records (Mabhala et al., 2021).

Only recently, a (small) group of papers has attempted to test the *causal* relationship between the level of homelessness and housing market characteristics. Fetzer et al. (2019) exploit quasi-exogenous variation in the affordability of rents due to a cut in rent subsidies for low-income benefits in the United Kingdom in April 2011. They document that individuals exposed to the cut were significantly more likely to build up rent arrears and face eviction. Using comprehensive district-level administrative data, they show that the affordability shock caused a significant increase in: evictions; individual bankruptcies; property crime; insecure temporary housing arrangements; statutory homelessness and actual rough sleeping, with the most notable rise in statutory homelessness among families with children. Along the same line, Collison et al. (2022) study the consequences of eviction for tenants using newly linked administrative data from two large cities in the US. They find that an eviction order increases homelessness, and reduces earnings, durable consumption, and access to credit. Effects on housing and labor market outcomes are driven by impacts for female and black tenants.

Based on this evidence, two possible lines of intervention to tackle the problem are the housing and the labor market. However, more rigorous studies can provide further insights.

Prevention and mitigation interventions

Rigorous evidence on the effectiveness of homelessness *prevention and mitigation strategies* has grown in recent years, though many gaps remain. Historically, policies to mitigate homelessness primarily focused on addressing immediate needs and basic requirements of homeless individuals. Both US and European policies were predominantly shaped by the *"Stair-Case System,"* in which homeless individuals had to demonstrate their ability to access standard accommodation. This often required years of preparation before they could be deemed "housing-ready." Attaining permanent housing was frequently contingent upon meeting certain conditions, such as demonstrating sobriety. Several non-experimental studies indicated that programs following the *"Stair-Case System"* reduced psychiatric symptoms associated with homelessness, but their impact on homelessness itself was marginal. Over time, this approach waned in favor of the *"Housing First"* approach, initiated in New York City in 1992 by Sem Tsemberis. The Housing First program provides apartments to individuals with fewer restrictions on the conditions they must adhere to. Rigorous evaluations of the Housing First program in Canada and France yielded

---

since better weather conditions make homeless people more visible and less vulnerable to mortality (Lee et al., 2003; Quigley and Raphael, 2002; Quigley et al., 2001).

mixed results (Aubry et al., 2015; Aubry et al., 2020; Lachaud et al., 2021; Tsemberis et al., 2004). The Canadian evaluation demonstrated that Housing First participants were more likely to secure housing and reported greater improvements in quality of life compared to those in treatment as usual (Aubry et al., 2020). However, no treatment effects have been found in subsequent evaluations of HF on health care utilization (Lachaud et al., 2021), criminal behavior (Leclair et al., 2019), substance use or psychiatric symptoms (Tsemberis et al., 2004) and mortality (Tinland et al., 2021). In line with the Housing First, Rapid Re-Housing (RRH) is another policy that has been rigorously evaluated expanding the general approach of providing immediate housing to non-permanent forms of assistance. RRH offers time-limited rental assistance and services to families and individuals experiencing homelessness. A forthcoming study by Cohen (forthcoming) in Los Angeles found that rapid placement of homeless individuals into housing programs significantly reduced the likelihood of returning to homelessness and criminal activity. However, he found no discernible effect on health care use. Two experiments with rapid re-housing programs are currently underway. Cash transfers have also been used in the past. Evans et al. (2016) evaluate a program in Chicago that provides temporary financial assistance with the goal of keeping individuals in their homes and out of homeless shelters. They find that one-time payments of up to $1500 greatly reduce the likelihood of homelessness. The estimated economic benefits exceed the estimated costs, with immeasurable psychological and physical benefits.

Sullivan and Sabety (ongoing) are testing the impact of the Rapid Re-Housing (RRH) program, combined with cash transfers, on individuals in the San Francisco Bay area. RRH offers a combination of temporary services that typically last between 6 and 24 months, such as housing search assistance, rental subsidies, and case management, plus a cash transfer to improve housing stability. They will measure the impact on homelessness, housing stability, financial security and other outcomes one and two years after study enrollment. Similarly, Gould (ongoing) is evaluating the effectiveness of direct cash payments as a supplement to rapid rehousing services in preventing homelessness and aiding the transition to longer-term housing stability. She has recruited between 400 and 450 families with children experiencing homelessness. Half will be randomly selected to receive a monthly cash payment of $1,000 for 12 months after they complete 18 months of rapid rehousing. Using administrative data, she will estimate the effects of this intervention on returns to homelessness, housing stability and rent burden in the 12 months after the payments end.

Final remarks

The evidence presented in this book suggests that economists have not traditionally viewed homelessness as a sufficiently persistent problem to warrant in-depth study. This idea has been well entrenched in the field. To the best of our knowledge, the earliest scholarly work by economists on homelessness was published in 1987 by Freeman and Hall, based on an undergraduate thesis. The next two papers appeared three years later by Quigley (1990) and Hill and Stamey (1990), but all of these early papers were published in interdisciplinary journals. After almost 40 years, the amount of economic literature devoted to the topic remained remarkably limited.

One of the main reasons for the limited empirical research in economics and social science is the lack of rigorous and comparative data collections.

In the pages of this book, through careful data search in various European countries, we have shown that homelessness is not a trivial phenomenon, but is alarmingly prevalent in many regions of the world. We also discuss that the economic and social costs of housing deprivation are enormous, affecting both individual well-being and society at large. Homelessness is associated with a wide range of adverse outcomes, including increased mortality and morbidity, increased involvement in criminal activity, and steep declines in cognitive and employment skills, which impose a heavy administrative and financial burden on public agencies and local governments.

However, to improve homelessness policies across Europe, countries should adopt a more standardized approach to data collection, aligning the frequency and methodology to ensure data comparability and reliability across different regions. Furthermore, having a centralized European database of homelessness statistics would facilitate better analysis and policy formulation. These steps are crucial to achieving a comprehensive understanding of homelessness at the European level and to tackling it effectively. Far from viewing housing vulnerability as an immutable feature of our social and economic environments, we demonstrate that empirical research on homelessness is possible. We outline a methodology for identifying and surveying homeless individuals in developed countries, and in doing so, we offer hope that economists worldwide will undertake outstanding research on this critical and pressing issue that characterizes contemporary societies.

Appendix Tables

Table 17   Data collections on homeless people at the national level – Panel A

Country	Years of data collections	Method of data collection	Observation period	Definition¹	Source
Panel A					
Austria	2008-2017	service-based admin	1 year	rough sleepers and sheltered	Fink (2019), ESPEN country report
	2008-2012, 2014, 2016, 2018	service-based admin	1 year	broad definition	National Social Report (2014); Feantsa Country Fiche (2018, 2017, 2020)
	2010-2020	service-based admin	1 year	broad definition	Statistik Austria; Feantsa Country Fiche (2020)
	1998	service-based estimate	1 year	broad definition	Eitel and Schoibl (1999), BAWO survey; Schoibl (2006)
Belgium	2022	PIT	1 night	rough sleepers	Fondation Roi Baudouin
Bosnia	2013	census	2 weeks	na	BiH Agency for Statistics; 2013 Census data
Croatia	2017-2018	PIT	1 night	na	Ministry of Social Affairs
	2013	service-based estimate	na	broad definition	Feantsa Country Fiche (2014)
Czech Republic	2011	PIT	1 day	rough sleepers and sheltered	Feantsa Country Fiche (2014, 2020); Volker Busch-Geertsema et al. (2014); Baptista et al. (2012)

Table 17   Data collections on homeless people at the national level – Panel A (Continued)

Country	Years of data collections	Method of data collection	Observation period	Definition[1]	Source
	2016	service-based admin	1 year	broad definition	Feantsa Country Fiche (2016)
	2016	service-based estimate	1 year	na	Feantsa report (2018)
	2019	service-based estimate	1 week	rough sleepers and sheltered	Ministry of labour and social affairs
Denmark	2007, 2009, 2011, 2013, 2015, 2017, 2019, 2022	service-based admin	1 week	broad definition (including with family/friends)	Benjaminsen and Christensen (2007); Benjaminsen (2009); Lauritzen et al. (2011); Benjaminsen and Lauritzen (2013); Feantsa Country Fiche (2014); National centre for social research
Estonia	2003-2017	service-based admin	1 year	rough sleepers and sheltered	Ministry of Social Affairs
	2017	service-based admin	1 year	rough sleepers and sheltered	Baptista and Marlier (2019), ESPN country report
	2021	census	1 year	na	Statistics Estonia
	2005	na	na	broad definition	Edgard and Meert (2006)
Finland	1987	service-based estimate	1 day	broad definition (including with family/friends)	Tiitinen and Ikonen (2003); ARA (2012, 2011, 2014, 2015, 2020, 2021, 2022)
France	2000	na	na	broad definition	Briant and Donzeau (2011); Feantsa Country Fiche (2014)
	2001, 2012	service-based estimate	1 week	broad definition	Yaouancq and Duée (2014); Yaouancq et al. (2013); INSEE (2001)

Table 17 Data collections on homeless people at the national level – Panel A (Continued)

Country	Years of data collections	Method of data collection	Observation period	Definition[1]	Source
	1999, 2006	census	na	broad definition	Richet-Mastain (2007)
	2017	na	1 night	broad definition	Feantsa Country Fiche (2017)
	2022-2023	na	1 night	rough sleepers and sheltered	Fondation Abbé Pierre
Germany	1999-2021	service-based estimate	yearly	broad definition (including with family/friends)	Feantsa Country Fiche (2014, 2017); BAG-W
	2022-2023	service-based admin	1 week	broad definition (including with family/friends)	Federal Statistical Office, Genesis (2023) / Feantsa report (2023)
Greece	2005	na	na	rough sleepers and sheltered	Edgard and Meert (2006)
	2009	na	na	broad definition	Feantsa Country Fiche (2014)
	2011	service-based estimate	na	broad definition	Feantsa Country Fiche (2014)
	2018	PIT	1 night	rough sleepers and sheltered	
Hungary	2005	service-based estimate	na	broad definition	Edgard and Meert (2006)
	2008-2012	service-based estimate	1 night	rough sleepers and sheltered	Gyori and Szabó (2012); Gyori et al. (2013); Feantsa Country Fiche (2014)
	2013-2020	PIT	1 night	rough sleepers and sheltered	Gyori et al. (2013); Feantsa Country Fiche (2014, 2016, 2020)

Note: (1) "broad" means a definition of homelessness including not only rough sleepers and sheltered homeless, but also at least one additional group from ETHOS categories 4.1-12 (such as, for example, people in women's sheters, people due to be released from penal or macical institutions, etc.) with the exception of people living temporarily with family or friends (ETHOS 8.1); "broad (including family/friends)" means a definition including all ETHOS categories 1.1-12, including people living temporarily with family or friends.

Table 18   Data collections on homeless people at the national level – Panel B

Country	Years of data collections	Method of data collection	Observation period	Definition[1]	Source
Panel B					
Iceland	2011	census	na	rough sleepers and sheltered	Statistics Iceland
Ireland	2011, 2016	PIT	1 night	rough sleepers and sheltered	Feantsa Country Fiche (2014); Central Statistics Office (2012, 2017)
	2014-2023	service-based admin	1 week	rough sleepers and sheltered	Department of Housing, Local Government and Heritage
	2002, 2005, 2008, 2011, 2013	service-based admin	yearly	broad definition	Housing Agency (2008, 2012)
Italy	2000	service-based estimate	1 night	broad definition	Fondazione Zancan (2000)
	2011, 2014	service-based estimate	1 month	rough sleepers and sheltered	Istat (2012, 2014); Feantsa Country Fiche (2014)
	2021	service-based admin	1 year	broad definition	Istat
Latvia	2009-2017, 2021	service-based admin	1 year	rough sleepers and sheltered	Ministry of Welfare
	2005	na	1 year	rough sleepers and sheltered	Edgard and Meert (2006)
Lithuania	2005	service-based estimate	na	broad definition (including with family/friends)	Edgard and Meert (2006)
	2005, 2011, 2012	PIT	1 night	rough sleepers and sheltered, broad definition	Feantsa Country Fiche (2014)
	2013-2022	service-based admin	1 year	broad definition, rough sleepers and sheltered	Statistics Lithuania; Feantsa Country Fiche (2016, 2019, 2020)
Luxembourg	2007	service-based admin	1 week	broad definition	Feantsa Country Fiche (2014)
	2008-2012	service-based admin	5 months	broad definition	Feantsa Country Fiche (2014)
	2013	service-based admin	1 year	broad definition	Feantsa Country Fiche (2014)

Table 18   Data collections on homeless people at the national level – Panel B (continued)

Country	Years of data collections	Method of data collection	Observation period	Definition[1]	Source
	2014-2016	service-based admin	1 year	broad definition	Feantsa Country Fiche (2017)
	2016	PIT	1 night	broad definition	Ministry for Family and Integration (2016)
	2017	PIT	1 night	rough sleepers and sheltered	Feantsa (2013); Ministry for Family and Integration
Malta	2013-2018	service-based admin	1 year	rough sleepers	ESPN country report (2019)
Netherlands	2003	service-based admin	na	broad definition	Edgard and Meert (2006)
	2009-2021	service-based estimate	1 day	broad definition (including with family/friends)	CBS (Statistics Netherlands); Feantsa Country Fiche (2020); ESPN country report (2019)
Norway	1996, 2003, 2005, 2008, 2012, 2016, 2020	service-based admin	1 week	broad definition (including with family/friends)	Dyb and Johannessen (2009, 2013); Dyb and Zeiner (2021)
Poland	2005	service-based admin	1 year	broad definition	Edgard and Meert (2006)
	2011	census	1 night	rough sleepers and sheltered	Feantsa Country Fiche (2014)
	2011, 2013, 2015, 2017, 2019, 2021	PIT	1 night	rough sleepers and sheltered	Feantsa Country Fiche (2014, 2017, 2019, 2020); Ministry of Family, Labour and Social Policy (2015)
	2012	service-based estimate	1 year	rough sleepers and sheltered	Feantsa Country Fiche (2014)
	2016	service-based admin	1 night	broad definition	Feantsa Country Fiche (2017)

Note: (1) "broad" means a definition of homelessness including not only rough sleepers and sheltered homeless, but also at least one additional group from ETHOS categories 4.1-12 (such as, for example, people in women's shelters, people due to be released from penal or medical institutions, etc.) with the exception of people living temporarily with family or friends (ETHOS 8.1); "broad (including family/friends)" means a definition including all ETHOS categories 1.1-12, including people living temporarily with family or friends.

Table 19 Data collections on homeless people at the national level – Panel C

Country	Years of data collections	Method of data collection	Observation period	Definition[1]	Source
Panel C					
Portugal	2005	PIT	1 night	rough sleepers and sheltered	Edgard and Meert (2006)
	2009, 2018-2021	PIT	1 night	rough sleepers and sheltered	Feantsa Country Fiche (2014); ENIPSA
	2013	service-based estimate	1 year	broad definition	Feantsa Country Fiche (2014)
	2016	service-based admin	1 year	broad definition	Feantsa Country Fiche (2017); ENIPSA
	2018		4 months	broad definition	ESPN country report (2019)
Romania	2017	na	1 year	na	ESPN country report (2019)
	2009		na	na	
	2011	service-based admin	1 year	broad definition	Feantsa Country Fiche (2016)
Serbia	2011	census	1 month	rough sleepers	ESPN country report (2019)
Slovakia	2016	service-based admin	2 months	rough sleepers and sheltered	ESPN country report (2019)
	2011, 2021	census	1 night	rough sleepers and sheltered	Slovak Statistical Office (2021)
Slovenia	2005	service-based estimate	na	broad definition	Edgard and Meert (2006)
	2012	service-based admin	na	rough sleepers and sheltered	Volker Busch-Geertsema et al. (2014)
	2016	service-based admin	na	na	
	2010-2019	service-based admin	1 year	rough sleepers and sheltered	ESPN country report (2019); Feantsa Country Fiche (2020)
	2020	service-based admin	1 year	rough sleepers and sheltered	Institute of Social Welfare
Spain	2016	service-based estimate	na	broad definition	Feantsa Country Fiche (2017)

Appendix Tables

Table 19 Data collections on homeless people at the national level – Panel C (continued)

Country	Years of data collections	Method of data collection	Observation period	Definition[1]	Source
	2005, 2012, 2022	service-based estimate	1 week	broad definition	Feantsa Country Fiche (2014); INE (2005, 2012, 2022)
Sweden	1993, 1999	service-based estimate	1 week	rough sleepers	Sahlin (2004)
	2005, 201-, 2017	service-based estimate	1 week	broad definition	National Board of Health and Welfare (NBHW)
Switzerland	2021	service-based estimate	na	na	University of Applied Sciences Northwestern Switzerland (FHNW)
Turkey	2011, 2018	na	na	rough sleepers	ESPN country report (2019)
UK	2006	PIT	1 night	rough sleepers	Edgard and Meert 2006
	2006	service-based admin	1 year	rough sleepers	Edgard and Meert 2006
	2019	service-based admin	1 year	broad definition	Feantsa report (2023)
	2010-2022	PIT	1 night	rough sleepers	Department for Levelling Up, Housing and Communities
Australia	2001, 2006, 2011	PIT	1 night	broad definition (including with family/friends)	Census of Population and Housing
	2016, 2021	PIT	1 night	broad definition	ABS
Canada	2001, 2016	PIT	1 night	broad definition	Statistics Canada
	2005-2018	service-based estimate	1 year	rough sleepers and sheltered	National Shelter Study
	2021	PIT	1 night	rough sleepers and sheltered	Canadian Housing Survey (CHS)
New Zealand	2018	PIT	1 day	broad definition (including people temp. living with family/friends)	Ministry of Housing and Urban Devevelopment

Table 19 Data collections on homeless people at the national level – Panel C (continued)

Country	Years of data collections	Method of data collection	Observation period	Definition[1]	Source
USA	2005-2020, 2022	PIT	1 night	rough sleepers and sheltered	Annual Homeless Assessment Report (AHAR) to Congress
	2021	service-based estimate	1 night	rough sleepers and sheltered	Annual Homeless Assessment Report (AHAR) to Congress

Note: (1) "broad" means a definition of homelessness including not only rough sleepers and sheltered homeless, but also at least one additional group from ETHOS categories 4.1-12 (such as, for example, people in women's sheters, people due to be released from penal or madical institutions, etc.) with the exception of people living temporarily with family or friends (ETHOS 8.1); "broad (including family/friends)" means a definition including all ETHOS categories 1.1-12, including people living temporarily with family or friends.

Bibliography

Introduction:
European Commission, 2010 European Commission. 2010. "A strategy for smart, sustainable and inclusive growth", Communication from the Commission, Europe 2020, Com (2010) 2020 Final, March 3, 2010.

Department of Housing and Urban Development (2022). *The 2022 Annual Homeless Assessment Report to the congress*. The U.S. Department of Housing and Urban Development, Office of Community planning and Development.

FEANTSA (2023). *Eight Overview of Housing Exclusion in Europe*. European Federation of National Organizations Working with the Homeless.

Chapter 1:
Australian Parliament. House of Representatives. Standing Committee on Community Affairs, & Morris, A. (1995). A report on aspects of youth homelessness. Australian Government Pub. Service.

Australian Bureau of Statistics (ABS). (2011). ABS Review of Counting the Homeless Methodology, Position Paper, August 2011

Australian Bureau of Statistics (ABS). (2012b) Information paper – A statistical definition of homelessness, Cat. no. 4922.0, Canberra: ABS.

Berk, R., Kriegler, B., & Ylvisaker, D. (2008). Counting the homeless in Los Angeles county. In Probability and statistics: Essays in honor of David A. Freedman (pp. 127-141). Institute of Mathematical Statistics.

Berry, B. (2007). A repeated observation approach for estimating the street homeless population. Evaluation review, 31(2), 166-199.

Bogard, C. J. (2001). Advocacy and enumeration: Counting homeless people in a suburban community. American Behavioral Scientist, 45(1), 105-120.

Busch-Geertsema, V. (2010). Defining and measuring homelessness. Homelessness Research in Europe: Festschrift for Bill Edgar and Joe Doherty, 19-39.

Busch-Geertsema, V., Benjaminsen, L., Filipovič Hrast, M. and Pleace, N. (2014). Extent and Profile of Homelessness in European Member States. A Statistical Update, EOH Comparative Studies on Homelessness, No 4, Brussels: FEANTSA/EOH.

Chamberlain, C & MacKenzie, D. (1992). 'Understanding contemporary homelessness: issues of definition and meaning', Australian Journal of Social Issues, vol.27, no.4, pp.274–97.

Chamberlain, C., & MacKenzie, D. (1998). Youth Homelessness: Early Intervention & Prevention. Australian Centre for Equity through Education, Corner Bridge and Swanson Streets, Erskineville, New South Wales 2043, Australia.

Chamberlain, C. (1999) Counting the homeless: implications for policy development, Canberra: Australian Bureau of Statistics, Catalogue No. 2041.0.

Chamberlain, C. (2014) Homelessness: re-shaping the policy agenda?, AHURI Final Report No. 221, Melbourne: Australian Housing and Urban Research Institute.

Cordray, D. S., & Pion, G. M. (1991). What's behind the numbers? Definitional issues in counting the homeless. Housing Policy Debate, 2(3), 585-616.

Culhane, D. P., Metraux, S., & Byrne, T. (2011). A prevention-centered approach to homelessness assistance: A paradigm shift?. Housing Policy Debate, 21(2), 295-315.

Department of Housing and Urban Development (HUD). (2008). A guide to counting unsheltered homeless people. Second Revision January 2008. Washington DC: Office of Community Planning and Development

European Commission, https://cordis.europa.eu/project/id/727112

Feantsa (2024a). ETHOS - European Typology on Homelessness and Housing Exclusion. Accessible at: https://www.feantsa.org/en/toolkit/2005/04/01/ethos-typology-on-homelessness-and-housing-exclusion (accessed 06 April 2024)

Feantsa (2024b) ETHOS Light - European Typology on Homelessness and Housing Exclusion, available at: https://www.feantsa.org/download/fea-002-18-update-ethos-light-003241744178868741919154.pdf (accessed 06 April 2024)

Homeless Emergency Assistance and Rapid Transition to Housing HEARTH Act of 2009, Pub L. 111-22. 123 Stat 1632. (2009)

Human Rights and Equal Opportunity Commission, & Burdekin, B. (1989). Our homeless children: report of the National Inquiry into Homeless Children. Australian Government Publishing Service.

Johnson, G., & Chamberlain, C. (2008). From youth to adult homelessness. Australian Journal of Social Issues, 43(4), 563-

McKinney-Vento (1987). Homeless Assistance Act, 42 U.S.C. 11431 *et seq.*

National Alliance to End Homelessness [NAEH] (2012), Changes in the HUS definition of 'homeless', Federal policy brief, January 18, website: http://www.endhomelessness.org/library/entry/changes-in-the-hud-definition-of-homeless

Neil, C. C., & Fopp, R. (1994). Homelessness in Australia: Causes and consequences (Vol. 1). Australian Housing and Urban Research Institute by arrangement with Victorian Ministerial

Pickering, K., Fitzpatrick, S., Hinds, K., Lynn, P., & Tipping, S. (2003). Tracking homelessness: A feasibility study.

Report of the Working Party on Homeless Men and Women. 1973. Canberra: Australian Government Publishing Service.

Rossi, P. H. (1991), *Down and Out in America: The Origins of Homelessness*, University of Chicago Press.

Sackville, R. (1976). Homeless people and the law: a report. Australian Government Publishing Service.

Sosin, M., Piliavin, I., & Westerfelt, H. (1990). Toward a longitudinal analysis of homelessness. Journal of Social Issues, 46(4), 157-174.

Stax, T. (2004). Possibilities and Limitations in Longitudinal Analysis of Homelessness Based on Information From Official Registers. 3rd meeting CUHP, Copenhagen, www.cuhp.org.

Sullivan, A. A. (2023). What does it mean to be homeless? How definitions affect homelessness policy. Urban Affairs Review, 59(3), 728-758.

United Nations Statistical Division (UNSD). (2008). Principles and Recommendations for Population and Housing Censuses, Revision 2, Statistical papers Series M No. 67/Rev.2

Williams, J. C. (2011). "Stand up and be counted": the politics of a homeless enumeration. Poverty & Public Policy, 3(3), 1-27.

Chapter 2:

Agans, R. P., Jefferson, M. T., Bowling, J. M., Zeng, D., Yang, J., & Silverbush, M. (2014). Enumerating the Hidden Homeless: Strategies to Estimate the Homeless Gone Missing From a Point-in-Time Count. Journal of Official Statistics, 30(2), 215-229.

Baptista, I., Benjaminsen, L., Pleace, N. and Busch-Geertsema, V. (2012) Counting Homeless People in the 2011 Housing and Population Census, EOH Comparative Studies on Homelessness, No 2, Brussels: FEANTSA/EOH

Benjaminsen, L. (2005). Udviklingen af omfanget af indsaten for de social udsatte grupper. En analyse af kravet om tilvaekst: Evauering af puljen til social udsatte i de 6 stortse byer - delrapport1. SFI - Det Nationale Forskningscenter for Velfaerd. SFI Arbejdspapir Nr. 04:2005 - "The development of the scope of efforts for socially vulnerable groups: An analysis of the demand for growth"

Berk, R., Kriegler, B., & Ylvisaker, D. (2008). Counting the homeless in Los Angeles county. In Probability and statistics: Essays in honor of David A. Freedman (pp. 127-141). Institute of Mathematical Statistics.

Berry, B. (2007). A repeated observation approach fo estimating the street homeless population. Evaluation review, 31(2), 166-199.

BFZ-C (2024), Built for Zero Canada. Getting to zero. Available at: https://bfzcanada.ca/getting-to-zero/ (accessed 05 April 2024)

Brakenhoff, B., Jang, B., Slesnick, N., & Snyder, A. (2015). Longitudinal predictors of homelessness: Findings from the National Longitudinal Survey of Youth-97. *Journal of Youth Studies*, *18*(8), 1015-1034.

Busch-Geertsema, V., Benjaminsen, L., Filipovič Hrast, M. and Pleace, N. (2014). Extent and Profile of Homelessness in European Member States. A Statistical Update, EOH Comparative Studies on Homelessness, No 4, Brussels: FEANTSA/EOH.

Caton, C. L., Dominguez, B., Schanzer, B., Hasin, D. S., Shrout, P. E., Felix, A., ... & Hsu, E. (2005). Risk factors for long-term homelessness: Findings from a longitudinal study of first-time homeless single adults. *American journal of public health*, *95*(10), 1753-1759.

Community Solutions (2018). Getting to proof points: Key learning from the first three years of the Built for Zero initiative. Available at https: https://community.solutions/new-report-reflections-from-the-first-three-years-of-built-for-zero/ ((accessed 05 April 2024)

Community Solutions (2019). Canada Announces Launch of Built for Zero. Available at: https://community.solutions/canada-announces-launch-of-built-for-zero/ (accessed 05 April 2024)

Community Solutions (2024). Built-for-zero. Methodology. Available at https://community.solutions/built-for-zero/methodology/ (accessed 05 April 2024)

Community Solutions (2024). By-Name data. Available at https://community.solutions/quality-by-name-data/ (accessed 05 April 2024).

Cousineau, M. R., & Ward, T. W. (1992). An evaluation of the S-Night street enumeration of the homeless in Los Angeles. Evaluation review, 16(4), 389-399.

Craig, T. K., Hodson, S., Woodward, S., & Richardson, S. (1996). *Off to a bad start: A longitudinal study of homeless young people in London*. London: Mental Health Foundation.

Dávid, B., & Snijders, T. A. (2002). Estimating the size of the homeless population in Budapest, Hungary. Quality and Quantity, 36(3), 291-303.

Department of Housing and Urban Development (HUD). (2008). A guide to counting unsheltered homeless people. Second Revision January 2008. Washington DC: Office of Community Planning and Development

Department of Housing and Urban Development (HUD). 2014. Point-in-Time Count Methodology Guide

Devine, J. A., & Wright, J. D. (1992). Counting the Homeless S-Night in New Orleans. Evaluation review, 16(4), 409-417.

Dunton, L., Albanese, T., & D'Alanno, T. (2014). Point-in-time count methodology guide. US Department of Housing and Urban Development. Available at: https://files.hudexchange.info/resources/documents/PIT-Count-Methodology-Guide.pdf (accessed 05 April 2024)

Edin, K. (1992). Counting Chicago's Homeless An Assessment of the Census Bureau's" Street and Shelter Night". Evaluation review, 16(4), 365-375.

Farrell, S. J., & Reissing, E. D. (2004). Picking Up the Challenge Developing a Methodology to Enumerate and Assess the Needs of the Street Homeless Population. Evaluation Review, 28(2), 144-155.

Fitzgerald, S. T., Shelley, M. C., & Dail, P. W. (2001). Research on homelessness: Sources and implications of uncertainty. American Behavioral Scientist, 45(1), 121-148.

Grainger, G. L. (2022). What tradeoffs are made on the path to functional zero chronic homelessness? Housing Studies, 1–22.

Henry, M., Cortes, A., Morris, S., Khadduri, J., & Culhane, D. P. (2013). The 2013 Annual Homelessness Assessment Report (AHAR) to Congress: Part 1, Point-in-Time Estimates of Homelessness.

Hopper, K., Shinn, M., Laska, E., Meisner, M., & Wanderling, J. (2008). Estimating numbers of unsheltered homeless people through plant-capture and postcount survey methods. American journal of public health, 98(8), 1438.

HUD Exchange (2024). Point-in-Time Count and Housing Inventory Count. Available at: https://www.hudexchange.info/programs/hdx/pit-hic/#hic-guides-and-tools (accessed 05 April 2024).

INSEE (2001). Survey homeless 2001. Available at: https://www.insee.fr/en/metadonnees/source/operation/s1267/processus-statistique (accessed 06 April 2024)

INSEE (2012). Survey homeless 2012. Available at: https://www.insee.fr/en/metadonnees/source/operation/s1268/presentation

Koegel, P., Burnam, M. A., & Morton, S. C. (1996). Enumerating homeless people alternative strategies and their consequences. Evaluation review, 20(4), 378-403.

La Porte, R. E. (1994). Assessing the human condition: capture-recapture techniques. BMJ: British Medical Journal, 308(6920), 5.

Martin, E. (1992). Assessment of S-Night street enumeration in the 1990 Census. Evaluation Review, 16(4), 418-438.

O'Callaghan, B., Dominian, L., Evans, A., Dix, J., Smith, R., Williams, P., & Zimmeck, M. (1996). *Study of homeless applicants*. HM Stationery Office.

Rossi, P. H. (1991), *Down and Out in America: The Origins of Homelessness*, University of Chicago Press.

Scutella, R., & Johnson, G. (2012). Locating and designing 'Journeys Home': A literature review.

Scutella, R., Tseng, Y. P., & Wooden, M. (2017). Journeys Home: Tracking the most vulnerable. *Longitudinal and Life Course Studies*, 8(3), 302-318.

Shinn, M., Weitzman, B. C., Stojanovic, D., Knickman, J. R., Jimenez, L., Duchon, L., ... & Krantz, D. H. (1998). Predictors of homelessness among families in New York City: from shelter request to housing stability. *American Journal of Public Health*, 88(11), 1651-1657.

Smith, A. S., Holmberg, C., & Jones-Puthoff, M. (2012). The Emergency and Transitional Shelter Population, 2010. US Department of Commerce, Economics and Statistics Administration, US Census Bureau.

Sosin, M., Piliavin, I., & Westerfelt, H. (1990). Toward a longitudinal analysis of homelessness. *Journal of Social Issues*, 46(4), 157-174.

Stark, L. R. (1992). Counting the Homeless An Assessment of S-Night in Phoenix. Evaluation review, 16(4), 400-408.

Tually, S., & Goodwin-Smith, I. (2019). Known, Housed. Supported: Aligning housing to the needs of people on the Adelaide Zero Project By-Name List: data, considerations and implications. Available at https: https://www.dunstan.org.au/resources/aligned-housing-research-report/ (accessed 5 April 2024).

United States Census Bureau (2024). How the 2020 Census Counts People Experiencing Homelessness. Available at: https://www.census.gov/library/fact-sheets/2020/dec/2020-census-counts-homeless.html (accessed 05 April 2024).

Weitzman, B. C., Knickman, J. R., & Shinn, M. (1990). Pathways to homelessness among New York City families. *Journal of Social Issues*, 46(4), 125-140.

Wong, Y. L. I., Culhane, D. P., & Kuhn, R. (1997). Predictors of exit and reentry among family shelter users in New York City. *Social Service Review*, 71(3), 441-462.

Wong, Y. L. I., & Piliavin, I. (2001). Stressors, resources, and distress among homeless persons:: a longitudinal analysis. *Social Science & Medicine*, 52(7), 1029-1042.

Wright, J. D., & Devine, J. A. (1992). Counting the Homeless The Census Bureau's" S-Night" in Five US Cities. Evaluation review, 16(4), 355-364.

Chapter 3

Australian Bureau of Statistics (ABS). (2023). Estimating Homelessness: Census. Realased 22/03/2023. Available at: https://www.abs.gov.au/statistics/people/housing/estimating-homelessness-census/latest-release (accessed 05 April 2024)

Avramov, D. (2018). Data Sources on Homelessness and Data Necessary for Needs-Based Research. In Coping with Homelessness (pp. 145-164). Routledge.

Batterham, D., Cigdem-Bayram, M., Parkinson, S., Reynolds, M., & Wood, G. (2022). The spatial dynamics of homelessness in australia: Urbanisation, intra-city dynamics and affordable housing. Applied Spatial Analysis and Policy, 15(4), 1021-1043.

Busch-Geertsema, V., Benjaminsen, L., Hrast, MF, & Pleace, N. (2014). Extent and profile of homelessness in European Member States: A statistical update. EOH Comparative Studies on Homelessness, No 4, Brussels: Feantsa/EOH.

Department of Housing and Urban Development (2024). AHAR Reports. Available at: https://www.hudexchange.info/homelessness-assistance/ahar/#2023-reports (accessed 07 April 2024

Edgar, B., & Meert, H. (2006). *Fifth review of statistics on homelessness in Europe*. Feantsa.

Horvat, N., & Coupechoux, S. (2023). *8th Overview of Housing Exclusion in Europe 2023*. Feantsa [on line]. Available at: https://www.feantsa.org/en/report/2023/09/05/report-8th-overview-of-housing-exclusion-in-europe-2023 (accessed: 01 April 2024)

Human Resources and Skills Development Canada, https://publications.gc.ca/collections/collection_2017/edsc-esdc/Em12-17-2017-eng.pdf

Rossi, P. H. (1991), *Down and Out in America: The Origins of Homelessness*, University of Chicago Press.

Chapter 4
ARA (2023). Report 2/2023: Homeless people 2022. Available at: https://www.ara.fi/en-US/Materials/Homelessness_reports/Homelessness_in_Finland_2022(65349)#:~:text=At%20the%20end%20of%202022,a%20decrease%20of%20185%20people (accessed 11/04/2024)

Benjaminsen, L. (2022). Homelessness in Denmark 2022. VIVE. Available at: https://www.vive.dk/da/udgivelser/hjemloeshed-i-danmark-2022-ozokjnvn/

Busch-Geertsema, V. (2010). The Finnish National Programme to reduce long-term homelessness. Synthesis Report. Hg. v. GISS. Association for Innovative Social Research and Social. Bremen. Online verfügbar unter https://www. google. com/url.

Busch-Geertsema, V. (2023). Homelessness in Germany, in: J. Bretherton and N. Pleace (Eds.) The Routledge Handbook of Homelessness, pp.316-323, Abingdon: Routledge.

Dyb, E. (2017). Counting homelessness and politics: the case of Norway. European Journal of Homelessness, 11(2).

EEAG (2012) "The Hungarian Crisis" in *The EEAG Report on the European Economy*, CESifo, Munich 2012, pp. 115-130.

Fruzsina, A., Teller, N., Fehér, B., & Kőszeghy, L. (2019). ESPN Thematic Report on National strategies to fight homelessness and housing exclusion. Hungary, ESPN Report, Directorate-General for Employment, Social Affairs and Inclusion. Available at: https://ec.europa.eu/social/main.jsp?catId=738&langId=en&pubId=8243&furtherPubs=yes (accessed 12/04/2024)

Gray, T. (2022), Homelessness and the pandemic Emergency measures during Covid-19: what worked in global cities?, Centre for Homelessness Impact series. Available at: https://assets-global.website-files.com/59f07e67422cdf0001904c14/623db6e695e2c41a94eeeab4_CHI.IPPO.Pandemic.pdf

O'Sullivan, E. (2022). Key Elements in Homelessness Strategies to End Homelessness by 2030: A Discussion Paper. European Platform on Combatting Homelessness. Publications Office of the European Union, Luxembourg.

Unal, U., Hayo, B., & Erol, I. (2024). Housing market convergence: evidence from Germany. Applied Economics, 1–16. https://doi.org/10.1080/00036846.2024.2315094

Chapter 5:
Acemoglu, D., Johnson S., and Robinson, J.A. (2001). "The Colonial Origins of Comparative Development: An Empirical Investigation." *American Economic Review*, 91 (5): 1369-1401.

Allgood, S. and Warren, Jr. (2003). "The duration of homelessness: evidence from a national survey," Journal of Housing Economics, Elsevier, vol. 12(4), pages 273-290, December.

Braga M., & Corno L., (2011). Being Homeless: Evidence from Italy, Giornale degli Economisti, GDE (Giornale degli Economisti e Annali di Economia), Bocconi University, vol. 70(3), pages 33-73, December.

CECODHAS (2012), "Impact of the crisis and austerity measures on the social housing sector"

CECODHAS (2009), "Financing social housing after the economic crisis"

Döring, H., & Manow, P. (2010). Parliament and government composition database (ParlGov).

European Commission, Eurostat, https://eur-lex.europa.eu/legalcontent/EN/TXT/?uri=celex%3A52010DC2020

European Union, https://www.eurofound.europa.eu/en/european-industrial-relations-dictionary/annual-growth-survey

European Union, Communication (COM(2010) 2020 final) – Europe 2020: A strategy for smart, sustainable and inclusive growth, https://eur-lex.europa.eu/legal-content/EN/TXT/?uri=celex%3A52010DC2020

European Union, https://ec.europa.eu/eurostat/web/interactive-publications/housing-2023

Robert E. Hall & Charles I. Jones, 1999. "Why do Some Countries Produce So Much More Output Per Worker than Others?," The Quarterly Journal of Economics, President and Fellows of Harvard College, vol. 114(1), pages 83-116.

North, D. C. (1990). Institutions, Institutional Change and Economic Performance (p. 33). Cambridge: Cambridge University Press.

Piliavin, I., Wright B.R., Mare R.D. and Westerfelt A.H. (1996). Exits and returns to homelessness. *Social Service Review* 70(1): 33-57.

Shelter (2008). What causes homelessness? https://england.shelter.org.uk/support_us/campaigns/what_causes_homelessness

World Bank, https://databank.worldbank.org/metadataglossary/world-development-indicators/series/IC.LGL.CRED.XQ

Chapter 6:

ISTAT, 2005

ISTAT, 2008

Australian Regional Labour Force Statistics, https://www.abs.gov.au/statistics/labour/employment-and-unemployment/labour-force-australia-detailed/latest-release

Bentolila, S. and Ichino, A. 2007, "Unemployment and Consumption. Near and far away from the Mediterranean?", Journal of Population Economics, vol.21, pp.225-289.

Johnson, G, Scutella, R, Tseng, Y & Wood, G 2015, *Entries and exits from homelessness: A dynamic analysis of the relationship between structural conditions and individual characteristics*, Final Report, Australian Housing and Urban Research Institute, Melbourne.

Wood, G, Batterham, D, Cigdem, M &. Mallett, S 2014, *Final report 1: The spatial dynamics of homelessness in Australia 2001–2011*, Australian Housing and Urban Research Institute, Melbourne.

Chapter 7:

ABS 2014, ABS (Australian Bureau of Statistics) 2014, Labour force: Australia, detailed - electronic delivery, cat. no.6291.0.55.001, ABS, Canberra.

ABS 2010, 2010, Australian statistical geography standard (ASGS): volume 1—Main structure and greater capital city statistical areas, cat. no.1270.0.55.001, ABS, Canberra.

Aubry, T., Nelson, G., & Tsemberis, S. (2015). Housing first for people with severe mental illness who are homeless: a review of the research and findings from the at home—chez soi demonstration project. *The Canadian Journal of Psychiatry, 60*(11), 467-474.

Aubry, T., Bloch, G., Brcic, V., Saad, A., Magwood, O., Abdalla, T., ... & Pottie, K. (2020). Effectiveness of permanent supportive housing and income assistance interventions for homeless individuals in high-income countries: a systematic review. *The Lancet Public Health, 5*(6), e342-e360.

Byrne, T., Munley, E. A., Fargo, J. D., Montgomery, A. E., Culhabe, D. P. (2013). New perspectives on community-level determinants of homelessness. J. Urban Aff. 35 607–625.

Burt, M. R (1992), Over the Edge: The Growth of Homelessness in the 1980s. New York: Russell Sage.

Burt, M. R.(2001). *Helping America's homeless: Emergency shelter or affordable housing?*. The Urban Insitute.

Cebula, R. J., & Saunoris, J. W. (2021). Determinants of homelessness in the U.S.: New hypotheses and evidence. *Applied Economics, 53*(49), 5695–5709.

Collinson, R., Humphries J. E., Mader N., Reed D., Tannenbaum D., van Dijk W., (2024). "Eviction and Poverty in American Cities," The Quarterly Journal of Economics, vol 139(1), pages 57-120.

Corno, L. (2017). Homelessness and crime: do your friends matter? *The Economic Journal, 127*(602), 959–995.

Early D. W. (2004) "The determinants of homelessness and the targeting of housing assistance", Journal of Urban Economics, 2004, Volume 55, Issue 1, January 2004, Pages 195–214.

Evans, W. N., Sullivan, J. X., & Wallskog, M. (2016). The impact of homelessness prevention programs on homelessness. *Science, 353*(6300), 694-699.

Fetzer, T., Sen, S., & Souza, P. C. (2019). Housing insecurity, homelessness and populism: Evidence from the UK.

Flaming, D., Toros, H., Burns, P. (2015). Home Not Found: The Cost of Homelessness in Silicon Valley. *Economic Roundtable Research Report*.

Freeman, Richard B., and Brian Hall, 1987, Permanent homelessness in America? Population Research and Policy Review 6: 3-27.

Hill, R. P., & Stamey, M. (1990). The homeless in America: An examination of possessions and consumption behaviors. *Journal of consumer research, 17*(3), 303-321.

Honig, Marjorie, and Randall K. Filer, 1993, Causes of intercity variation in homelessness, American Economic Review 83(1): 248-255.

International Labour Standards (2011). *ILO Manual on the Measurement of Volunteer Work* C189 - Domestic Workers Convention, 2011 (No. 189)

Jarvis, J., (2015) Individual determinants of homelessness: A descriptive approach, Journal of Housing Economics, Volume 30, Pages 23-32, ISSN 1051-1377,

Lachaud, J., Mejia-Lancheros, C., Durbin, A., Nisenbaum, R., Wang, R., O'Campo, P., ... & Hwang, S. W. (2021). The effect of a housing first intervention on acute health care utilization among homeless adults with mental illness: long-term outcomes of the at home/chez-soi randomized pragmatic trial. *Journal of Urban Health, 98*(4), 505-515.

Leclair, M. C., Deveaux, F., Roy, L., Goulet, M. H., Latimer, E. A., & Crocker, A. G. (2019). The impact of Housing First on criminal justice outcomes among homeless people with mental illness: a systematic review. *The Canadian Journal of Psychiatry, 64*(8), 525-530.

Lee, B. A., Price-Spratlen, T., & Kanan, J. W. (2003). Determinants of homelessness in metropolitan areas. *Journal of Urban Affairs, 25*(3), 335-356.

Mabhala, M., Esealuka, W. A., Nwufo, A. N., Enyinna, C., Mabhala, C. N., Udechukwu, T., ... & Yohannes, A. (2021). Homelessness is socially created: Cluster analysis of social determinants of homelessness (SODH) in North West England in 2020. *International journal of environmental research and public health, 18*(6), 3066.

Early, Dirk, and Edgar Olsen, 2002, Subsidized housing, emergency shelters, and homelessness: An empirical investigation using data from the 1990 census, Advances in Economic Analysis and Policy 2 (1), n.p.2

European Social Policy Network (ESPN) National strategies to fight homelessness and housing exclusion (2019). https://ec.europa.eu/social/main.jsp?catId=1135&furtherNews=yes&langId=en&newsId=9456

Quigley, John M., 1990, Does rent control cause homelessness? Taking the claim seriously, Journal of Policy Analysis and Management 9: 89-93.

Quigley J., Raphael S., Smoloensky E. 2001. "Homeless in America, Homeless in California", Review of Economics and Statistics, 83(1), 37-51.

Quigley, J., Raphael, S., and Smolensky, E. (2001). The links between income inequality, housing markets, and homelessness in California. San Francisco: Public Policy Institute of California.

US National Alliance to End Homeless (2017). https://endhomelessness.org

Raphael, Steven, 2010, Homelessness and housing market regulation. In Ingrid Ellen and Brendan O'Flaherty, eds., How to House the Homeless. New York: Russell Sage.

Tinland, A., Loubiere, S., Cantiello, M., Boucekine, M., Girard, V., Taylor, O., & Auquier, P. (2021). Mortality in homeless people enrolled in the French housing first randomized controlled trial: a secondary outcome analysis of predictors and causes of death. *BMC public health*, *21*, 1-12.

Tsemberis Gulcuf, Nakae (2004) "Housing First, Consumer Choice, and Harm Reduction for Homeless Individuals With a Dual Diagnosis". American Journal of Public Health

About the Authors

Michela Braga is Lecturer in the Departement of Economics at Bocconi University. She is fellow of Baffi-Carefin and fRDB, a research organization that promotes applied and policy-oriented research on labor markets and welfare systems. She obtained a Ph.D. in Economics from Università Bocconi in 2008, after having completed a Master of Science in Economics. She is involved in research activities in the field of economics of education, migration, social exclusion and extreme poverty. Since 2008 she has designed and managed censuses and surveys on homeless people in main Italian cities. She is also involved in anti-poverty policies evaluation.

Lucia Corno is associate professor in the Department of Economics and Finance at Cattolica University and the Executive Director of the Laboratory for Effective Anti-poverty Policies (LEAP) at Bocconi University. She received a PhD in Economics from Bocconi University in 2009 and she was graduate visiting scholar at the University of Berkeley and at the Institute for International Economic Studies (IIES) in Stockholm. Before joining Cattolica, Prof. Corno held academic positions at University College London and Queen Mary University in London. She is affiliated with J-PAL, a fellow of the Centre for Economic Policy Research (CEPR) and a full member of the EUDN (European Development Research Network). In 2019, she received an ERC Starting Grant to study the reasons behind the persistence of harmful traditions (i.e. female genital cutting). Prof. Corno constantly collaborates with International Organizations and governments in developing countries and in Italy to implement and evaluate the effectiveness of anti-poverty policies.

Paola Monti is Research Coordinator at the Fondazione Rodolfo Debenedetti, a research organization that promotes applied and policy-oriented research on labour markets, immigration and welfare systems in Europe. She holds a Master of Science in Economics from the University College of London and a degree in Economic and Social Disciplines (DES) from Bocconi University. She has an extensive experience in research, survey design and project management. In her professional role, she oversees complex research projects related to labour economics, immigration, social policy, and policy evaluation. She has managed a wide range of projects, including the "racCONTAMI" initiatives, a census and a survey of homeless people in Milan and Rome.